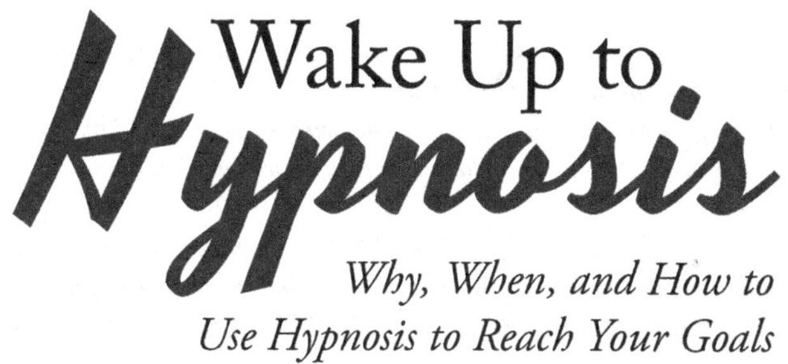

Barbara Powers, MSc, BDS

WAKE UP TO HYPNOSIS
WHY, WHEN, AND HOW TO USE HYPNOSIS
TO REACH YOUR GOALS

iUniverse books may be ordered through booksellers or by contacting:

iUniverse
1663 Liberty Drive
Bloomington, IN 47403
www.iuniverse.com
1-800-Authors (1-800-288-4677)

ISBN: 978-1-5320-8564-2 (sc)
ISBN: 978-1-5320-8566-6 (hc)
ISBN: 978-1-5320-8565-9 (e)

Library of Congress Control Number: 2019919680

Print information available on the last page.

iUniverse rev. date: 01/20/2020

PREFACE

My intention in writing this book is to shine a light on a specific process of the mind, the trance phenomenon, and to demystify and promote medical hypnosis. This book is the culmination of forty years of clinical practice and deep interest in clinical and research developments in a wide range of medical, psychological, and spiritual aspects concerning our physical and mental health, goals achievement, happiness, and welfare.

After having graduated in dentistry (Academy of Medicine, Wroclaw, Poland, 1971) and completing a specialization in oral surgery (1979), I soon recognized that having dental and surgical skill is only the main core for satisfactory treatment. We all know that dental procedures are quite painful and uncomfortable, causing distress to the whole family. Moreover, frequently patients were coming to the surgery with a wide range of personal problems which needed to be dealt with before the actual treatment could be started. The fear of pain frequently led to avoidance, and many patients came for treatment only to stop the unbearable pain. To convince the patient to behave otherwise, I found it necessary to learn how to create better bonds with my patients, in order to give more comfortable and more pleasant treatment. I moved to London in the United Kingdom in 1978. That was the time when medical hypnosis was widely recognized by academic centres and comprehensive courses were available to professionals in the medical, dental, and psychological fields. Curious about hypnotic pain control, I took the first opportunity I had to become engaged in the course leading to a diploma in medical hypnosis at University College London (UCL) in 1996. On completion of this course in 1997, I recognized that the application of hypnosis goes far beyond pain control. I was surprised to find that hypnosis is widely and successfully utilized in most medical and psychological fields not only to reduce the pain but also to facilitate postsurgical healing and minimize distress for patients. On top of this, it results in some cases in a smiling child promising to come back soon for a check-up. This new knowledge allowed me not only to successfully utilize hypnosis in various surgical procedures but also to practise hypnosis and self-hypnosis myself to improve my physical and mental health and achieve my goals. The combined experiences that I gained from treating patients from different geographical and social backgrounds and learning about the potential of the human mind were the most significant influences on my future interests and beliefs.

This passionate interest in the phenomenon of trance motivated me to become involved in deeper studies and research of medical hypnosis and the hypnosis phenomenon itself, leading to a Master of Science (MSc) degree in applied hypnosis from University College London in 1999. All these academic, clinical, and personal experiences presented in Part I and II erased any doubt from my mind that I had about hypnosis, and I saw it to be a powerful tool to be used in a wide range of applications by all of us.

In Part III of this book you will find chapters dealing with living a coma-like lifestyle, in which I express my observations about how our thoughts and emotions can build or destroy our destiny. In Part IV and V you can learn how practising self-hypnosis can help everyone gain control of their emotions, make better choices, and reach goals including taking better care of their mental and physical health.

I hope you will find these observations beneficial and that this book will help you to make steady improvements in your life to allow you to gain satisfaction in whatever you do.

ACKNOWLEDGEMENTS

To my late husband, Tony, whose great enthusiasm for and deep belief in my work was the essential fuel to accomplish my goal. To my dear daughter, Dagmara; my son-in-law, Keith; and my four wonderful grandchildren, Kathryn, Sarah, Benjamin, and James, whose presence supplied endless resources and proved how happy we as humans really can be if we let ourselves to be happy.

I would like to express my deep appreciation to all who helped me to complete this book: to my dear friend Terry for her kind support during the most difficult times when I needed a friendly hand and for her constructive thoughts on each chapter; to Laurie and her late husband, Scott, for correcting grammar and style, when they were experiencing the most difficult time in their lives; and finally to everyone who never doubted in my project and kept me going when dark thoughts started to melt my enthusiasm and belief.

CONTENTS

Part II
Inner Healing Powers

Part III
Master Self-Hypnosis: Be the Commander of Your Life Journey

Part IV
Find Your Present Position

Part V
Goals

LIST OF BOXES

INTRODUCTION

Winners believe that they will find a light in the darkness.

With the world's population increasing at an alarming rate, having exceeded seven billion in 2012, the demands of the twenty-first century are greater than ever, and we must be prepared for tougher competition in both our professional and personal lives. With these high demands, it is so very easy to turn down the wrong path when being exposed to many unfamiliar situations. I had witnessed every day that many of my patients were living with long-term stress, anger, unhappiness, fear and misshaped self-image. These conditions lead to poor health and disappointing performance on a daily basis, and in the long term block light and desire for positive change.

Many struggling with stress and excessive demands frequently surrender to depression, drugs, alcohol, or suicidal thoughts. Such conditions in turn further affect rational thinking and the ability to face everyday situations or solve problems, and the vicious cycle of misfortune continues. When this sort of thing happens, it can be very difficult to turn back onto the right path.

A few of the most common causes of making bad choices (or not making any choices) are low confidence, irrational thinking, and poor self-discipline, which may be the product of unrecognized long-term negative mind conditioning. Repeating bad choices in the long term leads to poor achievement and dissatisfaction with life. Frequently we hear from people who are trapped in an awkward situation that bad luck is knocking on their door. Unfortunately, this pattern of thinking only deepens negative expectations and does nothing to prevent repeated bad luck in the future. In such cases, the human spirit has lost its way and needs help to find its way back.

On the other hand, I had the pleasure of working with people facing difficult situations, as we all do from time to time, who somehow found the ability to go through tough times and overcome obstacles more effectively, make better choices, and move on to reach their desired goals. The highest achievers seem to have a natural ability to cope better with stress, and it is proven now that they tend to follow a unique positive pattern of thinking and are more open-minded, which enables them to spot new opportunities.

What is the difference between these two kinds of people? Do the latter have better skills learned from parents, teachers, and friends, or are they simply open-minded and trust their intuition? Probably the answer is both—and now you can be the same way if you are willing to step outside your comfort zone.

However, it is imperative to acknowledge that in order to be in better control of your destiny, it is necessary to increase your mental skill set, including improving your self-beliefs and developing effective coping and problem-solving strategies. We all know that to make a positive change, one cannot simply wish that it be so. Moreover, life brings different experiences to all of us every day, and we may lack the resources for dealing with some of these situations. Therefore, knowing how to use your mind's potential more efficiently, including the trance state of mind, will automatically increase your energy, self-image, creativity, and persistence to spot more opportunities along the way to reaching your goals. Learning positive and effective life strategies in hypnosis and self-hypnosis is the quickest and most comfortable way to make positive and long-lasting changes in your life. Whatever difficult situation you are facing, it may be just a matter of making a small change in your attitude and having the willingness to see the big picture in a different light (not merely what you want to see) to make the right change.

Therefore, I present the basic concept of conscious and unconscious mind processes for a better understanding of how hypnosis works and how you can benefit from it in order to have the freedom to choose your thoughts, feelings, and decisions. We all deserve to have the personal freedom to use our creative abilities to lead a rewarding life. We all have a choice; we can contribute something positive for future generations, or we can let ourselves remain trapped with negative emotions and destroy what our fathers and mothers built for us in the past.

I present many practical examples to show how the powers of the mind can be used to improve your health and personal life and increase the possibility that you will reach your dreams. You can learn how to deal with new challenges with confidence and to your satisfaction. This way you can be in a constructive mood all day long and start to think, "I can do it, and I deserve it."

I like to compare life to sailing a ship on the open ocean. We can allow ourselves to drift aimlessly across the open water, hoping that one day we will stumble upon paradise, but without plans and how to protect ourselves and our crew, we may encounter an unpleasant surprise and end up shipwrecked when coming upon stormy seas or shallow water.

Those who choose to be the commander of their lives know how to make a careful plan for the journey, taking full responsibility for the ship and being masters at keeping the united crew behind them at all times, regardless of the weather conditions. These types of people make confident decisions, use effective strategies, have good communication skills, and are up to date on the relevant data.

By reading this book, you will be able to recognize the potential of your ship, use the full potential of your mind as a navigation device to monitor your position, and enjoy sailing towards your desired destination. You will start to trust the resources of your unconscious mind and increase the possibility that you will achieve your goals in less time and with longer-lasting results.

Many people ask me, "Is it guaranteed?"

In my experience, it is. However, it is not magic—but it is the easiest, quickest, and cheapest way to achieve personal growth, learn beneficial approaches to life's experiences, and feel good about yourself and your ability to reach your goals. The final results will depend on how serious you are about improving your life. If you just "wish" you had a better life without taking any steps towards obtaining one, then it is less likely that you will get the results you seek.

When you know what you want and are willing to take responsibility for your life from now on and increase your skills to make better choices to reach what you desire, then you will make significant positive changes in your life.

By exercising and conditioning your brain for only a few minutes a day in hypnosis, you will develop a healthy balance between your body and mind, increase your energy, enthusiasm, and motivation to make positive changes in your life, and build something for yourself and others. The knowledge presented in this book is scientifically proven to be an effective way to increase your performance on a daily basis. It is based on various academic research, and my own clinical and personal experience. You can find a list of references at the back of the book for further reading.

Reading the book first will help you to understand the whole picture of what medical and psychological hypnotherapy means. In the first chapters of the book, you will find a simple explanation of how medical, dental, and psychological hypnosis is used in academic centres around the globe. This will help you to understand why, when, and how hypnosis is used by professionals and how it can help you or someone close to you.

In later chapters you will learn how to practise self-hypnosis to make steady, confidence-inspiring improvements in your life by achieving your goals one by one, whatever you are looking for. It will help you to be on the way to find yourself and expand your mind to achieve happiness and success.

Part I

Know the Ship You Are Sailing on Your Life Journey

One

A Short History of Hypnotic Phenomenon in Medicine

With appreciation to all whose unshaken belief in the mind's potential brought hypnosis to science for the benefit of all.

People have been puzzled by hypnotic phenomena for centuries. The power of trance and suggestion has been used purposefully, albeit perhaps without recognition, throughout the millennia. Both the positive and adverse effects were recognized a long time ago by churches and authorities for the purpose of gaining power and control. Belief in healing from the gods was very strong in the past and still is today. For this reason, temples were built and devotees were organized to pray for health, happiness, peace of mind, and serenity. Belief in prayer has always been very high regarding health and any other aspect of life. Witches, mystical rituals, and spells have been known for centuries. Happiness, health, and security were associated with wearing talismans such as tiger teeth and furs, among other symbols of power. Today many of us are still superstitious and alter our path when we see a black cat. Many of us are reluctant to accept a flight on the thirteenth of the month. Whatever the case may be, having only a little knowledge about hypnotic phenomena is the cause of many false beliefs about this state of mind and much of the controversy over practising hypnosis in the medical field.

Mesmerism (1500–1750)

The most creditably documented cases of practising medical hypnosis in Europe are found in the age of mesmerism. Franz Anton Mesmer (1734–1815), an Austrian physician, practised medicine in Paris beginning in 1778 and is known as the founder of medical hypnosis. His beliefs were shaped by his study of the influence of the moon and planets on the development of diseases. His belief known as "animal magnetism" was widely criticized by authorities.

Mesmer claimed that the universe's "magnetic fluid" in the human body could be blocked for many reasons and that unblocking the flow of the fluid would initiate the healing of any disease. In the beginning of his career, he used magnets to unblock these channels. Later he believed that the energy coming from his hands and eyes could restore the circulation of this fluid as well. This unusual controversial practice led the medical authorities of Austria to charge him with professional misconduct and prohibit him from practising. Persistent in his beliefs, Mesmer moved to Paris in 1778, where he continued practising individual hypnosis as well as group therapy, and where his practice gained in popularity.

The French Royal Commission did not approve of Mesmer's work either, and he was forbidden from practising not only in France but also in other countries for the rest of his life. However, his persistence and unshaken belief in magnetic fluid made a significant impact on other practitioners reacting to the new era of hypnosis science. Mesmer's work shined a light on one issue, namely that there are healing powers inside the human body, not just outside. It was proved at that time that Mesmer's animal magnetism or other, more natural methods would have the same outcome as an exorcism performed by Catholic priests to remove a devil from the body. The most significant discovery at that time was that imagination was recognized as part of the future of hypnotic phenomena, and that brought a totally new approach to trance and to the medical field. The technique spread to the United States, where mesmerism was used by Mary Baker Eddy (1821–1910) of the Church of Christ, Scientist.

The technique of inducing trance had an enormous impact on many medical and psychological practitioners across Europe and heralded a new era for medicine and research despite wide criticism from authorities.

Post-Mesmer (1830–1900)

Many practitioners continued practising hypnosis, frequently sacrificing their reputations and professions, and committed themselves to learning more about the potential of the human body and its inner healing mechanisms. Mesmerism was spreading across European countries. Utilization of hypnosis in treatment of many medical and psychological maladies was the centre of attention among professionals in Germany, E. Gmelin (1751-1809), and later K. C. Wolfram (1778–1832) in Berlin and across Russia, Britain, and the Scandinavian countries.

John Elliotson (1791–1868), professor of medicine at University College Hospital in England, was the first to practise mesmerism in England. Again, the inability to provide concrete evidence of the mind's potential for healing undermined the clinical results. Finally he was forced to stop his practice, despite having performed many successful operations using only Mesmer's technique of animal magnetism to eliminate pain.

Scotsman James Braid (1795–1860) from Manchester developed a new view on the science of mesmerism and hypnotic phenomena. He introduced the name of "hypnosis" (from the Greek word for "sleep") to describe this specific state of mind. His main belief was that hypnosis was the result of suggestion given to a person in a specific state of mind.

Braid was the creator of the classic method of hypnotic induction, *Eye fixation*, which is effectively used by many practitioners to this day. The message that there were effective hypnotic approaches to treat many medical conditions continued to spread rapidly among medical professionals and scientists around the world.

Another example of the negative attitude towards this new science can be seen in the claims of James Esdaile (1808–1859), a Scottish surgeon practising in India. He presented well-documented cases of the successful use of hypnosis to control pain in surgery. Again, his work was not accepted by authorities and therefore was never published. Miraculously, Esdaile's book *Mesmerism in India* was saved and is a highly valuable reference to learn about medical hypnosis in that era. Despite the repressive attitudes and the disappointments, other enthusiastic medical practitioners did not stop practising hypnosis.

Later, new findings were presented by people from different academic centres, and disputes were common between those subscribing to different schools of thought regarding hypnotic phenomena. Jean-Martin Charcot (1825–1893), anatomist and neurologist from the Salpêtrière School, believed that only hysterical patients were responsive to hypnotic suggestion and could benefit from hypnosis. Contrary to this was the Nancy School, with influential figures as A. A. Liébeault (1823–1893) and H. Bergheim (1840–1919), who explained that healing may be the result of suggestions. Professor Bergheim started to use direct suggestion to treat sciatica patients and significantly increased others' interest in using hypnosis to treat various psychological disorders.

One of the biggest movements to promote hypnosis was the First International Congress for Experimental and Therapeutic Hypnotism in Paris in 1889, which attracted medical and psychiatric experts from around the globe. The material presented at this congress had an influence on the famous psychiatrists Sigmund Freud and Josef Breuer (1842–1925), both of whom used hypnosis with psychiatric patients. At that time hypnosis started to be connected with psychology. Names connected with this trend are Pierre Janet (1859–1947) and M. Prince, who believed in the theory of dissociation of personality in hypnosis. Hypnosis was used to treat soldiers during World War I by English psychologist William

McDougall (1871–1944) and experimenter Clark Hull (1884–1952), the latter of whom wrote the book *Hypnosis and Suggestibility* in 1933.

John Milne Bramwell (1852–1925) presented well-documented cases of extraction of teeth with patients under hypnosis. His classic letter to a dentist is quoted in many books on psychology. He wrote to the dentist:

> Dear Mr Turner,
>
> I send you a patient with the enclosed order. When you give it to her, she will fall asleep at once and obey your commands.
>
> J. Milne Bramwell

The order was: "Go to sleep by order of Dr Bramwell, and obey Mr Turner's commands."

Bramwell's book *Hypnotism: It's History, Practice, and Theory* is proudly kept by many practitioners. The use of hypnosis was reported to have controlled pain in many medical procedures and to have calmed soldiers during the First World War and the Second World War.

The famous Sigmund Freud (1856–1939) introduced the metaphorical structure of the mind which included the unconscious mind and posed the ideas of unconscious access, free association, and dream analysis. Freud theorized that the conscious represents a fully awake mind state and that the preconscious is a partially conscious state of mind which can be restored to consciousness by turning one's attention. The unconscious mind holds memories, fantasies, and thoughts, which may not be available to consciousness. According to Freud, dreams are an altered state of consciousness—the "royal road" to unconscious mind activities.

Freud is well known for practising psychological and analytical therapy looking for the roots of problems in the early years of life. Freud's assumption was that some memories are repressed in the unconscious mind and have a significant impact on one's personal life. He believed that recovering these repressed memories in hypnosis may improve a person's health. This new point of view made a significant impact on the development of modern psychology. Moreover, Freud's model of the structure of mind is still the basis for scientific research into mental processes and hypnosis.

Freud's metaphorical structure of the mind as conscious, unconscious, and preconscious is the most widely recognized explanation of different mental processes, and the terminology is still used in modern psychology and science, including hypnotherapy.

However, all these clinical and academic thoughts about hypnosis and the conscious and unconscious mind were still controversial, and constant scrutiny by authorities diminished many practitioners' enthusiasm. Only a few practitioners used hypnosis in medical and psychological cases at that time.

The Dark Ages of Hypnosis (1900–1950).

Unfortunately, the benefits of hypnosis were once again disregarded because of the discovery of chemical anaesthesia. The use of chemicals and pharmaceuticals to relieve pain was blooming at the beginning of the twentieth century. These advancements came at the price of further undermining the power of the natural self-healing mechanisms of the mind.

The rapid global use of nitrous oxide to extract teeth, introduced by American dentists Dr Horace Wells and William Green Morton (1844) became very popular in dentistry and major surgeries soon after that. The effective drugs to control pain were efficient and quick to apply. Chemical pain control became an overwhelming phenomenon which spread rapidly around the world. Pharmacology was blooming at that time to treat most medical and psychological cases.

Despite this, many medical practitioners continued the search for clues as to the beneficial use of hypnosis. Because of their persistence, their sacrifices, and their sincere belief that hypnosis is a very effective tool for tapping into the mind's potential for resources, we can all benefit from their work today.

In the first few decades of the twentieth century, interest in hypnotic phenomena increased again because of new discoveries from extensive experiments in hypnosis conducted in scientific centres globally.

The significant experimental work on hypnosis was carried out by C. L. Hull (1884–1952), demonstrated in his book *Hypnosis and Suggestibility* (1933). This opened the window to many new discoveries and new literature. The "renaissance age" of hypnotism (1950) started to bloom.

With deeper research and increasing experience, scientists presented new theories, and the divisions between them started to result in different camps with a specific view on the main structure of hypnotic phenomena. Some schools believed that hypnosis is a special state of mind; others assumed that it is a normal state of mind responding to specific suggestion.

The second half of the twentieth century saw huge developments in psychology and neuropsychology. These new discoveries opened the door to the successful utilization of hypnosis again in medicine, psychology, business, human performance, and creativity, to name but a few areas. New interest was directed towards growing developments in behavioural psychotherapy, which again diminished the progress of and research into hypnosis.

Other scientists rushed to present new theories and assumptions about the conscious and the unconscious mind. Ronald Shor (1959) presented the theory of generalized reality orientation, claiming that hypnosis involves a shift from the conscious to the unconscious mind. Scientists started to recognize that hypnosis increases trust between a patient and the practitioner, improves the effect of therapy, increase creativity, and reduces pain and that hypnotherapy can be extended at home by practising self-hypnosis.

A very significant turning point was the introduction of the dissociated theory by Pierre Janet (1859–1947). Janet's new theory described the hypnotic phenomenon as a "dissociation of consciousness," a "splitting off" of ideas, thoughts, and emotions from consciousness.

Later, extensive work on dissociation was presented by E. R. Hilgard through his "hidden observer" feature of hypnosis. Around this time hypnotic mental processes started to be treated as a normal function, not as a pathological symptom. This encouraged others to present the neo- dissociation theory, which explains the therapeutic effect of introducing a new part of the ego to look at the present problem and accounts for the dissociation between the higher and lower levels of mind function.

The dissociated control theory of D. A. Norman and T. Shallice (1986) introduced -"executive ego" as a supervisory attentional system (SAS). All these theories assumed that hypnosis involves an altered state of mind.

New approaches started to arise from various medical centres, such as "regression in the service of ego" by Merton M. Gill and Margaret Brenman-Gibson (1959), the psychodynamic approach by E. Fromm (1992) and Nash (1991), and ego psychological theory, which shows a distinction between the primary and secondary processes of the mind as an altered state of the mind. Primary processes were presented as to early development, the emotionally driven unconscious, and image-based and creative processes. The secondary mind processes are those which develop later with age and are logical, conscious, and based on language.

It was recognized that hypnosis involves such features as absorption, ego receptive regression, increased imagery and holistic thoughts, and trance logic.

"Mind is the distinction between the conscious and unconscious mind and the division between conscious and unconscious processes is the best available clue to the structure of the mind."[1]

Different approaches to hypnotic phenomena were developed by R. W. White (1941) and schools of thoughts which assumed

---

[1] Philip N. Johnson-Laird, *Mental Models: Towards a Cognitive Science of Language, Inference, and Consciousness* (Cambridge, MA, 1983), 466.

that hypnosis is a natural state of mind and a socio-psychological phenomenon.

However, scientists' battle over the theories of hypnotic phenomena is still going on. There are now two main camps of scientists researching the function of brain and hypnosis phenomena. The first camp believes that the hypnotic experience is an altered state of consciousness and that some people are more hypnotizable than others by nature. This is a cognitive theory based on a number of concepts from classical psychoanalysis. The other camp believes that hypnosis is a normal state of consciousness (non-state theory) and that everyone can learn to be hypnotizable.

Many names and assumptions can be found in the increasing amount literature on hypnosis from that time:

- The "cognitive unconscious" which represents "mental processes which underlie cognition but are themselves not conscious (Kihlstrom, 1984, 1987).
- The deep grammar concept presented by Noam Chomsky (1982).
- The computer concept presented by David Marr (1982).
- Hypnosis as role playing presented by Theodore Sarbin et al.
- Suggestion and the use of cognitive strategies presented by Nicholas Spanos et al.
- Unfortunately, at that time another dark shadow on hypnosis was cast by the repeated misconduct of lay therapists, more outside the medical profession. The lack of any regulations and agreement among scientists gave rise to a lot of misconceptions. The perception of hypnosis has been further damaged by lay hypnotists and stage hypnotic performances and by the film industry portraying hypnosis as having destructive, mind-controlling abilities. The false beliefs and myths, and the fear that in a hypnotic trance a person's mind may be manipulated, still cast a shadow over the benefits of medical hypnosis. Their knowledge was limited only to a simple technique for inducing a trance, but the therapy applied

during trance was lacking in professional skill. Because of the many complaints and court cases, new strict regulations were introduced regarding practising hypnosis.

Now only professionals in the medical, dental, and psychological fields who have a specific professional registration and accredited training in hypnosis can apply hypnosis in practice in the area of their specialization. Professional organizations put a lot attention on a high standard of education and professional conduct during hypnotherapy. Because of that, many clinicians and psychologists have deepened their interest in hypnosis and new approaches were introduced.

Modern Medical Hypnosis

The Erickson era presented a modern approach to hypnotherapy and brought about the most significant hypnosis research and the clinical use of hypnosis around the world.

Dr Milton Erickson (1901–1980) was a psychiatrist. Many scientists and practitioners refer to him as the father of clinical hypnosis. His unique approach is very popular to this day and was spread through his many followers. Erickson's utilization model of hypnosis applies a naturalistic and personal approach to hypnosis, which emphasizes that the person seeking help needs to take responsibility and take action to make positive changes in his or her life. The therapist stimulates the person to take an active part in therapy and to find the best resources to solve the present problem, contrary to being an authoritative therapist telling the patient what to do.

According to Erickson, everyone is able to be hypnotized and benefit from hypnotherapy. Moreover, he believed that the therapist could use patient resistance as a tool for positive outcomes and to induce trance. For most therapies, the depth of hypnosis is not important and there is no need to use formal induction. Frequently Erickson used confusing suggestions and symptomatic and dynamic approaches. He believed that all symptoms could be positive and used in therapy to achieve the desired change.

Erickson utilized the patient's creativity and inner resources for a therapeutic purpose. He believed that everyone has "inner resources" to solve the present problem and that they can be reached by "tapping into the unconscious mind" for the release of them.

From that time on, the research into hypnotic phenomena increased, and hypnosis began being used in other aspects of life such as business, sports, the arts, and human performance.

Ronald Shor, in 1972, presented a new concept, namely that the contents of the unconscious mind may be available to the consciousness in some people. This means that we all can have closer contact with our unconscious mind while in a trance and benefit from its endless capability.

Hypnotherapy started to develop new motions when scientists overturned their assumptions and began to believe that hypnosis is a normal state of mind which is very useful in gaining close contact with the unconscious mind. Neurolinguistics programming (NLP) was created by two scientists in the 1970s, Richard Bandler (psychologist, mathematician, and computer expert) and John Grinder (assistant professor of linguistics at the University of California). Bandler was practising gestalt psychotherapy, and both he and Grinder analysed the communication patterns of famous therapists such as Fritz Perls (gestalt therapy), Virginia Satir (family therapy), and Milton Erickson (hypnotherapy). NLP programming quickly grew in popularity from the outset as it presented the central structures of successful human communication. This approach was immediately recognized in many fields such as education, therapy, management, and health and by other areas where the need for personal development and change was evident.

With new technology has come undisputable knowledge of how the human mind works. Hypnosis has been proven to be a useful tool in medical and psychological treatment. Brain scans show specific functions of the brain in a trance. The battle between scientists to find the exact mechanism showing how the human mind work continues. However, there is no doubt about the benefits of hypnotherapy in many disciplines from medicine to psychology to goal achievement. Now, we all can benefit from this knowledge and use the potential of our brains to improve health, performance, and creativity. Unfortunately, many of us are still fearful of experiencing a hypnotic trance even when we show curiosity about it. I hope my book will change your view on hypnosis so you can benefit from this normal state of mind.

Two

Gift from the Universe—the Mind

> There is a power and ruling force, which pervades and rules the boundless universe. You are part of this power.
>
> Prentice Mulford (1834–1891)

I would like to begin this chapter by expressing gratitude to Mother Nature for her most remarkable gift to all—the human mind. We all have different beliefs on the origin of the mind. Some believe it comes from God or the universe; others believe it is a product of evolution. It is normal that we take the processes of the mind for granted because we are not aware of them; they are automatic and protect us when we are asleep or awake without our conscious involvement. A more fascinating fact is that our mind is working on many different levels, one of these levels being trance, known commonly as hypnosis. Here the confusion starts, as hypnotic trance can be a scary concept for many and tends to conjure up images of a person "controlled" by someone else. This couldn't be farther from the truth.

Therefore, it is my pleasure to introduce you to the concepts of hypnosis so that you can enjoy all the benefits trance has to offer. Once you are more familiar with hypnosis and its associated terms, for example "trance and hypnotic suggestion," you may find it useful to practise self-hypnosis on a regular basis to improve your physical and mental health and boost your self-value and achievements within a short span of time.

In fact, hypnotic trance is not scary or dangerous. It is a natural state of mind which increases our learning ability and creativity and helps to maintain a healthy balance of mind and body. Unfortunately, despite the scientific proof of the safety and positive benefits of hypnosis in medical and psychological conditions, many of us are still reluctant to seek out medical hypnosis when we are looking for professional help.

Scientific research clearly indicates that there are very strong connections between the body's functions and the processes of the mind. This means that our thoughts and emotions can make physiological changes to our body function and vice versa. A simple example of this would be how our blood pressure and heart rate increase under stress and how they decrease amid conditions of relaxation.

This means that we can make both positive and negative changes to our health and to any aspect of our lives just by following our thoughts and emotions, which accordingly will influence our choices.

The question is, are we making the right choices? The facts show that we do not always make the right choices. Every day we see drastic examples of people losing control over their life's path, making wrong decisions which may damage their personal and family life.

Learning to feel good about yourself and having the feeling of being in control of your life can help you to stay focused on what is important to you. When you are open-minded, you are in a better position to see facts, not what you want to see in desperation, and to spot more options when facing difficult situations. By ceasing to worry, you will be on the right path to finding better coping strategies to overcome obstacles and prevent disaster. Otherwise, you may choose to live passively or in an illusion, exposing yourself to whatever life or others may bring to you, without having any control over it.

Making decisions in a rush without asking the question "Is it good for me?" or "Can I cope with all the consequences?" is familiar to many of us. We may be surprised by how quickly all our bridges collapse when we do this, leaving us with destroyed relationships, career, health, or finances. Sad to say, many of us have the tendency to repeat this mistake over and over again without learning from it.

The worst thing that we can allow to happen in our lives is to let the misfortune dance with us round and round. It is like trying to find the right rhythm to someone else's music and wondering why we aren't dancing to our favourite song. To have the freedom to make decisions and move in the right direction, it is necessary to stop the old music and start dancing to the music of your choice.

We now know that there is no need to block ourselves from having a rewarding life no matter what our current situation is. We all can learn to have a more satisfying life, be happier, and begin to be proud of our achievements. However, such positive changes must come from inside us. Our mind gives us the opportunity to make that choice. Good fortune stemming from "luck" is of short duration and never provides real satisfaction. Frequently we witness that people who have won millions on the lottery, although the money helps them to lead a more comfortable life for some time, do not necessarily see a change in the miserable lives they experienced before they won the money.

We have a choice: we can be miserable all the time and complain about our misfortune, or we can appreciate everything we have, create more of it, and enjoy life to the fullest.

Despite our different experiences and expectations, at the end of the day we all are looking for love, respect, and security. No matter how dark your past experiences are or what you want to accomplish, you can find the light and go towards it, or recover from a fall and start the journey again to reach your desired destination.

Knowing how to access your mind's potential by "tapping into the unconscious mind's resources," will help you to maintain a healthy balance between mind and body, control emotions, and increase creativity and performance.

Respecting yourself and others is second only to love, the powerful key to life mastery. Gratitude and good communication are a close third. By taking even the smallest step to make a change to an unwanted situation, you automatically open the door to many new opportunities. With time you will start to feel more confident and better able to do more every day to make a better tomorrow.

We can make a habit of adding something to somebody else's life. This is the most powerful feeling that a human being can experience. If all of us were willing to make just one positive change every day, even a very small one such as smiling at a stranger, then more than half our problems and stressful situations would just vanish by themselves.

So, let's find out what science says about hypnosis and the unconscious mind now, to remove the rusty false beliefs about hypnosis and gain the freedom to efficiently learn new skills that will help us make better choices.

Three

The Conscious Mind and the Unconscious Mind - What's the Difference?

Conscious was an essential component of everything that was mental or awareness of person mental state.

René Descartes

It would be difficult to understand the whole process of hypnosis without a basic knowledge of the structure of the human mind, which in the simplest explanation is made up of the conscious mind and the unconscious mind. The common fear is that the unconscious mind will "steal" our control.

For many of us, the unconscious mind is firmly connected with Sigmund Freud's practice of hypnosis at the beginning of the twentieth century. Despite his deep dedication, his controversial early work on the metaphorical unconscious mind with psychiatric patients left deep scars on the hypnotic phenomenon itself. Many of us to this day have negative images of the function of the unconscious mind.

Despite this, interest in the capabilities of the unconscious mind has existed throughout human history, especially in the medical profession. This is reflected in extensive research for more clues worldwide. The persistence of many medical practitioners started to bear fruit in the twentieth century, when science proved that the unconscious mind's potential could be successfully utilized to improve mental and physical health and human performance. Therefore, I present medical hypnosis and its benefits in a simple way to help you unblock the false beliefs about this natural tool that we all have.

Mind processes are very complex. We all have the ability to receive information from outside and inside the body. We are capable of filtering, memorizing, analysing, and selecting this information according to our needs and beliefs. We are able to visualize and imagine the past, present, and future. We have the capacity to learn new skills in order to secure constant growth and increase our coping strategies, survival skills, and creativity.

The terms conscious mind and unconscious mind together make up a useful metaphor for scientists to present the different states of the function of the human mind. Frequently the mind is compared to an iceberg with the tip of the iceberg above the surface of the water being the conscious mind and the bulky part beneath the water's surface representing the unconscious mind.

In the simplest structure, the brain has two main parts called hemispheres, which are different in their functions. The left hemisphere contains the conscious mind processes which develop along with our experiences with language, logic, and reality. The conscious mind allows us to be aware of who we are and of our surroundings and enables us to communicate with others. Its functions are in planning and judgement. For example, say you have an exciting idea for a business, but your conscious mind cools you down by thinking, "Ah, maybe it is not as good as I think." The conscious mind analyses what is good or bad for us and critically assesses any situation as a protective mechanism to eliminate threats to our comfort or safety. The conscious mind can only process a few things at a time. Therefore, when we are receiving a great deal of information all at the same time, our conscious will become preoccupied and more selective with regard to incoming information in order to concentrate on what is most important at that time.

However, when the conscious mind is overloaded with too much information for a long time, this condition may lead to mental conflict, for example confusion, irrational thinking, nervous breakdown, and addiction. A typical example is when we are overstretched with duties for a long time without a break. If this is not corrected, then more serious mental conditions such as depression and psychosis can develop.

In contrast, the right hemisphere involves unconscious processes which aim to protect and maintain our automatic body and mind processes. The unconscious mind controls automatic muscle movements and organ function (e.g. we are not aware of our heartbeat unless we pay attention to it). The unconscious mind processes also involve imagery, creativity, visualization, and goal achievement using very simple symbolic images. If we experience total silence for a considerably long time, our unconscious mind may create hallucinations to keep the balance in information processing. This is frequently experienced when someone is isolated for a long time, for example being held hostage. Such hallucination can be a survival tool for many.

The unconscious governs the automatic processes of everything that we learn, our well-mastered skills, from walking and reading to professional expertise. On the other hand, it also keeps us entrenched in automatic responses such as engaging in unwanted habits, repeating a negative thought pattern, making the same mistakes, living with phobias, repeatedly losing control over our actions, or maintaining bad habits such as nail biting.

Our life experiences are stored in the unconscious mind in the form of so-called "state bond memory", presented by Ernest Rossi, and the inner resources associated with these experiences may or may not be available to us at present and future times. Deep unconscious contents of the memory may be available to the conscious mind under different mental conditions, one of these being a trance. This means that everything we learn and experience is stored in our memory, and our memories are strongly associated with the emotional state of mind we had at the time of experiencing the related events. When we face similar situations, these memories will serve as a guide to dealing with things in a similar way (whether beneficial to us or not, depending on how we understand the experience).

All our past experiences are part of our precious inner resources for the present and for the future. It is like having an inner wisdom box which we can use anytime we need to deal effectively with similar events. When we are in trance, we are closer to the unconscious mind and have an opportunity to reach these inner resources more easily and search them to come up new ideas and solutions according to our needs. These past experiences stored in the memory can be reached easier during trance because the critical aspect of the conscious mind is temporarily on the side line.

For example, a very pleasant experience of meeting someone may be associated with the specific fragrance or music present during that meeting. In future, when we hear the same music or smell the same scent, we recall the pleasant feeling we experienced at that time.

However, sometimes the experience may be interpreted in a way that is not beneficial to us. The past bad experiences may be blocked, leading to poor or irrational reactions in similar situations in future. To have better outcomes in a similar situation, we need to change the way we deal with these experiences. For example, the fear experienced in the presence of someone in particular may be associated with the smell of cigarettes we perceived initially. In future, the same odour in any situation may bring back the feeling of fear, even if there is no danger present. A person can be stuck with such memories associated with that odour and have problems feeling safe in places with the smell of cigarettes.

In such a case, psychotherapy would be indicated to unblock such an association (the smell of cigarettes with being physically hurt) so as to allow the person to feel safe in all situations where there is the odour of cigarettes. This can be done by way of classic therapy, or it can be done much more quickly and with longer-lasting benefit by way of trance and unlinking the experience from the odour in the unconscious mind. More on this later.

It is important to recognize that what we have learned and experienced in the past has an influence on how we handle life events, (whether good or bad) in the present. These past experiences may be our greatest assets for now and in the future, or they may be our biggest enemy, trapping us in the past and preventing from moving forward.

However, with the beauty of our mind we can learn, unlearn, and relearn strategies to cope better with our constantly changing environment. We have the capacity to create, and the freedom to choose, better ways of dealing with unfamiliar situations. We can deal with these things in a calm manner instead of letting our life experiences cause us frustration, anger, or disappointment.

Learning new skills or unlearning undesired habits involves both conscious and unconscious processes. Some classic examples are walking, writing, brushing one's teeth, swimming, and driving—and any behaviour we do without thinking about it first.

Classic Learning Process

First Step: Unconscious Incompetence

Unconsciously we do not know that we don't know. Take learning to play the piano for example. The first tunes we play are chaotic, not in a sequence.

Second Step: Conscious Incompetence

This is the time when we consciously learn step by step and make mistakes. With practice, we put two tunes together, and then a third, and then the next one to make a melody, slowly but consistently.

Third Step: Conscious Competence

At this stage we improve the performance with practice. We start to enjoy playing, but we are still controlling the process by thinking how to do it right.

Fourth Step: Unconscious Competence

This is when the performance is well-accomplished. It happens when we start playing well and enjoy it without thinking about it.

It shows that we all use conscious/unconscious processes constantly without recognizing it. In hypnosis, the learning process is simplified as new ideas can be accepted directly by the unconscious mind. Information processes in the unconscious mind occur automatically without conscious involvement. This is the key element in therapy to make a desired change. If we want to learn a new pattern of behaviour or change bad habits, psychotherapy offers the classic pattern of unlearning old patterns first and learning new behaviour by way of repetition in the conscious mind until the actions become automatic to the unconscious mind.

The unconscious mind has greater potential than the conscious mind for processing all the information from the outside and the inside world. Relearning behaviours and learning new skills is quicker when the unconscious mind is directly involved. Once the new idea is accepted by the unconscious mind, a person will act automatically without the conscious mind having to be involved.

However, the unconscious mind does not recognize what is right or wrong. It simply follows your thoughts, emotions, and suggestions. Therefore, it is important to know the dominant thoughts, emotions, and suggestions you are exposing yourself to. This issue will be discussed in greater depth in the next chapters.

The mind and body must be in balance if one is to keep mentally and physically fit and if one is to be prevented us being exhausted and confused. When we feel good, there is no need to withdraw from the beauty of this world. It is natural that we enjoy the wonder of living.

However, to benefit from the great potential of our mind, both the conscious and the unconscious must cooperate to secure our health and security. In fact, they can work separately, or they can work together to some extent via a network of connections between them. Although there is communication between these two parts of the mind, some information may be exchanged only in a hypnotic trance.

If both parts of the mind are working together in harmony, then everything is in balance. When there is a conflict between the conscious and unconscious mind, it may lead to problems with both physical and mental health. Typical examples are living a passive life, actively engaging in an addiction, and practising bad habits.

Now we have the knowledge how to use both our conscious and unconscious processes more efficiently and increase our potential to reach our goals, from health to sports achievement.

Following is an example of initiating metal processes on the unconscious mind to reach a desired goal supported by strong emotions.

Reinforcing a Desire by Way of Strong Emotions

A particular eight-year-old girl from a hard-working family in the 1960s had little chance of going to a university. She had a very strong bond with her grandpa, who was unable to walk because of a severe illness. The two of them spent a lot of time in the garden, sitting on a bench in the shadow of an old apple tree. He was a master of telling fantastic stories. One day the girl cried when her grandpa struggled to take a few steps to get back home. Deeply distressed, she said, "I am going to be a doctor, and I will fix your legs." At the age of twenty-three, she completed her medical studies and started her scientific career.

The little girl's strong desire associated with deep emotional distress reached her unconscious mental processes. This suggestion was accepted directly by the unconscious mind, which initiated the automatic search for resources to reach the desired goal. She was able to sense all opportunities along her way for many years to accomplish her goal, and she never considered any other career. Her determination was so strong that no one and nothing could stop her from reaching her goal, despite a lot of obstacles and different advice along the way. Her unconscious search was unshaken, as she knew what she wanted, despite others' disbelief that she could not do it. What seemed to be almost impossible became reality.

In the next chapters, you will find how it is possible to reach a goal by embedding it in the unconscious mind so that you can follow those steps to achieve your goals, whatever they may be.

Four

Hypnotic Phenomena

> What this power is I cannot say; all I know is that it exists.
>
> Alexander Graham Bell (1847–1922)

The same can be said about hypnosis, during which we have closer contact with the unconscious mind. Neuropsychological studies in the twenty and twenty-first centuries brought remarkable new discoveries. Finally hypnotic phenomena are intensively studied and practised around the world. Academic studies proved the effectiveness and safety of medical hypnosis to facilitate many medical treatments, increase self-healing processes, speed up recovery from illness or injuries, treat mental disorders, and improve human performance.

So, what is behind this mystical "devil" of hypnosis?

Hypnosis in the original Greek means "sleep", but hypnosis is not sleep. It is not relaxation or meditation either. The imprecise name "hypnosis" has been used for such a long time that professionals decided to use this terminology for purposes of better communication when describing the particular state of mind of the trance. To make this whole issue easier to understand, I will describe the process of hypnosis in a simple way.

Professionals refer to hypnosis when discussing the treatment (medical hypnosis) or scientific research into hypnotic trance. However, for many people hypnosis may be confused with meditation or a relaxed state of mind, especially because many lay hypnotists and unprofessional therapists frequently avoid the word "hypnosis" so as not to scare the client. Hetero-hypnosis is when a person experiences hypnotic trance guided by another person. It may be a professional skilled person, a scientist, or a lay practitioner doing the guiding. In a medical centre, it is always registered professional who is using a set of specific suggestions (induction or cues) to help the subject experience hypnotic trance. The aim of this procedure is to enhance psychological therapy or medical treatment, obtain desired changes, or work on a goal.

Self-hypnosis is a process whereby one enters hypnotic trance by oneself. It can be initiated by verbal suggestion, visualization, imagery, physical touch, or sound cues without help from another person.

The brain functions are different in each of these states. This has been clearly shown on brain scans and other neurological tests. The mind works in a specific pattern according to the situations the subject is facing, such as high arousal; deep concentration; problem-solving; coping; relaxing; trance with its increased creativity, imagery, and resourceful states; and finally sleep.

An EEG of the brain shows different wave frequencies related to particular states of mind;

- Beta waves (14–28 cycles per second) occur in the normal, waking state of mind.
- Alpha waves (9–14 cycles per second) occur during relaxation and increase visualization and creativity.
- Theta waves (4–8 cycles per second) occur in trance during an unconscious state of mind with deep relaxation and mental clarity, enabling the reduction of pain and an increase in creative thinking and performance.
- Delta waves (1–4 cycles per second) occur during sleep.

Because the word "trance" causes goose bumps for many people, I would like to present the official scientific definition of a trance.

Definition of a Trance by University College London (UCL)

According to Michael Heap, clinical psychologist at Sheffield University,

"Trance is a waking state, in which our attention is detached from the immediate environment, there is a narrow focusing attention, and we are more open to suggestions. During a hypnotic trance, the conscious mind is preoccupied with focusing on outside information. Unconscious is more open and ready to accept the suggestion, without criticism from the conscious mind."

Official Formula of the British Society of Clinical and Academic Hypnosis.

Dr Michael Heap of Sheffield University said the following:

> Hypnosis—
>
> Facilitates the expression in conscious of cognitive activities (memories, thoughts, ideas, fantasies, affect), by relaxing the constraints on what is to be granted such expression at any time of free association, guided imagery, some form of meditation. This allows for greater availability of information, which may be more opposite to the situation, problem or task in hand which is habitually given priority for consciousness (creative problem solving, brainstorming, Erickson's idea of suspending one's habitual frame of reference).
>
> Facilitates the conscious expression of cognitions that are habitually denied this because of fear, guilt, and extreme sadness, associated with them (any psychodynamic therapy).
>
> Facilitates the processing of cognitive information, which is not sufficiently in form, which allows clear representation in consciousness (insight).

There is an ongoing debate among scientists regarding the processes in hypnosis; some believe that trance is a natural state of mind, and others think that it is an altered state of mind. Although it is important for scientific researchers to find the real mechanism behind trance, for the reader it is important to know that we experience trance every day without being aware of it and that you can learn how to benefit from this experience in many aspects of your life.

Some examples of experiencing an altered state, or light trance-like state of mind, are when we are reading, watching a movie, or sitting on a garden bench during a warm summer day and letting our minds flow freely. We all know the saying, "Step outside and take time before making a decision."

Hypnosis is a state of mind that allows us to experience trance and receive suggestion. This state of mind is a combination of many normal psychological and physiological processes, which allow us to experience trance. Trance brings us closer to the unconscious mind. It gently decreases conscious analytical and judgemental interference but does not eliminate the conscious mind's functioning while in this state of mind. During trance there is a shift of brain processes more to the right hemisphere with some effects on the physiological function of the body and mind. From a medical perspective, hypnosis is known to reduce stress and pain and to increase mental clarity, imagination, creativity, and performance.

When in a trance, we can better communicate with our inner selves, assess our experiences (past and present) without judgement or fear, and look at the big picture from a different perspective.

When the conscious mind is preoccupied and deeply absorbed in some task, the unconscious mind is processing all the information coming in. We may experience many different depths of hypnotic trance, from a light to a very deep trance, depending on our needs and desires.

Because trance is a natural process of the human mind, we are in control of it the whole time. Moreover, trance can only be initiated and terminated by ourselves, contrary to many beliefs. Another person, for example a hypnotherapist, may only guide us to experience this particular state of mind by making carefully selected suggestions. However, we still have the control to accept or reject the suggestion according to our understanding of it, as you will learn in later chapters.

We all experience trance differently, and each trance is different. We all have unique life experiences stored in our unconscious mind, and our trance experiences will depend on our culture and environment. How we respond to the therapist during trance will depend on our trust level, our past experiences, and our beliefs, as well on the emotional state we have at the time.

Hypnotic trance is an excellent state of mind that allows us to keep working on our thoughts and emotions, to find the real meanings of our past and present experiences, and to learn from those experiences. We need this particular state of mind to find new resources and ideas to deal with present situations.

Furthermore, we all need trance states and contact with the unconscious mind on a regular basis to reach many forms of natural body and mind mechanisms in order to let the body rest, repair damage, and renew cells and in order to find ourselves. Therefore, I like to describe trance as a "comfortable inner port" where we can anchor to recharge our batteries, have access to resources from our "inner wisdom box," and reinforce the functions of the body and mind by positive and constructive suggestion.

It is important to remember that trance is not a therapy, as is commonly believed, but is something that facilitates treatment. In the hypnotic state we can improve the cooperation between different levels of mental processes, or separate them to some extent, to find solutions to ongoing problems from a different angle.

The aim of any therapy in the hypnotic state of mind is to create positive changes in our health, behaviour, and thinking patterns. This will increase the possibility of achieving our goals, unlearning habits and learning new habits, and bringing about other desired changes. During hypnotic trance, changes are unlearned and relearned directly in the unconscious mind. By practising simple psychological strategies for a few minutes while in a trance, you can start every day with enthusiasm to work towards your goals and then go to bed appreciative of a productive day and with a vision for a rewarding day tomorrow. This will help you to gain energy and motivation to get through difficult times.

In the next chapter, I will briefly describe the meaning of some features of hypnotic phenomena.

Five

Trance Features

> Hypnotherapy in practice involves a variety of psychological processes of the mind and phenomena such as compliance, selective attention, guided imagery, absorption, relaxation, dissociation, expectancy, role-playing, and attribution.
>
> Dr Michael Heap, Sheffield University

Many trance features may be quite a bizarre experience for us. To erase any ideas that there is "black magic" behind trance, I will explain some of the trance processes in a simple way.

Selective Attention

Selective attention, one of the main features of hypnotic trance, occurs when we concentrate intensely on one issue at one time. "I am talking to you, but you don't hear me" is a familiar scenario to many of us when we are trying to get the attention of someone who is deeply focused on a different subject.

For example, when we are walking, we can see many things on the way: mountains, ocean, passing people, etc. At the same time, we are in control of where we are going and what we are doing, without thinking about it. We have the ability to choose what to observe and what to ignore. However, when we see something unusual, for example a fire, it will focus our attention automatically. At that moment the broader picture of the place will fade away and we will focus on that event with curiosity. Which scenario catches our attention depends on whether what we are seeing is something new, unexpected, and of interest to us.

This ability of the unconscious mind is used in medical hypnosis to induce trance so the subject may process the carefully selected therapeutic suggestion within the unconscious mind to achieve the desired change in patient thinking, behaviour, or body function.

Dissociation

In trance, there is a separation between the function of the conscious and unconscious mind to some extent. This process is known as dissociation. Scientists explain the process of separation in different ways. The most popular theory of dissociation is called "hidden observer," presented by Hilgard (1977), in which some part of the mind is "observing" trance experiences the whole time as an independent part of the mind.

According to this theory, when we experience trance, we are still in control of what's happening to us through our inner observer, and we can make decisions to stay in this state of mind or not. We can accept what is comfortable for us and reject any suggestion presenting danger or doubts about our comfort. This issue will be dealt with in more detail in the Chapter 6.

Dissociation is one of the main features of trance and is a very powerful tool in physical pain control and psychotherapy, especially when dealing with painful memories from the past. During a hypnotic trance, it is possible to re-experience both bad and good past events in a dissociated way. When recalling traumatic experiences, the subject can be detached from the uncomfortable emotions, making it easier to work on the problem. Without attached emotions, we can look at past unpleasant experiences in a more mature way, see the facts from a different perspective, learn from them, and make positive changes according to the meaning of these experiences.

On the other hand, the mind gives us the ability to associate experiences with our good memories from the past and use them for present needs. We can also learn from good memories, which may be a priceless therapeutic asset. It is possible to build a personal portfolio of positive constructive memories and effective coping and problem-solving strategies in order to use them as a reference to find a solution to a new problem. For example, we can recall an experience when we felt relaxed and calm during a class speech years ago and re-experience this feeling during a present important presentation.

Physiological Changes in Hypnotic Trance

Trance entails some physiological sensations and body experiences. The most common among these are muscle relaxation and slowed breathing, heart rate, and digestion. Body changes include different sensations and eye closure, fluttering, and watering. These conditions are safe and comfortable and are used to make desired changes such as relaxation of the body and mind and improved blood flow, heart rate, salivation, gastrointestinal function, and respiratory function according to patient condition and needs.

Catalepsy

This feature is one of the mystical elements of hypnosis. In fact, it is easy to explain from a physiological point of view as an inhibition of voluntary motion. It happens because in trance there is a feeling of deep relaxation and dissociation from the body, and the person may be reluctant to make voluntary movements and follow suggestions. In trance, natural and automatic processes occur, such as letting go, and because there is no critical aspect of conscious mind present, it is possible to obtain involuntary responses from a person in a trance. For example, the well-known hypnotic arm elevation, or arm catalepsy, is commonly used by stage hypnotists and scientists in clinical fields. In rare cases, it is used to induce trance, as well as to prove to the patient that he or she can influence his or her body by way of mind function in trance.

Analgesia

Analgesia is one of the most beneficial elements of hypnosis used in medicine. In trance, it is possible to make changes in sensation. It is possible to reduce pain or, when necessary, to create or increase pain, which is very useful for research purposes. Above all, it is used to teach the patient effective pain coping strategies for use at home. There are many different effective hypnotic approaches to dealing with both acute and chronic pain, which we will discuss later.

Amnesia

Amnesia is a mental process and another trance feature which people are afraid of. Although it is possible that a person in a trance may experience amnesia following hypnotic suggestion, it is a reversible process. Mostly this phenomenon is of great benefit for very specific therapeutic purposes (for example to ease posttraumatic suffering) and is useful in laboratory research. Whatever the reason, it is applied only with a person's full awareness.

Time Distortion

In hypnotic trance, there is a time distortion. Time may seem to slow down or speed up. We all know the feeling when we are waiting for an important message and the time seems to slow down, or when we are busy with a certain task and time appears to fly by. Time distortion is a very practical approach used in many psychological situations to help the subject to relax, clarify his or her thoughts, concentrate, etc.

Trance Logic

Trance logic is a state of mind where reasoning is different from what it is in the waking state. What would be impossible and illogical in a waking state may be possible during a trance. For example, the idea that you can fly may not be logical in an awake state, but in a trance, it is easy to imagine yourself, for example, as a child and experience such events as real. In such a case, the person is willing to undergo the transformation in time. Although it may sound a little scary, trance logic is a pleasant and safe tool used in hypnotherapy to help the patient go through the therapeutic experience, which is beneficial for many medical and psychological reasons. It is used to create therapeutic mental fantasies, induce deep relaxation, or find a solution to an ongoing situation without conscious judgemental influence.

Age Regression

In trance, it is possible to recall experiences from the past for therapeutic purposes. For example, the suggestion may be, "Go back in time to the age of six." It is possible to ask the person to travel back in time and experience past events, both positive and negative. This is useful in recovering good memories and experiences, as these can be very helpful in similar present and future situations. Moreover, such positive memories can be reinforced in a hypnotic trance and serve as future assets to deal with new experiences.

However, we should know that recovered memory during hypnotic trance does not necessarily represent the real facts of that experience. Therefore, memories recovered in a hypnotic trance are not be admissible in court as evidence in legal cases. However, reflection on trance memories might have great therapeutic value in helping the subject to find the different meanings of past experiences.

Age Progression

The ability to imagine the future is a very useful tool in therapy to make long-lasting changes in thinking, behaviour, and beliefs and to rehearse them for the future. This technique is used to check the progress of treatment and goal achievement. Age progression is used to guide the person to use the imagination and go into the future, for example, "See yourself the way you want to see yourself in future."

In trance, the person can move forwards and backwards in time because relaxation is deep and imagination and visualization is vivid.

Different scientists explain these phenomena in different ways. Some believe that our unconscious mind has the potential to predict the future. If this is so, then it is likely to be based on our experiences, beliefs, and desires.

Hallucinations

Hallucinations are for many of us the most bizarre among the significant features of hypnotic trance. However, knowing these natural phenomena helps us to recognize the unlimited abilities of our mind and body, as well the connection between them. Hallucinations can be positive or negative according to the suggestion applied. The different types are as follows:

- Auditory hallucination is when the person hears sound in the absence of any noise or does not recall sounds in the presence of noise. This is useful in therapy and in assessing the person's hypnotic ability and response to suggestion.
- Visual hallucination is when the person sees something that is not present or vice versa.
- Olfactory hallucination is when the person can smell something when such odour is not present, and vice versa. It is used in therapy to stop bad habits, for example smoking.
- Kinetic hallucination is when the person receives the suggestion to feel or not to feel some sensation. This is useful in pain control of any kind. It is also useful in cases of increased sensitivity, especially in children.

All the foregoing features are safe and very useful in medical hypnosis for the research, treatment, and/or prevention of many medical and psychological conditions. Other main mind processes such as visualization, imagination, and unconscious resources will be discussed separately in the following chapters.

Six

Hypnotic Suggestion

> Words can kill or heal. We have the power to accept or reject words.

The second major feature of medical hypnosis is suggestion received during trance. Trance without specific suggestion lets the mind to flow effortlessly. We are more familiar with this state of mind as meditation.

Many people believe that a harmful suggestion can be used during hypnosis to manipulate the hypnotized person. I have to say that those who believe this may be right and that those who don't believe it are right as well. It points to the most important question about suggestion in general, not only hypnotic suggestion. It is our ability to assess and make decisions which causes us to accept or reject suggestions as to everyday experiences.

To help the reader better understand this complex matter, I will present the facts about suggestion in general, and hypnotic suggestion and suggestibility in particular, throughout this book. Let's start with the official definition of suggestibility.

"Suggestibility is an individual person's ability to respond to suggestion."

The power of suggestion was recognized by religions and other authorities for centuries to gain power and control, both in positive and negative ways. A classic example of a widely accepted suggestion was the belief that a solar eclipse was a punishment from God. Nowadays people are more aware of the facts of a solar eclipse.

Any suggestion carries with it the possibility of bringing something positive or negative along with it or it could be received as meaningless.

Only by understanding the real meaning of suggestion and how it fits with our needs, we can we make a rational decision about it. The general rule is that only we have the power to decide which suggestions are good for us, and only we can make the decision which suggestions to accept or reject. It operates on the same principle as any other suggestion, regardless of where we are exposed to it—in a doctor's office during trance, while on the Internet, when with a friend, or when encountering a stranger. We select and analyse suggestions on conscious and unconscious levels and make decisions depending on how useful the suggestion is to us and on our understanding of the suggestion at the time.

However, if one's personal and moral values are not strong enough, or if one has low self-confidence, such a person may be prone to more easily accepting harmful or negative suggestions made by manipulators. For example, a vulnerable teenager from an abusive home may be more prone to accept something irrational as using drugs or alcohol to feel better. Others may accept the harmful suggestion to do something illegal or inappropriate out of fear of rejection or bullying.

Many adults are victims of manipulators as well. Those feeling very lonely may be trapped in the false belief that suddenly someone is offering them true love, where logically there is no basis for a healthy relationship. A person may fall victim of someone else's irrational plans and empty promises, as you will see in chapters 68–71, on addictions. Many people irrationally follow the suggestions of some "miracle organization," some clan, or an unprofessional adviser acting only for purposes of their own gain.

Every day we witness people irrationally accepting a suggestion when looking for a "miracle solution" to a problem. A typical example is when someone buys a "miracle remedy" for weight control which has the unpleasant consequence of heart problems or other medical problems.

Contrary to that, we also witness positive suggestions being rejected by family members, friends, and patients especially in relation to health when a person lives in denial and refuses to make any change or accept any help. A typical example of this is the refusal to accept the suggestion to change an unhealthy diet or lifestyle. Some people refuse to protect themselves from abusers. Others reject the positive suggestion that they would be in a better position if only they were willing to learn new strategies to deal with life in a more effective way.

Frequently, people repeat the same mistakes with the same negative results and still refuse to make any change to find a better way to do things.

You will find more on why we do this in Part II.

In fact, trance increase the ability to accept suggestions, which is a positive tool for medical and psychological treatment. And suggestion can induce a light trance. For example, we can be deeply involved in a discussion that we find interesting and detach ourselves from that issue.

Therefore, it is not a suggestion or a trance that we should be worried about but how confident we are to say yes or no to any suggestion made by those close to us, by our schoolmates, by our workmates, or by a stranger. What we accept or reject depends on our mental stability, moral values, and belief of what is good and what is bad.

However, the suggested idea is accepted only if it is believable to the person in a waking state and if it is in harmony with that person's interests. For example, if someone were to suggest that you jump into the ocean but you cannot swim, in a normal situation you would refuse to accept that suggestion. However, if you were an athlete and your goal was to win a gold medal in an Olympic competition, you may find the idea of practising in the ocean reasonable and beneficial to improving your skill as a swimmer.

In medical hypnosis, the purpose of using therapeutic suggestion is to obtain desired changes in thinking and behaviour, improve body function, and learn new skills according to patient needs. Specific suggestions are used to initiate trance, access the unconscious mind's inner resources, increase creativity, initiate desired changes during and after therapy, and end the trance.

The main benefit of hypnosis is that the therapeutic suggestion applied in a hypnotic trance is processed mostly with a little conscious judgement. An accepted suggestion in hypnosis, for example, "Stay calm," will be executed automatically. It is like muscle memory, for example when muscles hold the racket when playing tennis without thinking which muscle to use first. We simply hold the racket.

Say you are good swimmer. You will be able to swim until some drastic change happens, such as near-drowning or injury, to prevent you from swimming because of the fear that it may happen again. Such conditions (fear) can be changed by way of proper suggestion during hypnotherapy to remove the blocking element of fear and apply new suggestions, for example the benefits of swimming, directly to the unconscious mind.

Medical hypnosis should be carried out only by fully registered medical or psychological professionals. If you have a stomach problem, you wouldn't go to a witch doctor for advice, would you? But some people do; they reject a professional's suggestion and accept a nonprofessional's, for example another irrational diet. In any such case it is a personal choice. The possibility of misconduct by professionals during hypnosis is very rare, about the same as in any professional field without trance, so you should know that you are in a good hands.

In Part II, you will learn how to protect yourself from a harmful suggestion from outside as well as from negative autosuggestions. You will learn how to build your strength to make better choices with confidence.

Types of Hypnotic Suggestion

It may be of interest to those readers who want to self-hypnotize to know that there are different forms of hypnotic suggestion. Any one suggestion is carefully chosen by the practitioner according to his or her preferences. Following are examples of common suggestions used in medical and psychological hypnosis:

- Direct suggestion—"Close your eyes."
- Indirect suggestion—"Some people choose to close their eyes for better concentration."
- Positive suggestion—"You can relax your mind and body now."
- Authoritarian suggestion—"You will stay calm."
- Permissive suggestion—"You may close your eyes when focusing if you wish."

Hypnotic Induction

Hypnotic induction is a series of hypnotic suggestions made to initiate an experience of trance. There are many different hypnotic induction methods. Hypnotic inductions may be short or long, slow or rapid. Most of them focus on deep relaxation, breathing, and feeling well, directing the subject's awareness to his or her inner sensations, perceptions, thoughts, emotions, and memories.

Some hypnotic inductions are more traditional in style. For example, authoritative inductions, commonly used until the mid-twentieth century, use a direct form of suggestion. Many of us still have the old image of hypnosis where the hypnotist uses a chain watch, a pendulum, or another device to "put someone to sleep." However, these old traditional methods are not used in modern professional therapy. In fact, there are cases where there is no need to use a formal induction process to enter a trance, for example with children or with people who have certain medical conditions.

Types of Hypnotherapy

All the features of trance and suggestion are used as tools in the treatment of medical and psychological conditions and in any discipline where change is required in body function, behaviour, thinking, emotions, or creativity. As was mentioned earlier, an unconscious automatic process governs our body functions and controls our well-conditioned skills and habits. Therefore, if we want to change some of these things, we need be aware of them first, before learning the new automatic behaviour. This fact is used in medical hypnosis for the treatment of particular conditions or to enable a person to learn new skills in the unconscious mind according to one's needs and wishes.

In medical, psychological, or dental hypnosis, trance and suggestions are used to initiate positive psychological and physiological therapeutic changes. Hypnosis is used safely in human performance, sport, business, art, and many other disciplines.

In clinical sessions, patient and practitioner will agree on the suggestions leading to obtaining the desired goals. The practitioner may use direct suggestion, meaning that the patient passively accepts what to do to obtain the desired change.

These days, a naturalistic style of induction, introduced by the famous psychiatrist Milton Erickson, is much more popular. This style of induction and hypnotherapy is more permissive and doesn't require a formal hypnotic induction and "mystical rituals" to initiate trance. In this type of therapy, indirect suggestions are used to tap into the resources of the unconscious mind. This means that the patient must play an active part in searching for the best solution to his or her problem. The number of Erickson's followers increased rapidly around the world, ushering in a new era of medical hypnosis.

Which method is better?

Both are very powerful and effective. Each type of induction and therapy does the job and should be selected according to the personal preferences of the therapist and the patient.

A good practitioner will choose the style of suggestion and therapy which is more familiar and useful to the patient. We all have preferences, and everyone will experience the induction and therapy in different ways. Some will prefer the authoritative approach, just following the suggestions; others will fancy a more active style which stimulates the unconscious mind. I hope that knowing these facts about hypnotherapy will help you to feel more confident when discussing your preferences with a practitioner, if one choose to experience this state of mind.

Part II

Inner Healing Powers

In this section, you will learn what medical and psychological science has to say about the natural self-healing mechanisms of the body and mind. I present the placebo phenomenon, and the power of hypnotic therapeutic suggestion on the initiation of diseases and on healing processes.

You will learn how our beliefs, thinking patterns, emotions, imagination, visualization, and creativity can influence both the healing process and psychological changes.

Seven

Mind and Body Healing Reversal System

> Face towards the perfect image of every organ and the shadows of disease will never touch you.
>
> Robert Collier (1886–1950)

One of the most appealing presentations of the self-healing processes is by clinical psychologist E. L. Rossi (1986). In his book *Mind-Body Communication in Hypnosis*, he cites research from many medical centres explaining the connection between mind and body and how they influence each other's functions.

Deep interest in self-healing and "miracle cures" has been evident since human history began. The same is true of "evil spells" and "deadly suggestion." Belief in a connection with God and the universe is a shared reference point in group therapies and individual self-healing. Pilgrimages and healers still attract millions of people around the world.

The Bible describes many miracle healings, pointing that unconditional love and blessings have given hope and strength to millions of sufferers for more than two thousand years. Clinicians have witnessed and analysed miracle cures, such as returning to life after clinical death and making a full recovery from leukaemia, multiple sclerosis, and other serious medical and mental problems, and have no problem showing a scientific basis for these things.

In many of these cases, people report adopting a mind-set that they are healthy or using imagery to destroy the illness. Any form of belief in supernatural powers has the same history; naturally, we want to believe that there is a form of higher power to protect and save us.

In the last three decades, scientists have presented more evidence that brain processes can influence body function and that body function may create changes in our moods and mental condition. This means that our mental processes can initiate both the healing process and the malfunction of our body.

One of the greatest discoveries of the connection between the mind and body was by Ivan Pavlov, a Russian scientist who observed increased salivation in dogs triggered by the sound of a bell. This was the result of repetition, leading to a conditioning process between the mind and the body: the sound of a bell gave rise to the memory of feeding, which caused salivation without food being present.

The same type of thing happens when we think about lemons: our salivary glands create saliva when we see a lemon or smell one. We all know that listening to our favourite music; participating in aromatherapy or massage; watching an interesting movie; or simply hearing a kind word from another person make us feel better. In a similar way, our inner thoughts and the words or visual imagery we use are very powerful and have the capacity to initiate physiological changes or healing responses in our body organs.

Recent studies in immunology and pathology clearly show an active reversal process between the mind and body function. Genetics and biology research has brought new discoveries proving that genetic defects can be prevented or corrected, contrary to long-held belief.

The connections between mind and body processes are supported by anatomy and physiology and by extensive neuropsychological research. There is no doubt now that body processes, both physiological and pathological, are influenced by the mind processes via the nervous, hormonal, and immune systems and biochemistry. These facts may explain many "miracle healings" and well-documented cases of recovery from severe illnesses. What scientists are looking for is the exact mechanism of healing and what boosts and inhibits these natural processes of healing.

For me, the most important aspect is that recent scientific facts on healing are in line with all these spiritual and cultural beliefs, as well as with the laws of physics. This means that we can connect and use unconscious and conscious mind processes more effectively. From there, it is up to our imagination and beliefs, to where and with whom we are, and/or to how we are connecting to God, the universe, energy, or the mind with its unlimited unknown processes.

In fact, healing processes are working all the time. Every day we can observe the powers of self-healing and the function of the immune system and other protective processes. For example, bleeding from a cut stops itself within minutes, the wound closes within a few days, and the skin cells renew systematically. Viral infection heals within a few days, and bruises disappear within days. Fractured bones seal themselves (the surgeon only places the ends of the broken bone in the right position). What we don't know yet is how the mind exactly does these things, but we know that it happens.

However, we know now that medical hypnosis can increase our self-healing mechanisms and prevent many diseases and mental conditions. Now you have an opportunity to learn how to increase your self-healing processes and improve your physical and mental health. (See more about this in Section III.)

Power of Placebo Phenomenon

The placebo effect has been known for a long time in clinical scenarios as well as in the movies. Again it works in both directions: it can initiate the healing process or cause pathological changes.

Placebos make up 50–60 per cent of any healing process. This is a strong evidence of how powerful our beliefs are in initiating either healing or disease.

We all are exposed to stressful situations from time to time. There will be times when we are more vulnerable and might be trapped, feeling hopeless, disappointed, or frustrated. We all could be metaphorically lost at sea, desperately looking for lights indicating that land is close. But believing that we have an inner power to make positive changes will help us to stay healthy.

Other important factors that influence the healing process are motivation and determination to recover. Some patients will not show signs of recovery because they no longer see happiness in their lives. If a person's mind is filled with negative thoughts about illness and recovery, then the healing power of his or her body will be inhibited, and deterioration in health will soon follow.

Another reason for poor recovery is the secondary gain from being sick. Such an attitude may not be truly recognized in the conscious mind by some patients. The reason for such beliefs may involve physical or emotional burnout, seeking an escape from overwhelming responsibility, seeking attention, or having better living conditions in the hospital than are present at home.

In contrast, those who are more optimistic and motivated to recover will look for any type of help to improve their condition. Believing that they are given a miracle medication, they have a much higher possibility of getting better due to higher expectations and a more positive mind-set that this will work.

There are many documented clinical cases of miraculous recovery without conventional treatment. All such patients used a mind-set ranging from removal from a stressful environment, to deep relaxation, to dietary changes, to the elimination of negative emotions and thoughts. There is increasing scientific proof and a common belief among clinicians and scientists that the strength of faith, optimism, self-belief, motivation, and determination is the main factor in the self-healing process.

Therefore, having balance between body and mind function is essential to good health. Using logic in everything we do is important too, as is the ability to control our emotions. This means that having a well-balanced diet, a positive attitude, an active lifestyle, and regular rest for the body and mind is crucial to staying healthy—not just empty words.

Contrary to this, ignoring signals from the body and mind (intuition) may bring unwanted results. Learning about recognizable natural body signals may be a matter of life and death, or a matter of having happiness versus a miserable life.

Medical hypnosis is a natural way of improving and maintaining healthy body and mind processes. It is pleasant and free from side effects. Some people have the ability to use their natural defensive mechanism and follow their intuition; others may have to learn how to increase the healing powers of their body and mind before they can follow the signals their body and mind send.

"I Am a Healthy Man"

My grandpa always was saying that he was well. He never saw a doctor throughout his whole life. However, he always paid a lot of attention to eating fresh, good-quality food, and every day he had a nap in the fresh air for at least thirty minutes. He never used any medication and believed without any doubt that he was perfectly healthy. He died of natural causes at the age of ninety-three.

Eight

Power of Healing Suggestion

> When the end has been suggested, the subconscious finds means for its finalization.

The power of healing suggestion has been recognized for centuries. Spells have been popular subjects for movies and books. Suggestion can change body and mind processes in both directions, good and bad. There are many well-documented cases of healing and pathological changes in the body initiated by a believable suggestion. Sudden pathological changes, even death, have been seen in many voodoo cases. For example, Ernest Rossi presents the case of rapid physiological changes in a healthy boy who responded to a spell cast by a witch doctor. There drastic changes in the body function put his life in danger until the spell was recalled, bringing all physiological functions back to normal within minutes. There was no other explanation except the boy's deep belief that the spell would work.

There is no doubt among scientists that the power of suggestion is one of the main features utilized in medical hypnotherapy. Moreover, a healing suggestion is effective when it is used in a hypnotic trance, as well as without hypnotic intervention. For example, reassuring loving words from a mother to a child in distress work as a magic pain reliever, don't they?

As I mentioned before, suggestion itself can lead to a weak trance. During hypnosis, suggestions aiming to cause the subject to make the necessary change in body and mind function are applied directly to the unconscious mind. When a healing suggestion is accepted, it will act automatically.

To reinforce the therapy, a posthypnotic suggestion is given to extend the effect of the hypnotic suggestion, for example, "From now on you will feel confident in any situation."

The process of healing via suggestion is based on well-known laws of suggestion.

Four Laws of Suggestion

Law of concentrated attention—the idea which tends to realize itself in this way is always the idea on which spontaneous attention is concentrated.

Law of auxiliary emotions—when the idea is enclosed in powerful emotions, it is more likely that the idea will be suggestively realized.

Law of reverse effort—when the idea exposes itself in the mind, so it raises all the conscious effort it can muster to counteract the suggestion, which will actually run counter to the subconscious wishes and tend to intensify the suggestion.

Law of subconscious teleology—when the end has been suggested, the unconscious finds the means for its realization.

This law of suggestion apparently indicates that when the desire is created in the unconscious mind, it will automatically put your attention to it and initiate the process of searching for the right information to accomplish the suggested goal. The searching process is reinforced by deep emotions, high motivation, and having a final date of accomplishment. Any other suggestion, especially a contradictory one, not only will be rejected or ignored but also will reinforce the unconscious idea. It means that in hypnosis the goal can be reached in a shorter time.

I would like to present a clinical case of full recovery after a severe heart attack by a patient who refused to accept the illness.

Positive Thinking and Recovery

A man of seventy-three suffered a severe heart attack, affecting more than 40 per cent of the heart muscle. At the time, he still was practising dentistry, playing tennis three hours every day, and competing in national tennis tournaments. At the time of his heart attack, it was discovered that he had a heart defect (namely a hole in the heart wall) from birth which had never been diagnosed. Contrary to professionals' predictions that he would need full-time help, three weeks after being treated in hospital he returned to his work and played tennis day by day. He told me, "I am going to enjoy my life to the fullest for as long as I can." Three months after the devastating heart problem, he was winning second and third place in senior groups at national tournaments. A year after that, at the time of the writing of this book, he was still practising dentistry, enjoying tennis, and travelling across Europe. Five years after that he had a stroke that paralysed his right side and affected speech. After three weeks he was playing big ball with the intention of playing tennis again within a few weeks. When asked, "How do you feel?" he replied, "I am well and don't expect any different." He kept his promise.

This example illustrates the person's deep unconscious desire and positive self-suggestion to be healthy again. His high motivation and determination to continue his beloved work and to enjoy tennis were the dominating factors in his healing and recovery process. He totally rejected the thought of being unable to enjoy his life.

Practical application of the law of suggestion during self-hypnosis is discussed in Part III.

Nine

Unconscious Processes Utilized in Medical Hypnosis

The secret of the mastermind is found wholly in the use of imagination.

Christian D. Larson (1874–1962)

The Unconscious Mind's Inner Resources

In the previous chapter I mentioned that some exchange of information between the conscious and unconscious mind occurs only in specific situations. Our present problems or particular behaviour may have a root in past experiences, which may have been "framed" or "suppressed" according to our understanding of the event at that time. When we experience hypnotic trance, we have better access to the resources of the unconscious mind, which may help us to find solutions to ongoing problematic issues. It is like opening the inner wisdom box to use our assets when we need them. In trance, it is possible to recall experiences, memories, thoughts, ideas, or fantasy, including those which may not always be available at a conscious level. Moreover, accessing the contents of the unconscious mind allows us to review past experiences without the emotional aspect we had at the time they happened.

Recalling past events lets us see those events in a different way, learn from them, take the best from them, or just find their real meaning. Our past experiences could be associated with negative emotions such as fear, anger, sadness, or jealousy. Correcting the negative attached emotions during hypnosis may change the troubling behaviour or feelings within a shorter time than it would take for therapy without hypnosis.

On the other hand, happy experiences are associated with positive emotions such as worthwhileness, joy, love, gratitude, delight, and peace of mind. Good memories are very powerful future reference points, and knowing how to use them may improve how we behave and feel. See more about this in Part III.

Mostly we have a combination of emotions, but when an extreme experience occurs, it may lead to a long-lasting imbalance of thoughts and feelings. For example, the irrational behaviour may be persistent in adult life because some event in the past was misinterpreted by our childlike limited reasoning capability or because, when we were in distress, we did not have sufficient information to process the event. Recalling feeling good during a past performance, exam, or social event can boost a person's confidence for public appearances at present or in future.

Moreover, the unconscious mind has a creative imagination and visualization ability, needed when positive experiences from the past are limited or blocked for some reason. I would like to explain how these aspects work for us.

Imagination processes are the products of the complex creative ability of the unconscious mind. Images can be tangible or intangible or may come in symbolic form such as pictures, sounds, or feelings. They have no boundaries in logic, time, and space. Imagination processes of the unconscious are free from the analytical, judgemental processes of the conscious mind. Creative imagination can be described as that which converts a fantasy or dream from imagination to reality. Repeated images trigger the unconscious to search for the best resources to accomplish the desired outcome.

The unlimited ability of the unconscious mind to create different images when searching for resources to reach our goals is a powerful tool in medical hypnosis. Imagination is widely used in psychology to make positive changes in thinking and behaviour. Imagination is very effective at making changes to unwanted habits and improving self-image, self-esteem, creativity, and human performance. There are well-documented cases of people who were held captive for a long time used imagination to get through this seemingly hopeless situation.

Imagination is a powerful tool used by professionals to treat many medical conditions. There is the well-known work of Carl Simonton, an oncologist, and Stephanie Matthews-Simonton, a psychologist, who practised the use of imagination in conjunction with a conventionally treatment for patients with breast cancer. One example of this technique is to imagine a warm or cold hand used to alter the sensation of pain. Different images can be utilized to initiate the removal of some pathological lesions such as tumours, to cause skin changes, or to relax blood vessels to lower blood pressure.

Because in a hypnotic trance there is no critical conscious involvement, the imagination has no boundaries when seeking to choose the best resource to solve the ongoing problem. Also, the unconscious mind is able to create new imagery based on our thoughts. Repeated images of what we want sent to the unconscious mind will initiate the unconscious search for information to reach our goal. For example, imagining yourself remaining calm and in control during an important exam will help you to overcome panic and stress in a real scenario. Even if you have never before experienced such a positive feeling, you can mimic one belonging to your favourite character.

Still, the final result depends on many other factors, such as your motivation, beliefs, and imaginative capability. Therefore, in more serious situations, the guidance of a professional practitioner is advised to help you assess all these factors for a successful therapy. Moreover, to prevent illness, reinforce treatment, or increase the process of recovery, many important factors will be addressed during hypnotherapy, such as a healthy lifestyle, genetics, beliefs, psychological conditions, and attitude. To find a practical use of the imagination, see Part IV.

Ten

Visualization

> At the beginning of each picture, there is someone who works with me towards the end, I have the impression of having worked with a collaborator.
>
> Pablo Picasso

Visualization is mental imagery building on a previous experience. It is another powerful tool that helps to maintain a balance between body and mind. Positive visualization has been scientifically proven to be very useful in the treatment of a wide range of disease. Many clinicians use visualization as an adjunct to conventional treatment or as a solo therapy.

Visualization can initiate the healing process. It is also used aiming at changes in many medical and psychological problems. It is necessary in the planning process as well. Imagination and visualizations features are very powerful elements in hypnotherapy and are used for many purposes ranging from pain control to treatment of many medical conditions, including cancer and a variety of psychological conditions. Imagery and pictures are very powerful mind processes that improve human performance. They are very effective tools used in sports or the arts. Also, they can be utilized in any aspect of our lives, especially in reaching any goal.

Visualization therapy is based on the science of cybernetics (from the Greek: "steersman"). Introduced by physicist Norbert Wiener, it deals with positive and negative images in relation to goal achievement. According to this belief, patience and trust in intuition are crucial to complete any task. If the process of the unconscious mind is distracted by conscious analytical, critical, and judgemental influences, it will bring doubts upon that image and the unconscious will stop working towards the final desired outcome.

Wiener presents a classic example of how a baby learns to reach for a pencil. According to his beliefs, muscles receive negative or positive messages according to the position of the pencil. It is an automatic process involving many steps of motion before the task is completed. This example shows step by step the attempts to do this without conscious planning, namely making a zigzag-like pattern first until the pencil is reached.

The same processes occur each time we want to accomplish a goal, be it obtaining better health, making more money, having a better relationship, or baking the best cake ever.

The cybernetic theory of Maxwell Maltz, an American plastic surgeon who wrote the book *Psycho-Cybernetics*, is known in the medical field. According to Maltz, any goal created in our mind can be reached, and any obstacles or mistakes along the way will be corrected automatically by the unconscious mind, until the final result is reached.

Therefore, when working on any goals, it is important to learn to trust your unconscious mind and let it find the way to reach the goal. As long as you keep the precise picture of what you want in your mind, the goal will be accomplished sooner or later, depending on other factors involved in this unconscious process. Being in a good mood and staying positive on a daily basis will definitely reinforce the process to reach any goal.

Did you ever meet someone who said, "I just had a feeling that it will happen"?

Did what the person was referring to happen? In most cases it did.

During hypnotic trance, visualization can be very vivid. We are all different when it comes to experiencing sensations. Some people are more visual, whereas others use the auditory, kinetic, olfactory, or taste senses. But most of us can visualize orange, hear our favourite music, smell peaches, taste lemon, and feel the coldness of ice or the soft fur of a cat.

According to neurolinguistics programming, the dominant sense a person relies on is reflected in the language the person uses to express his or her mental processes. We can identify it by listening to what kinds of words they say, for example "I see," "I hear," or "I feel." It is interesting to know that matching other people's dominant sense helps us to communicate with them, and this element is used efficiently to build a bond between therapist and patient.

When we have a well-constructed final picture of what we want, automatically our energy increases, along with the determination and self-discipline to focus on that goal. Therefore, if a sportsman genuinely believes that he will beat a standing record, he raises the possibility that he will, until something shakes this belief.

Hypnotic trance reinforces the picture in the mind and initiates the unconscious mind's search for resources. Visualization and imagination can be practised in a waking state but is more powerful in relaxation and hypnotic trance. Contrary to some beliefs, everyone has the ability to visualize and imagine. We all can recall what our room looks like or create a story.

The more detailed the picture or image we have of that which we desire, the better the signal that is sent to the unconscious mind to find the way to achieve that image. The unconscious understands simple images only. It is not logical and will direct our thinking and behaviours according to the picture we present to it.

If the picture and image is positive, the unconscious mind will work in that direction. It is as Aladdin said: "Your wish is my command." You can say it too. However, if the picture is negative, Aladdin will still bring what you are asking for. Therefore, it is important to control your thoughts and the images and pictures of what you want daily. Hypnosis will reinforce this process significantly. You will find practical approaches to visualization in Part IV.

Eleven

Medical, Dental, and Psychological Hypnosis

Natural forces within us are the true healers of disease.

Hippocrates (*c.*460 BC–*c.*370 BC)

Now I would like to introduce you to common medical and psychological conditions for which the hypnotic approach is clinically proven to be beneficial. This chapter is just a guide to what may be achieved by adding hypnotic trance to conventional treatment.

Based on my clinical experience, I believe that the following information is valuable to help you understand the benefit of using hypnosis for a medical condition. Medical hypnosis is effectively practised in academic and clinical centres around the world, so you can find such a centre locally. Some readers may find this chapter to be too detailed and repetitive. If you find this to be the case for you, then skip ahead to the next chapter.

The previously discussed connection and reversal loops between the mind and body function are used to treat a variety of medical and psychological problems such as cancer, heart and circulation problems, obesity, immune system impairment, and digestive disorders. They can also be used in sexology and gynaecology.

Clinical psychologists might use hypnotic trance to enhance psychotherapy in patients with conditions such as phobias, personality disorders, low confidence and self-esteem, addiction, depression, and posttraumatic stress disorder, among many others. Hypnotherapy is effective in making changes in thinking and behaviour and helps people learn new skills to have a more successful life.

As I discussed in previous chapters, any therapy which involves hypnotic trance utilizes all the features of hypnotic trance including suggestion, imagination, visualization, creativity, and fantasy, among many others. In a hypnotic trance, the person looking for an improvement in health is more open to new suggestions and possibilities. She is better motivated and is willing to follow carefully selected therapeutic suggestions aiming to treat the disease and bring about a quick recovery.

Those who are willing to let go and enter a hypnotic trance experience deep relaxation. The therapeutic work is done directly in the unconscious mind.

First, the therapy will concentrate on elimination of all present pathological changes and any negative attitude preventing the desired outcome. One's creative ability during hypnotic trance is unlimited, and the use of visualization and imagination will initiate change, reinforce body and mind function, and aid in healing and recovery. At the end of treatment, the patient learns how to use self-hypnosis at home in order to improve quality of life and be independent.

Medical hypnosis can be carried out without changes to the conventional treatment or may be carried out as a solo approach (without any medication), as is practised in surgery to control pain. Patients practising self-hypnosis are more active in their treatment and thereby increase their belief in their own healing potential.

However, to realize a significant improvement in mental or physical health, patients need to make some changes in lifestyle and improve their self-discipline motivation, which are not easy things to do, as many of us know. However, with hypnotic interventions, it will be easier to make such changes within a short span of time because all the supporting elements will be automatically built in with the therapy.

Controlling emotions is another aspect essential to treatment and recovery, as is the patient's positive attitude. Both will be significantly improved with hypnotherapy. The more realistic hope we give to the patients, the better results we can expect (the placebo effect).

Although hypnosis is a natural, safe, and efficient process, it is important to seek medical treatment from registered medical practitioners with accredited qualifications in medical hypnosis. They have the necessary skills and knowledge to properly diagnose and treat medical or psychological conditions and to determine what type of treatment would be best for the patient.

In the next chapter, you will find more details on conditions that respond to medical hypnosis.

Twelve

Other Medical Uses of Hypnosis

Stress, the Immune System, and the Hypnotic State of Mind

We all know that stress has a strong influence on the function of the immune system. In contrast, happy feelings support our immune system, helping to prevent disease and aid in recovery from illness.

Our emotions and thoughts can change the processes in each cell in the body. There is communication between the brain and the body. When we are under stress, the brain sends information via neural messages to hormonal messengers, which send the signal to the hormonal (endocrinal) system. When this happens, steroidal hormones are released from the adrenal glands, which in turn influence the function of body organs.

When our body is exposed to a dangerous situation, acute pain, or an emergency, the hormonal system increases the release of adrenaline, which leads to rapid physiological responses aimed at helping us to survive. The whole sympathetic nervous system is elevated, and the parasympathetic nervous system slows down. Because of this, blood pressure rises, the heart beats faster, muscle tension increases, and breathing becomes rapid. It is the well-known fight or flight response.

This response is essential to our survival when we are exposed to danger. However, if stress persists for a long period of time, the function of the immune system will be considerably diminished and work against us. We frequently hear that stress is a silent killer. This idea is supported by science and clinical research concluding that chronic stress leads to many serious medical problems.

Selye's Adaptation Syndrome.

In 1978, Dr Hans Selye discovered that the secretion of corticosterone from the adrenal glands in a person with chronic stress significantly weakens the immune system. Selye's Adaptation Syndrome

When we are under chronic stress, the immune system loses the power to protect the body, and pathological changes occur. Stress affects self-healing factors in the blood, such as white cells and especially T-lymphocytes, which are responsible for the production of antibodies and other healing proteins. With the immune system repressed, the body are more prone to fungal, viral, and bacterial infections. A weak immune system's response to an intruder from the outside is insufficient to fight the invasion, which may lead to the development of a variety of illnesses and diseases such as cold, flu, cancer, stomach ulcer, heart disease, obesity, diabetes, and dermatological problems.

Damage to one organ for a long period will cause extreme changes in the function of other organs. Over time, if the condition is untreated, the healthy balance of the body will be disturbed. Complications and secondary problems will occur and weaken the body even more. When the body functions are insufficient, we feel ill and experience and increase in frustration, leading to more damage.

Chronic stress increases the danger of losing control over our emotions and diminishes our judgement, which leads to irrational actions and choices. Under prolonged stress we are more prone to turn to an unhealthy lifestyle and experience addiction, depression, negative attitude, suicidal thoughts, and many other severe conditions. Prolonged mental and physical illness leads to personal and professional problems. The cycle will continue unless something happens to restore the balance of the body and the mind.

Therefore, to maximize the strength of the immune system, it is important to reduce stress levels on a daily basis. When all the body's functions are in balance, the natural defence mechanisms are stronger to prevent illness or to fight a disease that already affects us.

Even when intruders (germs) invade our cells and infection develops, a healthy immune system will have the power to destroy the antigens by way of the body's natural defences, namely antibodies. The intruder will be destroyed within a reasonable time, and all damaged body cells will be repaired quickly by self-healing mechanisms.

Medical hypnosis is very effective in stress control, and trance is a relaxing experience in and of itself. Simple psychological techniques applied during trance to reduce the stress will eliminate negative thoughts and emotions. During trance we can learn better approaches to dealing with the same stressful situation in future. The therapy will be aimed at improving our ego and our coping and problem-solving strategies as well.

When we are in a calm and controlled state, pressure is released from the immune system and recovery starts to occur. Creativity, imagination, and hypnotic suggestion are used to increase the potential of our immune system during hypnotherapy and long afterwards.

You can learn how to control stress in Part III.

Allergies

Asthma and other forms of allergic reactions are serious conditions of uncertain aetiology. When an allergen is present, the immune system's function of producing antibodies is disturbed, and when the triggering antigen is present, serious reactions to body functions occur, causing severe symptoms such as difficulty breathing.

Medical hypnosis is clinically proven to be effective in the treatment of allergic conditions. The patient will feel more in control over the illness and will experience improvement in the function of the whole body. Medical hypnosis creates the perfect conditions to learn new skills to control body function, such as breathing evenly and staying calm during allergy attacks. Staying calm will automatically help to control symptoms and allow the sufferer to take the necessary actions, for example starting controlled breathing to increase oxygen supply.

Moreover, working on the unconscious mind gives us the opportunity to discover the trigger points and unblock or find inner resources necessary for self-healing and allergy prevention.

If you suffer from any form of allergy, ask your doctor about medical hypnotherapy to help reduce your suffering and put you in a position of having better control over this serious condition.

Skin Disorders

Dermatological disorders are difficult to treat because for many we still don't know the aetiology. However, many skin changes have an immunological component.

Many, if not all, skin problems respond exceptionally well to treatment when the sufferer is in a hypnotic trance. Hypnotherapy reduces the suffering, improves the healing of the skin, lowers the amount of medication needed, and decreases the duration of the problem. Imagination and visualization is used to heal the lesions and is effective in reducing itching, pain, and discomfort associated with skin problems, whether benign or cancerous. By way of appropriate hypnotic suggestion, it is possible to increase the blood flow to the skin and improve the conditions for healing. The skin, like any other organ, constantly repairs or replaces damaged cells. Therefore, hypnotherapy can reinforce healing and renewal.

Patients with skin disorders frequently suffer from a poor self-image, low self-esteem, and low self-confidence. During hypnotherapy, effective coping strategies can be learned to reduce the mental aspect of the suffering. Hypnotic intervention is effective and safe to use, but as with any other condition, a medical practitioner must exclude any serious underlying conditions and supervise the therapy.

Blood Pressure

Blood pressure is another silent killer, along with stress. The two conditions are connected, and the aetiology is still not fully known. However, there are known many factors which increase the risk of this chronic condition. Some of these are dysfunction of organs like the kidneys and heart, dysfunction of the blood vessels, and conditions such as diabetes and obesity. Other proven factors leading to high blood pressure are stress, an unhealthy lifestyle, addictions, caffeine use, and alcohol use. The consequences of high blood pressure are common and include haemorrhage, stroke, and heart problems. Although there are many medications available to control blood pressure, they present side effects which may cause heart and circulation problems, allergies, weight gain, skin problems, and malfunction of other organs.

Fortunately, it has now been proven by research that psychological approaches can modify blood pressure. These approaches can be reinforced in a hypnotic trance. Self-hypnosis is very useful and easy to apply. Many features of hypnotic trance, such as imagination, visualization, and creativity, are easy for the patient to learn. Self-hypnosis helps to eliminate the trigger factors, helps to improve lifestyle (such as diet), and helps to reduce stress. When self-hypnosis is used effectively, the amount of medication a patient takes to control blood pressure can be reduced or in some cases totally eliminated. We all have difficulty sticking to new habits from time to time, but hypnotherapy will increase our motivation and determination to stay on the right path. However, high blood pressure requires constant assessment and cooperation with a practitioner. Therefore, you must never stop any medication without consulting your doctor first.

Gynaecology

Medical hypnosis becomes more popular every day in gynaecology, where it is used to treat cancer, control pain during and after surgery, lessen the side effects of chemotherapy, and control bleeding, among many other things. Hypnotherapy reinforces the treatment and considerably shortens the therapy, including recovery time. The amount of medication after medical procedures may be significantly reduced, and the patient can return to normal life much quicker than without hypnotic intervention. Moreover, hypnotherapy offers a psychological approach, improving mental conditions, reducing discomfort, and improving the ability to cope with ongoing problems. If you are concerned about any of these conditions and would like to be treated with hypnosis, ask your doctor for a referral to a recognized medical centre.

Birthing with Hypnotherapy

Birthing with hypnotherapy is increasing in popularity these days. Hypnotherapy improves the comfort of the mother and creates better conditions for the new-born baby and medical staff. Stress is considerably controlled, and the whole procedure is much easier to manage, including any complications such as infection or bleeding. There are good hypnotic programmes run in clinics for pregnant women and for aiding in labour. Hypnotherapy helps prevent postnatal depression and leads to a more rewarding beginning for the new family. The mother feels more confident and better prepared for the critical days when she recognizes that from now on, she is entirely responsible for the well-being of her baby. Ask your doctor how you can join group therapy for this purpose.

Fertility

Hypnotherapy is proven to be effective during diagnostic procedures and in the preparation of the patient before and after procedures. It is also successful, in keeping a healthy balance during pregnancy. The therapy concentrates on stress control, weight management, pain, elimination of other medical and mental problems, and bleeding control. Visualization may be the tool of choice to reach the desired outcome. Treatment with hypnotic trance will improve patient comfort and posttreatment recovery and keep mind and body in balance. The improvement in psychological condition due to hypnotherapy is very much appreciated by both doctors and patients.

The foregoing are only examples of medical conditions in which hypnotherapy can make huge changes in patient comfort. If you suffer from any medical condition, ask your doctor about hypnotherapy.

Thirteen

Dental Hypnosis

Dentistry is usually associated with significant discomfort for the patient and dental staff. Despite significant improvements in technology, the levels of pain and stress are still considerable, preventing many people from visiting the dentist on a regular basis.

Dental hypnosis is very effective in any dental specialization, helping patients to complete the necessary treatment in a more comfortable way and increasing the dentist's chance of seeing the patient in future for a check-up. Hypnosis intervention in dentistry can be used as a solo approach or in conjunction with local anaesthesia. Patients can be prepared for such treatment before or during the dental visit.

Hypnotic trance and hypnotic suggestion help to control bleeding, excessive salivation, and physical discomfort during treatment. Fear, such as the fear of needles, water, lying flat during treatment, drills, noise, choking, and losing control, is a common problem seen in dental practices. Hypnotherapy will eliminate such conditions and improve the patient's comfort and feeling of being in control.

Surgical procedures, from simple tooth extraction, to major jaw surgery, to cancers of soft tissues and bones, can be carried out with a patient in a hypnotic trance. Treatment time and postoperative care are reduced considerably, as is the number of painkillers needed after treatment. Hypnotic intervention is useful in pain control during conservative treatments such fillings, removing calculus, and polishing the teeth. Read more in Chapter 14: Hypnotic Pain Control.

Hypnotherapy will help the patient accept new dentures or orthodontic appliances. This relaxing approach facilitates the treatment of habits such as nail biting and bruxism (grinding of teeth) and reduces painful muscle tension.

Learning to control pain, emotions, anxiety, and stress by practising self-hypnosis makes the treatment much more pleasant for the patient and the dental team during the treatment and afterwards. Above all, in many cases, having effective pain and anxiety control may be the only way for the dentist to see the patient again, complete the necessary treatment, and prevent total damage to dentition. The foregoing are just a few examples of how hypnotherapy and self-hypnosis can improve the effectiveness and comfort of complicated conditions and treatments.

Children Dentistry and Hypnosis

The benefits of using hypnosis with children during dental treatment are enormous. Hypnosis makes the treatment stress-free and painless. Children can enjoy the treatment because painful injections can be avoided and the number of chemicals used can be reduced (or eliminated altogether).

Comfortable, pain-free dentistry will help the child come for regular care with a smile. It is the little patients that are the most sensitive to dental procedures, and hypnotic intervention solves many problems for the child, the dentist, and the terrified parent. Children can be prepared before and during treatment by hypnotic therapeutic stories geared towards different dental interventions.

Children are extremely responsive to hypnotic stories and metaphors; therefore, trance can be initiated without formal hypnotic induction. There is an unlimited number of therapeutic stories used in dentistry. It only depends on the dentist's imagination. A child's imagination and ability to be absorbed in a story or metaphor is very high, especially from the ages of five to twelve. Imagination and metaphors are a very powerful tool in treating children, including those with the most severe cases of cancer of the mouth and other systemic syndromes.

Children are very cooperative in following suggestion such as, "Let's make a hole in a tooth to hide the rabbit from the fox that is chasing it." They show deep involvement in a story, so much so that they dissociate from the dental procedure, allowing the dentist to complete the treatment successfully and see the smiling face at the end. The most important thing is that children love it.

In a similar way to the foregoing applications, medical hypnosis may be used in surgery and in all other medical fields for things such as simple medical procedures, laboratory tests, and posttreatment recovery.

Fourteen

Hypnotic Pain Control

You have the power within your mind to switch the pain on and off. We all are familiar with pain stemming from different sources and the suffering it causes.

Hypnosis has been used successfully to control pain in clinical fields for centuries. It is one of the most researched aspects of medicine and psychology as well.

However, the potential of the mind to control pain has been diminished by the discovery of chemical pain control, one of the most significant achievements of the last century. Chemicals have been used to obtain general anaesthesia in surgical procedures. Analgesics commonly known as "painkillers" are used to control pain. No opioid painkillers combine antipyretic, analgesic, and anti-inflammatory actions. The most common of these are paracetamol and aspirin. Another group are the opioid analgesics. Listing in order from the strongest to the weakest, these include diamorphine (heroin), morphine (methadone and dextromoramide), pethidine, dihydrocodeine, codeine, and dextropropoxyphene.

However, we are now aware of the very serious side effects of these painkillers when they are used for a long time. It is commonly recognized that painkillers create dependence and present the risk of severe damage to organ function. Painkillers, narcotics, and alcohol are used by millions of people around the globe to self-medicate from physical or emotional pain, putting them in danger of addiction and death. Sadly, every day young people die from various drug overdoses. Statistics show an alarming number of seventy thousand people losing their lives to addiction in the USA in 2018.

Unfortunately, painkillers are easy to find over the counter and also by prescription. The problem of overprescribing is serious around the world. Also problematic is the mental and physical damage affecting millions of people around the globe. You can find more information on this issue in the chapters on addiction (68–71) in Part IV.

With this growing problem, it is wonderful to have adequate pain control without side effects through hypnosis. Clinicians and scientists have presented well-documented cases showing that hypnotic pain control is very efficient and safe. Hypnosis can be applied to control both acute and chronic pain. It is easy to use for adults and children, especially those who require repeated painful medical procedures over an extended period, for example with diabetes.

To control pain efficiently we need to understand the mechanism behind it.

The most significant theory of pain is the gate control theory of Ronald Melzack and Patrick Wall (1965). According to this theory, pain consists of two parts: the first part is informative (sensory pain), and the second part is motivation-affective (suffering pain). Therefore, effective pain control should deal with both these aspects of pain at the same time.

Pain can be of different character and duration. According to this, there will be a different approach to deal with it. Many professional books are available discussing how to control pain. Here, I describe two main types of pain, acute and chronic pain, and how hypnotherapy helps to control it. I also provide a guide on how children can benefit from medical hypnosis to control painful conditions.

Acute Pain

"Stop the pain."

"Your wish is my command," said Aladdin.

Acute pain is associated with many medical procedures, from minor to major surgical operations and dental procedures, and postoperative pain is common in medical offices. Pain can be induced as well for research in laboratory settings. The most common acute pain is caused by accidental body injury, pathological tissue damage, or medical procedures. In medical terminology, any pain lasting up to six months is recognized as acute.

Hypnosis can be used to obtain general anaesthesia and analgesia as a solo agent or in conjunction with anaesthetic/analgesic chemicals. Solo hypnotic pain control is used mostly when there is a contraindication to chemical integrations. Examples are medical conditions such as heart problems, high blood pressure, blood disorders such as haemophilia causing uncontrolled bleeding, and acute infections.

The most frequent utilization of hypnotic pain control is for minor surgical procedures, dental surgeries, tooth extraction, scaling, diagnostic procedures, painful injections, and skin dressing changes. Postoperative pain and discomfort are well-controlled by hypnotic intervention. Hypnotic pain control reduces the time of healing and recovery and the amount of medication needed. Moreover, the patient can learn self-hypnosis for a way to control pain at home long after the surgery.

This form of pain control is convenient for the patient as well as for the medical team. It makes treatment more relaxed for everyone and reduces the amount of chemicals in the body.

Fifteen

Hypnotic Control of Chronic Pain

Pain killers may kill the pain and the body. Hypnosis smooths and controls both.

In the medical field, any pain lasting longer than six months is recognized as chronic pain. There are many medical conditions associated with pain, and many people have to rely on painkillers every day. Examples of some causes of common chronic pain are arthritis, rheumatism, phantom pain, headache, multiple sclerosis, musculoskeletal problems, injuries, and cancers. With time, stronger prescription drugs are needed in order to achieve effective pain control, and these stronger drugs bring with them several side effects, damaging many organs and causing an imbalance in physiological and mental processes. Depression, suicidal thoughts, and addictions are common, and the number of patients with these devastating conditions is increasing around the world.

There are psychological techniques which are scientifically proven to be effective in pain control. On top of this, patients can benefit from hypnosis to control pain, and by practising self-hypnosis they can be more independent. Also, they can use it anytime they need to.

Moreover, the psychological and hypnotic approach to controlling pain is free of chemicals and effects such as addiction and financial burden. Everyone can take advantage of this effective psychological pain control technique. It can be applied during a hypnotic trance to reinforce its effectiveness considerably. Hypnotic pain control can reduce the intensity of pain, as well as its character and duration.

Phantom Pain

During a home visit for dental treatment, I found that my patient was depressed and complained of chronic phantom pain since he'd had his leg amputated at the knee. Without thinking long, I simply suggested, "Maybe you can try to imagine that you have a tap on the thigh which you can switch on and off. Just use it to regulate the intensity of the pain and find a level you can feel comfortable with. You can use it just like a water tap."

On the next visit, I was surprised to see a happy man. He told me that at first he had taken my suggestion as a joke, but later he tried it and it worked. Now he is able to control the pain to a level which feels much more comfortable. Moreover, he reduced the number of painkillers he took by half in the first months, and later he had stopped taking them entirely.

This is just one example of how the simple suggestion of using the imagination can be effective in pain control even without hypnotic trance. However, results will vary according to underlying problems, patient beliefs, patient motivation, and the patient's attitude towards learning the skill of pain control. Therefore, it is important to seek out a professional practitioner to eliminate any obstacle in the way and take full advantage of this hypnotic phenomenon.

Hypnotic pain control is a pleasant experience. It is easy to apply, free from side effects, and affordable. However, hypnotic pain control must be used only when the origin of pain is known. For example, headache may be the result of stress or a brain tumour. Covering the pain without knowing the cause may lead to serious consequences.

Self-hypnosis can be learned at the beginning of hypnotherapy and continue to be applied at home. Moreover, the patient will learn coping strategies and can improve his or her mental state by creating a positive image of the future.

The most popular techniques used in a hypnotic trance to relieve pain are dissociation, relocation, and altering the character of the pain. Methods used to deal with pain are distraction, directing the attention to more pleasant experiences, watching comedy, mentally blocking the pain by imagination and visualization, and symptom substitution.

Classic examples of hypnotic pain control are glove anaesthesia. All these methods are easy to learn with professional supervision. For pain control, deep hypnosis is not necessary because the patient's motivation and determination to feel better is high in most cases. Therefore, self-hypnosis to control pain is easily used by the patient anytime and anywhere.

Sixteen

Hypnosis and Emergency Cases

As we know already, during trance it is possible to regulate body functions significantly by way of suggestion. There are many everyday situations where knowledge of hypnosis and the power of suggestion can save lives.

When people are in shock, they are in an altered state of mind. Therefore, they accept suggestions without criticism, especially those suggestions aimed at helping. We can apply specific hypnotic suggestion to ourselves in urgent situations, or we can apply such suggestions to someone else in emergency cases. Common urgent situations include heart attack, acute asthmatic episode, laryngospasm, bleeding, or panic attack. Giving a straight suggestion to someone at the scene of the accident might be a matter of life or death. Ordering a suffering person at the accident scene to breathe calmly, relax his or her muscles, or stop the bleeding may change the outcome of the situation. Examples of such suggestions are "Stop the bleeding," "Breathe calmly," "Relax. Relax deeper and deeper," and "Stop the pain."

As we learned in a previous chapter, staying calm can have a strong influence on the physiological functions of organs including the brain. The same mechanism is activated in an urgent situation. By applying a suggestion, we may stabilize the person's condition until paramedics arrive to help.

Hypnotic suggestion proves to be efficient in controlling bleeding during surgery and dental treatment and in many other emergency cases. Suggestion can regulate or shut down the blood vessels and stop the bleeding. Patients involved in a drastic situation will respond to any suggestion, including guided imagery and reassurance that everything will be OK or that help is on the way. Such mental support may help the patient to find the necessary motivation to keep going and control the situation. This approach is commonly used by doctors and nurses in emergency rooms with undoubtedly positive results.

Children and Medical Hypnosis

Many children require very painful medical procedures on a regular basis. From my experience, there is no better gift scientists and clinicians can offer them than effective pain control.

Hypnotic pain control is a very effective alternative we can offer to a scared and suffering little patient. It has it all—it is pleasant to apply and is free from side effects. It will help the child to have more comfortable medical procedures, will speed up recovery time, and will bring back their smile.

Children suffering from diabetes need daily painful injections. During surgery, dental treatment, diagnostic procedures, or cancer treatment, including chemotherapy and its side effects, hypnosis can make an enormous difference to a child. It offers a broad range of therapy and treatment, providing physical comfort, helping to building better coping techniques, and improving general well-being. It is easy to teach children the "magic pain removal" technique, for example the "magic finger", because a child's imagination is undisturbed.

Classic clinical hypnotic inductions and terminology are not used with children. Hypnotic pain control requires only metaphor, or a favourite story suitable to the child's age, to engage the child in the hypnotic state. Modelling the child's TV heroes is commonly practised to capture the child's attention and then apply therapeutic suggestion or accomplish treatment. Therapeutic stories can initiate better healing, make the recovery much more pleasant, and reduce the need for chemicals.

Seventeen

Sport and Hypnosis

> People do not need to know the details or means of reaching goals; they just have to be able to picture the goal.
>
> Maxwell Maltz

The processes of the mind and the natural laws described in previous chapters are proven by science to enhance human performance. Hypnotic trance increases this effect and therefore is widely used in sports and creativity and for many other applications, including business goals.

In various sport disciplines, the hypnotic approach is practised by top athletes to reach their peak performance. There is strong evidence showing that the hypnotic approach and visualization increases sports achievement significantly (see A. H. Morgan, the Stanford Hypnotic Clinical Scale, 1979; William S. Kroger, *Clinical and Experimental Hypnosis*, 1977; and N. Katz, 1984). According to the McKinney study, 5 per cent of performance depends on equipment, 20 per cent on physical condition, and 75 per cent on mental approach.

Professor of sports psychology at Sheffield Hallam University Ian Maynard used hypnosis to prepare the Great Britain sailing team for the Athens Olympics. They were trained in goal setting and used visualization, imagery, dissociation, and positive distraction techniques to enhance their performance. The sportsmen had been asked to visualize themselves running while they were in fact not moving. Amazingly, the results showed that all their muscles were working as in real action. This fact proves how powerful visualization is, and therefore this technique is now widely used by athletes around the world.

The Mental Training Program (MTP) is one of the most effective techniques for improving performance. Research proves that any performance can be increased by making goals and practising psychological approaches. The best results are achieved by focusing on both physical performance and mental activity to increase attention and emotional control so as to reduce stress and anxiety. Other factors boosting performance are biofeedback, mental rehearsal, relaxation, meditation, and hypnosis.

The most common hypnotic programmes which are used to improve human performance involve the following:

- creating a clear picture of the goal and a precise time frame to accomplish it
- having a clear motivation to improve persistence to achieve the goal
- increasing self-belief and self-trust to reach the desired goal
- learning emotional control to stay calm but maintaining the tension essential to compete
- improving self-discipline in order to be persistent until the goal is reached
- improving coping and problem-solving strategies to overcome obstacles.

All the foregoing elements are important to achieve any goal. They are described in more detail in Part IV.

A very popular and easy to follow technique to improve any performance is the inner way of learning by Edwin A. Locke. He describes simple steps to improve any performance:

1. Be aware of present performance. For example, if someone wants to improve cross-court shots in basketball, first it is necessary to know how these are executed.

2. Visualize the new way of doing something. Having a clear image of the goal in your mind will automatically involve different muscle groups and body positions necessary to do it right.
3. Practise this new technique in a calm manner free from criticism and doubt until you feel confident with it.
4. Trust yourself and let the unconscious accomplish the goal.

As we learned before, by visualizing we are sending the precise image to the unconscious mind of what we expect in the end. The unconscious mind then will search for necessary resources to find the shortest way to accomplish the desired goal, even if it will be a zigzag course, as it often is. Therefore, it is paramount to trust yourself and your unconscious, knowing without a doubt that sooner or later, the final desired outcome will come. Learning to "let it happen" without doubts and criticism is the critical point in goal achievement to eliminate the influence of the conscious mind. Otherwise, the results will be different.

For example, an athlete practising for the Olympics may be bombarded with his or her own ideas as well as different opinions and judgemental comments from the coach, the rest of the team, friends, et al. Such a situation may trigger frustration and confusion, leading to poor performance.

We all know the old saying "The harder we try, the harder it goes." We know now that such an approach presents the risk of shaking one's self-image and self-esteem, only to bring more disappointing results.

Whatever we want to achieve, improve, or change, the most effective way to do it is to stay calm, trust ourselves, and be persistent until the desired performance is executed comfortably in an automatic fashion, without our consciously thinking about it.

Repetition leads to excellence, and if something is not right the first time, we have the ability to learn and do the right thing to achieve the desired outcome.

Working on the unconscious mind in hypnotic trance will improve self-discipline, self-esteem, and determination to reach any goal in a much shorter time than when working with the analytical and judgemental aspect of the conscious mind.

The greatest sport stars have used hypnotherapy to prepare for the Olympics. This approach to improve human performance is growing in popularity. Hypnotic techniques are made up of natural human abilities and therefore are legal to use, compared to the illegal use of many forms of chemical substances to improve performance.

Unfortunately, the use of stimulants is still reported frequently, with the devastating results of stripping many athletes of their medals and their dignity and blocking the natural potential of their brain's activity.

We need to recognize that honesty is important not only in sports but also in all aspects of our lives if we want to find satisfaction at the end of the day. Feeling good about ourselves and our achievements is a great asset and the best source of positive energy we have.

Being on good terms with ourselves will pay dividends, especially when rainy days come.

Learning to do the right thing in childhood and early competitions is the basis for future success. Therefore, my intention is to sensitize young people especially to seek the real value of achievements and competitions, bringing them the feeling of being excellent at something. We all can improve our achievements just by learning how to use the potential of the unconscious mind more effectively.

Real competition and honest play is the main reason we love the atmosphere of the Olympics. The Olympic Games always have an enormous influence on the whole nation. An even deeper impact on young people is witnessed during the Paralympic Games. One thing is for sure: we would not spend hours of our precious time and as much of our money to see which stimulants were better.

The real spirit of sport is only evident in honest competition. Such a victory will stay long with the winner and in the history of human performance.

Eighteen

Art and Hypnosis

Suppress Stress, Release Creativity

Creativity is a product of the processes of the unconscious mind and is based on our inner and outer experiences of both mind and body. The unconscious mind stores all our experiences and the information coded in our genes. The human mind is powerful and able to create unlimited ideas, especially when we tap into this power.

Hypnotic trance reduces stress, which lets the mind flow effortlessly to enhance the creation of new ideas. All geniuses seem to be in an altered state of mind, closer to unconscious mind function, when they create their greatest masterpieces. The greatest composers such as Mozart and Beethoven created their music in a trance-like state of mind. In Michelangelo's words, he had the image of his work inside his mind before he created the masterpiece. Painters such as Pablo Picasso, Vincent Van Gogh, and Claude Monet were most creative when working in an altered state of mind. Therefore, hypnosis is very useful in art. Many artists rely on intuition most of the time. It seems that the final product of their work is the result of the unconscious mind's ability to create when there is a degree of detachment from the artist's close surroundings and when there is a deeper involvement with the activity of the inner mind, free from criticism.

It seems that geniuses create excellent products without making mistakes, compared to highly skilled people who need to make numerous corrections before the product is satisfactorily finished. We know that all geniuses focus intensively and concentrate during the process of creation until the product is completed.

Dance and any other performance can benefit from hypnotic intervention for the same reasons. Music and other disciplines involve unconscious creation, and artists have the ability to tap into the unconscious mind for new images and ideas. Therefore, hypnosis is very useful in art. As stated, many artists rely on intuition, so the use of imagination and visualization expands their creativity as happens in hypnotic trance.

Are great creators different from us and cleverer than we are? Do they have a greater ability than the average person to access the resources of the unconscious mind resources and their creative potential?

Probably they do, but could we learn to be more creative? Probably we could.

There is still much to learn before we can answer those questions, but we do know enough to start making significant improvements to our creativity and performance. We are all capable of creativity on some level. With practice and learning, creativity will increase. We all have done some painting, or built a sandcastle, or chosen different clothes for various occasions. Moreover, we all experience the processes of an altered state of mind at different times and different levels without our awareness. For example, you may remember an experience of sunbathing, staring at the horizon and being miles away, when suddenly an idea shot into your mind and you felt the urge to act on it straightaway.

During the creative process, the logical and critical aspects of the conscious mind are not involved, so the created image is free of any reasoning limitations. However, we know that creation is a complex matter involving different levels of the mind.

Creativity comes from the unconscious, but in what form it is stored in the unconscious is a question still to be answered. The power of creation is unlimited, and it may be just a matter of having stronger beliefs and finding the proper button to push for more intense unconscious creativity. Trance brings us into closer contact with the unconscious mind and gives us the opportunity to tap into resources. Expand your inner creativity by using trance; don't shrink it by using stimulants.

Your unconscious has the power to create, and with unshaken belief, your unconscious will deliver what you are looking for. Self-hypnosis is the perfect way to have closer contact with your unconscious mind, where you will find new resources and increased creativity.

Nineteen

Business and Hypnosis

Tap into the Unconscious Mind for New Ideas

For many years, hypnotic approaches have been used in business. There are many groups or individual courses based on this issue, and they are becoming more popular every year. There are well-known neurolinguistics programming (NLP) courses around the world where you can be trained in hypnotic approaches used in personal development and business. More on this can be read in the books on NLP by Richard Bandler and John Grinder. .

The NLP programme is widely used to reach goals. The main assumption is that our bad habits or unwanted behaviour and thinking patterns can be unlearned and "reframed" with more efficient ones. Bandler and Grinder also stress that communication skills are crucial in approaching life situations. Following NLP programming, the main keys to success are writing goals and making plans to achieve them. These skills can be learned individually or in group hypnotherapy, each of which utilizes a different psychological approach.

Any therapy will aim towards self-esteem and self-confidence, emotional control, and learning new strategies. Group therapy is successful in helping people reach goals and improve communication. Brainstorming is used to gain new ideas. These techniques are based on assumptions that new ideas come when the mind is in a prolonged period of silence, for example when sitting in a park or in a totally quiet room for twenty to thirty minutes. We all know the feeling of needing time to be by oneself.

Hypnotherapy in business, in addition to other forms of therapy, will help us review our many life experiences, look at them from a more mature angle, and help us understand them. And we will find that if a change is needed, we can alter our thinking and behaviour accordingly. Tapping into unconscious mind for new resources is the key to making improvements in whatever we do. When problematic situations occur, we need to be willing to see the big picture, not just a fragmented one which keeps us in our comfort zone. Having the true picture of the troubling situation, we can not only discover more options for solving the problem but also improve our sense of taking responsibility for it. At the same time, our attitude towards what we do and our respect for others will be improved as an important factor necessary to succeed in both personal and professional life.

Twenty

Safety of Hypnosis

> We can do more harm by being ignorant of hypnosis than we can ever do by the intelligent use of hypnosis and constructive suggestion.
>
> Dr David Cheek, gynaecologist and follower of Milton Erickson

Despite evidence from research and successful therapies around the world proving the effectiveness and safety of hypnosis, hypnosis still suffers from a bad image. Many of us still show deep concern about the possibility of mind manipulation. The fact is that most misconceptions about hypnosis derive from movies, lay hypnotists, and stage hypnotism. The most common fear is about losing control over one's body and mind, being manipulated, or being trapped in a trance.

The fact is that it is not trance or suggestion we should be worried about. Trance is a natural state of mind, and we all use it every day to some extent. We are bombarded with suggestions from different sources, some bad and some good, all the time. What matters is how we deal with them and how confidently we say either yes or no in our daily experiences or during hypnosis.

It is part of our natural defence system to act in line with our beliefs and desires. Moreover, we accept or reject any suggestion while in a trance according to our beliefs on that issue when we are in a waking state. When a suggestion in hypnosis is too confusing or bizarre and contradicts a person's beliefs, it will raise the person's conscious attention to the question "What is going on?" Such suggestion will be ignored by the unconscious mind, at least until further explanation of its purpose is provided. For example, you will consider jumping into freezing water only if someone needs help and you believe that you have the ability to help; otherwise, you will say, "Are you kidding me?" and refuse such a suggestion.

As I mentioned before, suggestion can cause a weak trance when we focus on it, and in trance we are more suggestible, but not to such an extreme that we will be confused about whether what is suggested is positive or negative or will cause us to cross the line of dignity. From a clinical, laboratory perspective and from my personal experience, the person in hypnosis always has the capacity to recognize what is going on, recognize the bizarre suggestion, assess the situation, and take appropriate action if necessary. What suggestions we accept depend on our personal beliefs, moral values, and confidence.

Therefore, when we are mentally weak, have a poor self-image, or are going through difficult times and feeling hopeless, such condition may have a strong influence on our choices. We know that desperate people jump into many things without reasoning first or are willing to accept others' expectations without question.

Irrational thinking and behaviour may arise for many different reasons, for example low confidence, poor problem-solving strategies, a feeling of insecurity, or fear of being rejected. A person who is constantly exposed to hopeless situations may be more amenable to any suggestion, without reasoning, for example believing that he or she is useless.

On the other hand, every day we witness people who refuse to accept positive, constructive suggestions from professionals, family members, or friends and unknowingly create more problems for themselves. This will happen when the suggestion presents some uncertainty of change or discomfort about doing something new. It may concern health, bad habits, or addictions, where people are engaged in repeating activities that bring about the same unwanted outcome, but they still refuse to accept suggestions to make positive changes regardless of their state of mind in either a waking state or hypnosis.

For example, people easily accept the suggestion to use drugs to reduce stress, despite knowing the risk of addiction and brain damage, but they refuse the positive suggestion to stop using drugs. Such a response clearly shows irrational thinking and wrong-headed decision-making. Refusal to admit that one is losing control over his or her thoughts and emotions is a typical example of being afraid to make a change. It is commonly seen that patients who need professional help to clarify the mind-body mechanisms show this type of "false protection" and refuse to make a constructive change to thinking and behaviour. Such rejection of a suggestion is called "resistance to suggestion."

In hypnotherapy, resistance is one of the most challenging things to overcome in order to have a positive therapeutic outcome. On the other hand, resistance is yet more proof that we are always in control of our decisions during trance and make the final decision. The main challenge for a professional is to convince the patient to be willing to try new constructive approaches and experience the positive outcome.

Medical hypnosis should be conducted only by professional medical, dental, and psychological practitioners who have only one goal in mind: to use the knowledge to help the patient. If someone feels lost amid their life events and can't find their way back, what would be safer for such a person than to go through relaxing, pleasant hypnotherapy skilfully run by a person who trained for years to help other people restore balance to mind and body function?

To avoid patient resistance to positive therapeutic suggestion, the skilled practitioner will spend time building a rapport and gaining trust. The practitioner will explain the therapeutic plan in detail. For example, the practitioner may propose gradually changing negative thoughts and emotions, followed by applying positive affirmations and suggestions to rebalance beliefs, thoughts, and feelings, at which time the positive change will start to be executed automatically in the unconscious mind.

Another important fact to be noted is that no one can induce trance against our will. We have the ability to enter and terminate trance at any time we wish. For example, when there is an urgent situation such as a fire, the person in hypnosis can end the trance immediately and take appropriate action. In hypnosis we do not lose control. In fact, during trance we hear everything around us and can make our own decisions and dictate our own responses according to our wishes.

Sometimes I have noticed during therapy that patients are reluctant to follow the instruction to terminate the trance. The common reason for this is that they simply enjoy the trance very much and want to stay in this pleasant state of mind for a longer or want to complete what they were working on during trance. They can and will wake up in their own time, feeling great.

Loss of memory (amnesia) is another misunderstanding about hypnosis. In fact, memory loss may occur temporarily during hypnotic trance when such suggestion is accepted by the person in a trance, but such memory can also be recalled. In hypnotherapy, there is little need to use this technique unless there is a specific purpose for it. In a laboratory setting, it may be used for research with participants who are willing to experience it. Subjects undergoing such experiences understand that it is temporary amnesia and that it is safe for them to participate. Again, it is still up to them whether they wish to follow the therapist's suggestion or not.

The "hidden observer" described in a previous chapter is further proof that we are not totally isolated during a hypnotic trance. This dissociated part of the mind is observing the whole process and all the experiences (as it always does), and helps to "protect" the person by advising whether to stay in the trance or terminate it. Like happens during sleep, there is a protective mechanism to wake a person from trance when something requires their full attention.

Although hypnosis is safe, it is strongly advised not to use hypnosis when driving a car or operating other machines. Deep relaxation may affect your ability to concentrate on the task. Moreover, it is a personal therapy and should be used only in safe and comfortable conditions. It should be considered only to make positive changes in medical conditions, mental health, or human performance. Hypnosis should not be used for fun or to foolishly manipulate others, as in cases of bullying.

If you feel that you have had bad experiences in your life, self-help may not be enough, especially when dealing with unhealed dramatic experiences. Ask your doctor for help.

Scientists and other professionals have used hypnosis successfully for years with the aim of improving the treatment and comfort of people with many medical and psychological conditions. It minimizes or eliminates the need for chemicals and reduces the time and cost of the treatment. It helps to improve your feelings about yourself and to build a strong personality and values.

Medical, dental, and psychological hypnosis is regulated by recognized professional organizations around the globe. You can find the list of them at the end of this book.

Many of us do not make use of the benefits of hypnotherapy by avoiding it, not knowing that medical hypnosis uses our natural mental abilities. Being afraid of using the mind's natural processes is like feeling uncomfortable in one's own skin.

Now I will leave it to you to make a decision about medical hypnosis. You can either use it or lose it.

Following are some clinically and scientifically proven facts on the safety of hypnosis:

- Only you decide whether to experience trance or not.
- In hypnosis people do not lose control; they are aware of what they do and who they are.
- A hypnotized person can terminate the trance at any time by themselves.
- Medical hypnosis is safe and pleasant.
- Light hypnosis is sufficient for most therapies.

You may find some reassurance from experts' views on the safety of hypnotherapy, as follows:

- "As to self-induction, many thousands have learned it. I have yet to hear a report of any bad results from its use."
  —Leslie La Crème, psychologist, and authority on hypnosis

- "We have never observed any harmful influences on the patient, which could be described in the method of hypnotherapy. Or any tendency towards the development of unstable personality, weakening of the will or pathological urge for hypnosis."
  —Dr William S. Kroger, author of *Clinical and Experimental Hypnosis*
- "Hypnotism is a natural phenomenon; there is no known deleterious effect from its use."
  —Dr Louie P. Thorpe, professor emeritus, University of Southern California, author of *The Psychology of Mental Health*

Safety of Hypnosis

Hypnosis is a procedure during which a health professional researcher suggests to a client, patient or subject, to experience changes in sensation, perception, thoughts or behaviour. The hypnotic context is established by an induction procedure. Although there are many hypnotic inductions, most include the suggestion of relaxation, calmness, well-being, and imagination of pleasurable experience. People respond to hypnosis in different ways, some describe it as an altered state of consciousness, others as a natural state of focused attention in which they feel very calm and relaxed. Most people describe it as a pleasant experience. Some people are more responsive to suggestions; others are less. They remember what happened during the trance. Hypnosis makes it easier for people to experience suggestion, but it does not force them to have this experience.[2] American Psychological Association

---

[2] Executive Committee of the American Psychological Association, Division of Psychological Hypnosis, *Psychological Hypnosis: A Bulletin of Division*, 3/2 (Fall 1997), 7.

"Can I Be Hypnotized?"

This is the second most common question regarding hypnosis. Many people believe that they cannot experience trance. To clarify this, let's start with an official formula about hypnotisability. Only your willingness has the key to your unconscious mind.

Hypnotisability

Hypnotisability describes a personal capacity to experience trance and changes in automatic activities of the brain to achieve the desired goals, learn, create, or simply clarify thoughts and recharge the body and mind.

In fact, we know that some people are more hypnotisable than others. There are also different opinions among scientists regarding the exact mechanism of hypnosis and who can be hypnotized. However, all agree that the ability to enter trance is influenced by many factors such as a person's beliefs, life experiences, personal motivation, and expectation. The person's strong desire to achieve a goal or make an expected change will increase the chance of positive results.

However, from a clinical point of view, most of us can benefit from hypnotherapy, and for a medical or psychological purpose, only a light trance is required to obtain the desired change.

Moreover, there are simple to follow psychological tests to assess a person's hypnotisability and suggestibility which will be applied before hypnotherapy starts.

Some people enter hypnosis very easily just by letting go. Others may be reluctant at first, still unconvinced that they want to be hypnotized. One's decision to accept trance or not is based on the beliefs one has about hypnosis and the person applying hypnosis. If we feel confident, we may easily let ourselves to experience hypnotic trance, or if we have thoughts of doubt, we are likely to reject the suggestion to enter a trance. People with trust issues may need guidance to resist their fear and to find the motivation to seek a positive change in their lives. Patients after a trauma may have difficulty relaxing and accepting the suggestion to make the desired changes.

However, a skilled practitioner will spend time building patient trust and eliminating resistance. In most cases, full explanations of the nature of trance, suggestion, and expectations are sufficient to carry out successful hypnotherapy. If this is not enough, the patient may have a more serious reason for resistance and, being already in professional hands, will benefit from a full assessment of the conditions and appropriate steps needed to regain health.

Twenty-one

Hypnosis in Unprofessional Hands

> Hypnotic suggestion is as powerful as fire; it either can bring healing or may burn when misused.

We need to remember that hypnosis is not a therapy as is commonly believed. Therefore, when hypnosis is used as an adjunct to therapy for medical or psychological conditions, it is logical that only a medical or psychological practitioner specializing in medical hypnosis should provide it. I repeat that it is not hypnosis we should be concerned about, but the danger posed by an unqualified or disingenuous therapist or a destructive suggestion applied to you by an unskilled person. It may be harmful or, in the best-case scenario, simply not beneficial to your condition and a total waste of your time and money.

Claims of patients being assaulted by professionals and clinicians using hypnosis are extremely rare and no different in character than claims involving other professional or nonprofessional misconduct. Therefore, each case must be investigated by authorized professional and ethical standards organizations, instead of generalizing such misconduct.

We need to remember that it takes on average five to six years of broad study and continuing postgraduate education to be a medical or psychological specialist. Medical and psychological practitioners must be registered with their respective professional councils, and even those using hypnosis as part of their practice must be registered with one of the hypnosis societies and prove that they undergo continuing education and adhere to standards of professional conduct.

I will go back to the main question: is there any danger posed by using hypnosis?

I would say yes, there are a few conditions when hypnosis is used by a person who has no knowledge of what they are doing, especially when working with fragile people. Another misuse of hypnosis is making it the topic of unhealthy jokes.

Highly skilled and ethical professionals apply hypnotic trance for one purpose only: to enhance the therapy or treatment necessary for the patient's benefit. They not only have the skill to treat the condition but also know how to use hypnosis to reinforce the necessary treatment.

You wouldn't go to an uneducated person to reduce your blood pressure, would you? Use your logic, trust your intuition, and seek professional help.

Stage Hypnotism

Stage hypnotism is known to many of us and has been performed in many countries. It is entertainment, and the hypnotists usually are well-skilled in inducing hypnosis. Stage hypnotists are masters of acting and know how to choose a subject who is willing to respond to the act and who will obey the suggestion given during trance (or not in trance) to make the show successful.

Simply put, stage hypnotism is a magic show performed by someone who knows the whole act behind it. A typical example of such an act is when a volunteer is asked to be a chicken. The hypnotized (or pretending to be hypnotized) person acts like a chicken. In fact, that person voluntarily obeys the hypnotist's suggestion to do so because he or she accepts the idea in the first place and is willing to act on it.

In recent times, as the ethical side of stage hypnosis has become controversial, stage hypnotism is restricted in many cities and banned in some countries such as Norway and South Africa to protect the dignity of individuals, rather than as a statement regarding the safety of hypnosis.

The Home Office Panel of Experts in the United Kingdom has reported on its findings that stage hypnosis is relatively safe, but the Panel still would like to see a clear code of conduct (Dr M. Heap, Sheffield University).

Twenty-two

Pros and Cons of Hypnotherapy

Therapy without hypnosis is like dinner without dessert.

Benefits of Medical Hypnosis versus Non Hypnotic Therapy

The benefits of medical hypnosis are widely recognized by scientists and clinicians around the world. There is increasing evidence from neuropsychological research that hypnotherapy enhances the treatment, reduces the time required for treatment, speeds up recovery, and offers a mode of comfortable psychological support for the patient, something that is frequently missing during any illness or recovery. Medical conditions are treated in a wide context to establish the patient's physical and mental well-being, not just to deal with the unpleasant physical discomfort. It is a powerful therapy to learn new strategies and reframe unwanted thoughts and behaviours associated with any disease or mental condition. Hypnotherapy is very effective in changing old habits and starting a person on the path to a healthier lifestyle. Such therapy can increase healing abilities, improve motivation, and increase the belief that the patient will get better. It focuses on controlling negative emotions, reducing stress, improving well-being, and learning new coping skills and problem-solving strategies. Learning how to improve and maintain the balance between mind and body function and how to return to independent life after illness will make a significant change to a person's lifestyle.

Medical hypnosis, in general, is a relaxing, pleasant experience, free of negative emotions and pain. Results are long-lasting, and the amount of medication and post hospital care is reduced significantly, as is the cost of treatment. Posttreatment care can be extended by practising self-hypnosis at home, giving the patient a more comfortable recovery period and greater independence. Once mastered, self-hypnosis will help with many issues such as confidence, emotion control, and goal achievement. You can learn why, when, and how to use self-hypnosis in Part III of this book.

Individual vs. Group Hypnotherapy

Individual therapy is much more beneficial than group therapy, as the whole programme is prepared according to individual needs. Patient responsiveness to suggestion and therapy is assessed, after which time the therapist can make a full treatment plan. Creating a good rapport will help the patient understand the whole process of hypnotherapy and respond better without fear of the unknown. This treatment is becoming more popular every day, helping with many psychological issues and helping people learn better coping strategies.

However, group therapy can be very successful when directed by professionals. This method is popular for helping patients to go through or recover from a serious medical problem such as cancer, diabetes, asthma, multiple sclerosis, physical disability, or addiction. Group therapy provides the patient with the opportunity to meet people who have similar experiences and needs. Having new friends who understand and share one's own experiences is always very rewarding and can help get a person back on their feet.

Self-Hypnosis

For clarification, I provide an explanation of other hypnosis terminology:

Hetero-hypnosis is when a person experiences hypnotic trance guided by another person. It may be a professional skilled person, a scientist, a lay practitioner, or friend who has the skill to apply hypnotic inductions. In a medical centre, it is always registered professional who is using a set of specific suggestions (induction) to help the subject experience hypnotic trance. The aim of this procedure is to enhance the therapy in order to obtain desired changes or work on a goal.

Self-hypnosis is when a person enters hypnotic trance by themselves. At the end of hypnotherapy, the patient is instructed on how to use self-hypnosis to extend the treatment at home.

Mostly, they follow the suggestions or cues practised beforehand with a practitioner during hypnotic trance. It could be self-suggestion ("Relax") or another simple repeated technique during therapy to initiate a trance experience, previously learned.

Self-hypnosis is very useful to extend the therapy at home. Once mastered, it can be used to improve fitness and make improvements in any aspect of life. It is especially effective in working on confidence, improving coping strategies, and reaching goals.

Standard self-hypnotic programmes are of high value in making self-improvements to reach the desired goal. They help to improve understanding of the importance of building human values and improving self-discipline and responsibility. Self-hypnosis may be the starting point for someone to make a significant change in thinking and make better choices. Many of us need a deeper understanding of some past experiences to make different decisions and be in better control of our thoughts and feelings. Self-hypnosis is useful when contact with a medical or psychological hypnotist is impossible.

The next part is an extended guide on how to practise self-hypnosis. Practising self-hypnosis for a few minutes every day could lead to a significant change in your attitude towards life, your emotions, and your expectations in general, which automatically will have an influence on your choices. It will help you to expand your understanding of the basic things required for well-being and success. It will clarify the difference between living with automatic negative self-suggestion and making constructive suggestions to improve your life. You can learn how to assess your present situation and start a new journey at your command.

SAY MY NAME

BEETL JU E

NO KILLING

Part III

Master Self-Hypnosis: Be the Commander of Your Life Journey

Twenty-three

Comfort Zone

> Danger of being in a "prolonged comfort zone" is slipping into a coma.

Now that you know what scientists and other professionals have to say about medical hypnosis, I would like to introduce you to self-hypnosis and explain why, when, and how to use it to make positive changes in your life.

To make changes, first we need to fully understand what we need to change and why we were in the unacceptable position in the first place. Frequently we are not fully aware of, or else we deny, the truth of our present situation. Therefore, to help you better recognize the common mistakes people make every day, first I will illustrate the most frequent conditions which require attention before one attempts to make any change. Only by doing this can we prevent making the same mistakes again and again, leading us to wonder why we are in the same position and saying, "This always happens to me." As I explained before, hypnosis will not change anything, but having a clear picture of what you want to change and what you want instead will help you to be in a better position. Carefully prepared desires and goals presented to the unconscious mind during trance in self-hypnosis will do the "magic" and facilitate the process of desired change or reaching a goal. This way you will be able to make steady and positive improvements in your life, instead of dancing to the same old out-of-tune music.

Therefore, for educational purpose only, I share with you my clinical and personal observations of how easy it is to turn in the wrong direction or to live a passive lifestyle. Bear in mind that it is a magnified picture to show how an unrecognized or ignored negative attitude towards everyday experiences can badly affect not only the life of the individual life but also the life of the whole family and the community, sometimes for generations. However, I have no intention to judge or criticize anyone in any way.

As an oral surgeon, I have been providing dental services in one of the oldest parts of London, just a few minutes' walk from Parliament and Big Ben. Since the first day of my practice, I noticed a certain significant behaviour of our patients, in contrast to my experiences working in other places in the United Kingdom and other European countries.

In this area crime was seen frequently. This has a particular influence on many teens, who believe that their future depends on how knowledgeable they are about underground culture and the world of drugs. Young people are the first to volunteer to be involved in illegal activities in order to make a quick buck, only to abuse alcohol and other drugs to release their fear at the end of the day. From time to time, one of these people would disappear, and we only heard that they were "in the house." Others paid the highest price, their lives cut short by a drug overdose or a shoot-out on the street.

One day, my receptionist went to buy lunch, only to come back two minutes later, announcing to everyone that there had been an armed robbery a few minutes earlier. There was no panic; no one was surprised. Someone said, "Oh, love, just go to the next store at the corner!" Such experiences were normal for them and passively accepted by the whole society.

On another occasion the local senior police officer said, "We worry about you girls here. You never close the door. We wonder how you have survived so far." A few days after that, my nurse and I were attacked just outside the practice in broad daylight. It was very interesting to see how everyone left everything behind and rushed to help us without hesitation. The community was shocked and felt guilty about this incident, feeling that they had failed to protect members of the community. From that day on, there was always a "big brother" looking after us discreetly when we left the office and walked to our cars. Those who watched over us were local workers, shoppers, and other members of the community. They all knew us, and they knew all about us. Although it was a bizarre experience for me, for some reason I and my co-workers felt safe knowing that they accepted us as member of the family.

Getting back to my dental practice, I found that treatment was often the last thing on a patient's mind. Only several toothaches could change their minds to sit in the dental chair, with a loud announcement: "I am scared and won't let you touch me, but I do want snow-white teeth." Although this is a typical statement in all dental surgeries, in our place the patients really meant it! They made any excuse to avoid an appointment with telegraphic speed. One day we had to postpone one patient's visit for a few minutes so I could collect my glasses from a local optician. To our surprise, no other patients came for their appointments that day—everyone had gotten the message that "the dentist is blind today."

Punctuality was non-existent; patients simply came for treatment when it was convenient for them. Any suggestion to improve this situation was stopped by a quick response: "But I can't," or "I won't bother," or "It is not for me."

Others were convinced that they knew what they wanted to do, but they were not aware of what they didn't know. They just modelled their parents, siblings, neighbours, and community by repeatedly making wrong choices or not making choices at all. Drama and the abuse of alcohol and drugs were the best-mastered survival strategies. Irrational thinking and bad choices were seen on a daily basis. The whole community's lifestyle was far worse than that of any active community. Regarding adaptation to the global flow, people had low expectations for their lives—or no expectations at all. Our reception was always full of patients preoccupied with chatting for hours about being unfairly treated by other members of their family, the government, and the rest of the world.

The general community strategy was to master dealing with the "devil they knew" and refusing to make any attempt to make positive changes. They simply made a comfort zone of the uncomfortable situation they were living. They didn't understand that by saying, "I can't," "I won't bother," and "I don't care," they were barricading themselves behind a closed door and preventing themselves from having any opportunities. They believed that the way they were living was normal, and to my great surprise, my staff and I almost started to feel that it was normal as well.

However, it was difficult for me to understand the reasons behind this specific adaptation to everyday experiences. Living in the centre of the world, it was like the whole community accepted a coma-like lifestyle and was frozen in time. I wanted to know what made the community so resistant to any change. What kept them from accepting any positive influence from the rest of the world to grow and make some steady improvements in their lives?

Soon, I recognized that to achieve my goal of securing the dental health of my patients, I would face a big challenge to maintain high standards and meet their specific expectations. I was desperate to find the answer to why they lived with such a negative attitude towards everything. I was looking for the best and quickest way to wake my patients to the knowledge that there is a better way to live and increase their motivation to go for it, including taking better care of their dental health.

Some may ask what all this has to do with dentistry.

In fact, it has a lot to do with dentistry. Dental health involves not only fillings or stopping a toothache. Dental health is strongly connected to the whole body and mind. It has an influence on, or is a result of, many medical conditions and psychological conditions. Poor education and lack of motivation and ambition are common reasons for neglecting one's dental health. Conditions such as diabetes, digestive problems, chronic pain, heart disease, infectious disease, are just a few commonly seen in dental practices. Low confidence, depression, chronic negative emotions and thoughts, poor energy frequently puts the dental visits away. Unhealthy lifestyle, as poor eating patterns, sleep deficits, addictions, physical and mental abuse and many other psychological conditions can cause people to abandon a positive, constructive, and active lifestyle, which leads to neglect of their dental health as well.

Did I find the answers? Probably not all of them, but for sure I learned a lot by attending postgraduate courses, including courses in medical and dental hypnosis at London College University.

Soon I recognized that the majority of my patients were the silent victims of a dysfunctional society, not knowing how to do things better. They grew up inside a closed, untouchable, tightly knit community, feeling comfortable in an uncomfortable zone.

We all know that there are many places around the world where education is at a low level, such as some parts of Africa, some parts of Asia, and many developing countries where children and young people must survive in terrible conditions.

That is true, but the difference between these places and certain depressed neighbourhoods in First World countries is very significant. In London, schools are free to everyone, and full support is given to anyone to find proper schooling and career opportunities. The social support system is one of the most effective in the world, healthcare is free, and there are many well-organized youth centres offering full support for education.

So, what happened there? Why have so many rejected the benefits of such a unique system?

Because they are used to living a coma-like lifestyle without a positive guide to follow to make constructive plans for tomorrow, they don't want to hear that life could be different if only they were willing to make a small effort and change their comfort zone. They don't know that changing their thinking to "I can" could open the way to a more rewarding and independent life. They do not understand that passive living through the generations has prevented them from having a constructive and more satisfying life. They missed the opportunity to learn from past experiences in order to deal more efficiently with similar situations. They do not believe that they can live, and deserve to enjoy, a better life.

I recognize how easy is to accept a passive life and live in fear of the unknown, trapped in a comfortable cocoon and stuck in destructive beliefs, thoughts, and emotions. The comfort zone is known to all of us. We are in a comfort zone when we acquire the skill to do something effortlessly with full confidence and pleasure. It is the same feeling whether we bake the best cake or perform the most complicated surgery. However, after some time of enjoying our expertise, it is the normal process of the mind to search for new ideas, to go with the flow, and to expand our life experiences. Simply, we all need to take our skills and experiences to the next level and build new comfort zones at that different level. Building new comfort zones through our lifespan gives us satisfaction and good feelings in everything we do.

For example:

- A tennis player who is comfortable with forehand will, in time, need to learn new strokes.
- In business, it is necessary to move a company to a higher level of quality.
- In professional life, we need to move out from our comfort zone to expand our knowledge.
- People in healthy relationships need to form new strong bonds in time.

The problem starts when someone chooses (either consciously or unconsciously) to stay in a comfort zone for a prolonged period of time. I like to compare life experiences to sailing on the ocean; it might be the most rewarding and enjoyable trip, or we might be drifting in the ocean during stormy weather, in fear of when disaster will strike.

Unfortunately, the facts show that many young people lose their way, not even reaching open waters. Others repeatedly make mistakes and drift round and round in the same place, wondering why they are always off course and unable to reach the desired port.

The natural laws of physics show that nothing lasts forever, which means that eventually our comfort zone may become uncomfortable. There may be situations where our previous successful and comfortable actions do not work anymore, and we may start to wonder what is happening in our life. This may occur when we take things for granted and stop working on new challenges. Being unaware that we are living a coma-like lifestyle is like exposing ourselves to long-term negative conditioning and self-destructiveness. When feeling hopeless, we may start to believe that misfortune is dancing with us and furthering our unhappiness. This is the critical point when negative habitual thinking and behaviour may start to build up.

Unfortunately, this can happen to anyone, to any family, to any community, and anywhere. Every day we see people lost on their life journey, hopelessly exposed to stormy weather. Some survive; some don't. It may be you, or someone close to you, struggling to support yourself and your family, or being stripped of dignity and drowning in the endless emotional pain of "misfortune". When we can no longer see the lighthouse on our journey, we may lose control over our decisions. Panic and desperation lead to irrational thinking and making mistakes over and over again. Consequences may be serious and destroy the belief that you can sail safely again.

It is like all your senses are blocked and you passively accept the present uncomfortable situation. There is no doubt in my mind that the passive way of living is very costly and affects the quality of life of many charming and big-hearted people who remain trapped in their cocoons with frozen beliefs, which prevent them from make positive changes in their lives.

I write this book in the hope that someone, somewhere will be jarred out of their uncomfortable comfort zone and start off on a more rewarding life journey. The use of self-hypnosis with simple psychological techniques built in can change many people's lives significantly. There are many people of all ages around the globe who are cut off from any medical or psychological help, and this book could wake a person to the belief that there is a better way of living and that anyone can learn it.

Twenty-four

Rising Star

There is an old saying that all roads lead to Rome.

In contrast to a passive life, I would like to share with you my amazement upon observing how some members from the same frozen-in-time community refused to be "put into a coma". I had the privilege of meeting a small but exceptional group of extremely ambitious young people there. They were like a light in the darkness, and their deep belief that they could be successful in their lives seemed to have come from nowhere. Nobody was giving them support, but they had a clear vision that life could be better.

I Know Who I Want to Be

One day, a sixteen-year-old girl came for a treatment with her alcoholic mother, who was drinking a beer in the reception. The girl felt very embarrassed and said, "I am sorry." We had a chat later regarding this experience, and I said that her priority should be to concentrate on building something positive for herself. From that day on, she visited the surgery frequently and shared with me and my staff her ambitions and school achievements. She also told us how difficult it was for her to see her drunken mother and take care of her two younger brothers. When she asked about dental assistant courses, her mother went ballistic, shouting, "Girl, stop dreaming. You'd better ask for a cleaning job instead."

The girl did not ask for a job, but she asked many questions about different courses. Soon she took a part-time job in a local shop and attended evening classes at the local college. Later she was accepted for a grant to study chemistry and successfully completed her degree. She started her scientific career at London University. She was growing in the same community, but her senses were looking for other opportunities along the way. She widened her horizon to see everything that such a place as London had to offer.

This is an example showing that if we put our mind to achieving something, there is always a way, but we must be willing to look for all opportunities. This girl had the natural ability to see the opportunities. She was willing to ask for and accept help and follow her clear vision of what she wanted, despite the fact that she had to fight to achieve freedom from her destructive environment.

This case shows clearly that we all have a choice. We can let ourselves live a coma-like lifestyle and accept everything that comes with it, even when we do not like it, or we can take the opportunity to learn how to have what we want and be a rising star.

Whatever we do makes an impact on our lives, on the lives of those around us, on the earth, and on the universe. We all have different experiences and needs, but at the end of the day we all want to be loved and feel secure and satisfied. However, to have what we want to have, or to be what we want to be, we need to be familiar with the fundamental conditions that lead us to make the right choices and become willing to learn from our mistakes.

Like weather, which is changing all the time, our lives are constantly in flux, and so far we are unable to control the rain or the physicals laws of the universe. But we have our minds and the ability to think of how to protect ourselves from disaster and how to prevent disaster next time.

Interestingly, some people seem to have better coping and problem-solving strategies, regardless of their past experiences. They are better prepared to go through any difficult time. Somehow, they find the way to stay calm and maintain their dignity in any situation, and they have the persistence to make the things right, whatever it takes. They can find the way to repair any damage done along the way and prevent similar disasters in future. They seem to be more confident and open-minded to recognize what is wrong and what is right and a better ability to adjust to any situation by learning from their own observations and judgements. They also are likely to have more respect for basic morals and ethics.

Some people think that they are either lucky or unlucky. However, there is no such thing as luck. Only some people are born with the ability to use the potential of their conscious and unconscious minds better than others. They rely on conscious logic and judgement and trust the instincts of their unconscious mind and its resources. Others learn more effective life strategies to make improvements to their present situation. This book serves as an intensive guide for you to do the same. I do believe that everyone has space for improvement or can find the spark to start a better life regardless of what happened in the past.

Sometimes we need to wake up, start to believe that we can be as successful as others, and go for it. Others need to receive a wake-up call to leave their comfort zone and create a new one. We all can improve our skills and be more open-minded to experimentation and have fun with it. We can find better solutions to overcoming the obstacles we face along the way and move forward on our journey. By having better strategies, we will be able to pick up fruits we couldn't reach before and remove the decayed ones. Feeling confident helps to ask questions and find the answers to them. Having a clear picture of where you want to be in the future is one of the ways to reach that place and enjoy it once you're there.

However, to better understand how to get on the right track, we need to know what is happening in our life in the first place. We must be able to make positive changes, instead of repeating things that did not work before.

Therefore, I would like to open this section of the book with some questions:

- Do you really know who you are and who you want to be?
- Do you really know the reasons behind any disappointments in your life?
- Do you slip into a coma-like lifestyle during the daytime and suffer insomnia at night?
- Are you trapped behind a closed door, not knowing what to do next?

If your answer to any of these questions is yes, then ask what keeps you there. Perhaps it is fear and or the belief that you can't do better.

Think about these questions to make a good start now. Life brings different experiences every day, and we have to be better prepared for it. Our life journey depends on how we approach life events, what coping strategies we use, and our ability to fulfil our needs. According to our life circumstances and what we believe, our thoughts and actions may be creative or destructive towards our lives and everything around us.

Beliefs, thoughts, and emotions are the main engine of making decisions, and the fact is that only we can decide what we are willing to accept or reject in life.

Therefore, first I would like to stress how important it is to come to know yourself better and discover your true talents and ambitions. According to what you find, you will seek out different opportunities and make different choices, believing that they are the best.

Many of our decisions are directed by past experiences, knowledge, beliefs, and personal goals. But we all have a choice to give love to our family and friends and be successful workers and dedicated professionals. Or we may choose a destructive lifestyle, one full of negative actions towards others and especially towards ourselves.

Only by learning to deal with life events actively can we be successful commanders of our ship. To reach balanced mental health

we need to improve our self- acceptance, self- valuation, have better relationships with others, and the environment, and be mindful of purpose of life and growth. Our success depends on our inner strengths, self-trust, self-image, self-esteem, and ambitions, and our persistence to reach what we want.

Each chapter in this section serves as a guide to the basic skills you need to master if you want to make positive changes in your life. At the same time, understanding the importance of obeying natural laws will make your life path safe and rewarding. Therefore, first I will take you step by step through the most common causes of being off track, confused, and hopeless with the habit of repeating bad choices and thereby damaging your life and your family. In later chapters, I will guide you to discover your present position and how to get back on track and start enjoying sailing under your own command to your desired destiny. At the end of this book you will find a full script of hypnotic program, to start practising self-hypnosis, including what therapeutic goals you want to achieve during the session.

Readers may notice some repetitions in each parts of the book, which were intentionally inserted to have a clear picture of the discuss topic.

Twenty-five

Self-Hypnosis

> Most folks are as happy as they make up their minds to be.
>
> Abraham Lincoln

There is something unique inside each of us that is yet to be discovered. The ability to experience hypnotic trance is a universal gift that Mother Nature gave us so we could be in better control of our bodies and minds. Knowing the processes of our mind and its unlimited potential better will increase our creativity and resources not only to survive but also to reach our goals.

Life experience shows that when we try something new, after a short period of enthusiasm, doubts tend to fill our mind and the process of learning something positive is broken, leaving us at square one. Typical examples are trying to stop wasting your time, overeating, or losing your temper. When what you are trying to stop doing happens again, your frustration increases, leading you to lose control over your thoughts and emotions even more. At this point, the cycle of unfortunate events moves even faster. Your motivation starts to fade, and you may be reluctant to try something new.

Sometimes people become stuck in the false belief that they can't do better. "I want this, but I can't do that" is a typical thing we hear from people who are attempting to make a positive change such as stopping smoking, improving their relationships, overcoming addiction, or performing better in business.

However, there is a better way to be free from all unwanted habits, irrational thinking, and uncontrolled behaviour and to stop repeating the same mistakes.

As I presented in an earlier chapter, the hypnotic state of mind can facilitate desired changes and achievements. A hypnosis session can be carried out by a person who guides another person to enter a trance. This could be a practitioner applying hypnotic induction to the patient who is willing to experience trance with a specific aim to work on a specific change or goal.

Self-hypnosis involves the same procedure, but the person working on achieving desired goal enters a hypnotic trance by themselves. Self-hypnosis is a very useful tool to extend hypnotherapy at home to maintain health and boost self-healing mechanisms and well-being. It is the quickest way to make positive changes in one's thinking, feelings, and beliefs. It is especially effective in working on confidence, improving problem-solving strategies, finding resources to solve problems, increasing creativity, and improving performance.

Learning to use self-hypnosis will speed up the process of unlearning unwanted habits and learning new coping and problem-solving strategies. It is a natural state of mind which lets us be closer to the unconscious mind and its processes and resources that are vital to our health, survival, and ability to achieve. Hypnotic trance increases our contact with the inner self, making it is easier for us to find out who we really are and assess our present position.

With experience, during hypnotic trance, it is possible to tap into the unconscious mind to access our inner resources to find a solution to the ongoing questionable situation. These inner resources may be based on our past experiences, and we can learn from them. When such positive resources are out of reach, our mind has the capacity to find a different resource, as the unconscious has unlimited creative ability. By learning how to rely on your unconscious resources, you will be in better control over your decision-making, creativity, performance, and goal achievement.

Practising self-hypnosis may prevent many disappointments and help you to find the right track again if you drift off course during stormy weather. It is the most convenient way to adjust to ongoing worldwide changes and situations of any sort and will help you to go with the flow. It is a useful way to stay calm in all situations and see the true picture in a more mature way.

Learning healthy, constructive techniques while in a trance will help to improve your self-image, ability, and judgement. When in a trance, we can improve our motivation and persistence to make necessary changes to anything that we want to change about ourselves. Newly learned patterns of positive thinking and behaviour will have longer-lasting results as they will be processed directly by the unconscious mind in an automatic way.

Therefore, I call upon young people especially to wake up to hypnosis and benefit from its potential to lead you to a more pleasant and more rewarding life. You can be in better control of your life journey from the beginning and make the right decisions to reach what you want.

Everyone can learn how to use self-hypnosis. When mastered, it can be used at anytime and anywhere you need to be in control and make steady improvements in your life. Feeling better about yourself helps you to look for more opportunities, as well as improves performance in school, in your professional life, in sports, or in art. You can better prepare yourself for everyday tasks such as exams, interviews, and public speaking and learn to negotiate any deal with confidence. Above all, you will be more confident to say yes or no to any situation in line with your beliefs, instead of pleasing others.

A few minutes with your unconscious mind every morning will increase your energy and motivation to have a creative, successful day. Whatever your starting point is and regardless of your past experiences, this will enhance your belief that you can sail successfully and enjoy your journey, regardless of weather conditions. But above all, it could open the door to happiness and better relationships, increasing your appreciation and your gratitude to yourself and others.

This daily practice will help to restore a healthy balance between the body and mind after a busy day, initiate the restoring and healing processes, and increase energy for the next day's activities. A few minutes before bedtime will help you leave any unfinished business behind and make positive plans for a successful tomorrow. This way, there will be no storm in your head and you will sleep like a baby without the need for sleeping pills.

Sometimes we need to wake up and be open-minded to new ideas or willing to ask for help from people who have experience with the issue we are facing. When all bridges are crumbling, you need to see why this happens in the first place and take the necessary steps to stop it.

Like in sailing after a damaging storm, we need to anchor ourselves from time to time to recharge our energy, repair any damage, make new plans, and prepare the ship with new equipment before taking the next step of the journey. Sailors must adapt to weather conditions and need to update their navigational skills if they are to be responsible for the safety of the ship. Commanders must have high moral and ethical standards and must stand behind the crew in any situation. They need to make decisions confidently and in a calm way. They know where they are sailing and why. This way they secure the excitement of the crew and the safety of the ship for the entire journey. We need to do the same if we are looking for a better life.

Let's turn now to the more technical side of entering a trance and making positive desired changes. To practise self-hypnosis you need to follow a few simple steps to experience trance in which you can apply specific previously selected suggestions to obtain the desired goal. Here, I merely explain each step, but the whole script is presented at the end of the book.

First - induction and deepening. A set of induction suggestions must be applied to initiate trance, followed by two sets of suggestions to deepen the trance. Induction suggestions mostly aim at relaxing the body and causing you to concentrate on your breathing, as is presented in Chapter 33 and Chapter 72. For deepening the trance, pleasant imagery can be used, but the most popular images are of a garden, a valley, the beach, or stairs (see more in Chapter 51). Other hypnosis features described in Part I can be applied.

Second - ego strengthening. When a person is in a trance, suggestions of self-image, ability, and well-being are added to improve the person's self-beliefs and feelings. See examples in Chapter 33.

Third - application of therapeutic or goal suggestion. It is the stage where specific therapeutic or goal suggestions are applied and, if they are believable to you, they will be accepted by the unconscious mind. Therapeutic suggestions are given to bring about positive changes in a person's feelings, thoughts, beliefs, or perceptions.

You can take an active part by learning how to build your own therapeutic or goal-oriented suggestions by reading the next chapters. At the end of each chapter, I provide examples of specific suggestions for each particular issue to give you an idea of what suggestions to use. Each chapter presents different elementary issues important to making positive changes in your life and reaching your goals one by one. You can say, "I stay calm in all situations," "I always look for the true picture of any situation," and "I always look for the best solution in a calm and mature way." Or you can join a few suggestions together as each one is the result of the previous one.

For example, working on anger issues, you can use the following suggestion: "By staying calm, I can see the true picture of my present unpleasant situation, which helps me to find the right way to solve the problem in a more mature way and with a better final result." Working on improving your eating habits, you can say, "I choose a healthy diet because it increases my natural self-healing mechanisms and automatically improves my well-being."

This stage of trance can be used to apply suggestions to a personal goal, for example, "I will complete my course by June 2019" or "I will buy a new house in January 2020." "Upon completion of my course, I will get a well-paying job, and because of that, I will buy a house in 2020."

Take a time to be more familiar with this process. Practice makes perfect, so start to enjoy self-hypnosis anywhere and anytime you need it.

Fourth, - post hypnotic suggestions. Any goal or accepted therapeutic suggestion can be reinforced by posthypnotic suggestions which aim to extend the newly obtained changes lasting long after the termination of hypnosis. Such reinforced suggestions will act in an automatic way, like skating or swimming, once mastered. For example, any change you work on today in this special relaxed state of mind will cause your unconscious mind to act automatically when appropriate, long after you terminate the trance.

Posthypnotic suggestions or cues are given as well to allow you to re-experience trance anytime you need to. One commonly used combination consists of breathing suggestions, relaxation, and a verbal or physical trigger point. These are practised a few times during hypnosis. Such suggestions that trigger the hypnotic state in future may be as follows:

- Each time you, (I) wish to experience the pleasant feeling of relaxation and peace of mind as you are experiencing it now during this special state of mind, you can take a deep breath in and then, when breathing out, say to yourself, "Focus now." Immediately you will find yourself in special place where you can relax your body and mind to increase body and mind healing mechanisms or to work on any personal goal as you wish.
- Any suggestion such as "Relax" or "Go inside" combined with any physical gesture, for example putting a thumb and index finger together, putting your hands together, or making a fist, will automatically initiate the state of mind where you can extend the therapy indicated by a practitioner or work on a personal goal.

Fifth - termination of trance. It is a set of suggestions is given to terminate the trance. Taking the benefit of everything you learn and experience in this relaxing state of mind, as is the case now, you can end this session when you are ready just by counting from one up to 5. With each number of the count up, you are more awake. On the count of five, your eyes are wide open and you are fully awake, ready to go back to normal daily duties, feeling refreshed and feeling good about yourself. Start counting now: one (waking up), two (becoming more aware of reality), three (continuing to wake up), four (almost awake), five (wide awake, feeling good about yourself and feeling good inside yourself).

Remember, learning new skill takes a time, but practising it will bring the desired results within a short time.

Again, it is important to remember that hypnosis is not a therapy; it only increases the speed of learning directly by way of the unconscious mind. I said before that hypnotherapy is safe, and this is true. However, if you send a meaningless or harmful wish, the result of the hypnosis will reflect that. The most important part of hypnotherapy is to use the appropriate suggestion. Then it will deliver what you are asking for. "Your wish is my command," said Aladdin in the classic children's story. Your unconscious mind will respond in the same way if you send a clear picture of what you want.

Therefore, I present the most fundamental of the natural laws for you to secure a comfortable fit with the rest of the world wherever you are. These will help you to recognize how important it is to remember that your beliefs, emotions, and thoughts govern your choices and actions and remind you to make the necessary adjustments. This may be the starting point for you to make a significant change in your thinking and to make better choices. Many of us need only a deeper understanding of some past experiences to make different, right decisions and be in better control of our thoughts and feelings.

Moreover, from clinical experience we know that many people may have a problem following simple suggestions, for example to relax or to feel comfortable. People who never experienced love may have a problem giving love. Those living in constant fear have trouble relaxing. Someone with bad past experiences may not know what it is like to feel comfortable or confident. A suggestion to have a good relationship will not work if the subject does not understand the basic fundamentals of a relationship. Something that seems to be obvious for some will be difficult for others to follow, provided they even know what it is.

Therefore, to fully benefit from practising self-hypnosis, it would be beneficial to read this book first to the end, to gain the whole picture of the all steps necessary to make positive changes in physical and mental health and have better results in achieving goals. Whatever you are looking for, it is important to know exactly what you want to achieve during trance and to use the right suggestions.

I started this section with a presentation of how our thoughts, emotions, and beliefs shape our destiny. I did this in order to make the reader aware of the common reasons people remain stuck in a comfort zone. Although it may feel that we all know them, but do we react to them in the right way? Therefore, I will go step by step to build your confidence, create your goals, and learn fundamentals to start a new, more rewarding life. I support each issue by offering a suggestion which can be used later when working on self-hypnosis. The purpose of all these suggestions is to help you make positive changes in your thinking and in your feelings about yourself and the rest of the world and to help you reach your goals.

With experience you will be able to add your own important therapeutic/goal suggestion(s) according to your needs. Have a notebook and pen ready to make a list of your goals and exercises, which you can build into your self-hypnotic programme.

If only one reader should find the light in the darkness, then this will bring me the greatest satisfaction, but I know that there is more than one lost at sea, looking desperately for a way to reach a safe port. Take the benefit of the hard work of the professionals who sacrificed their careers to present evidence of the benefits and safety of hypnosis. Thanks to their strong belief in this natural gift, we can use it safely today to its full potential, helping to improve not only our own lives but also the lives of those around us.

Twenty-six

The Power of Thoughts

Thoughts can light your way or keep you in darkness. Thoughts, emotions, and beliefs are connected and influence each other; therefore, throughout the rest of the book, I will refer to them as the "Trio Mind".

First, we should acknowledge that extremes in belief, thought, and emotion are acceptable only when there is a reason for it. For example, confused and illogical thoughts and emotions can be expected when grieving, when experiencing pain, or when in a dangerous situation. Wild excitement is justified when someone has been accepted to university, won the lottery, has fallen in love, etc. However, there is no healthy balance of Trio Mind when one is unrealistically optimistic or pessimistic. Every day we see people living with anger or sadness, as they have been doing for a long time without any significant reason for it. It is not logical to believe that we are worse than others only because someone else said so. There is no positive thinking, or no thinking at all, that things will be OK when everything is going the wrong way, without taking positive steps to turn the tide and go in a different direction.

Thoughts are the mental processes influencing our decisions and moving the chain of the Trio Mind. An enormous amount of different thoughts run through our heads, thoughts responding to past and ongoing experiences or future expectations as we search for the best outcome. It is important to remember that all our thoughts have a definite meaning in our lives and that none must be ignored. They reflect our experiences and are our tools to cope with different life situations. Most of us take the time to apply reason to our experiences or ask for advice. The more information we have, the easier it is for us to find what is more logical, beneficial, and believable. Bigger issues require a larger investment of time to find the right answer, but finally our thoughts will send us in a direction to deal with whatever the issue may be.

Depending on our experiences and how we understand them, our thoughts may be positive and constructive or negative and destructive. The ability to control our thoughts is a survival, coping, and problem-solving mechanism. Frequently we do not recognize that we have the freedom to make up our own thoughts, regardless of our present or past experiences. Acquiring the ability to control our thoughts will help us to build personal values, confidence, and judgemental abilities and reach our goals.

Having been exposed to different experiences every day, we most likely grew up with a mixture of different thoughts. When going through pleasant and unpleasant situations, the human analyses every situation and forms its own opinion.

However, the danger comes when we let negative, irrational, or catastrophic thoughts run rampant for a long time. In such cases we encounter the danger of filling our mind with stormy seas.

Whatever you think of first thing in the morning is mostly what will stay with you all day long. It may be denial thoughts as "Maybe it wasn't too bad or something better will come along," as we see with a person in a coma-like condition, or perhaps it is whispering, "I am useless, I can't, I don't care," etc.

The law of the sea is straight and logical: assess any problematic situation as fast as possible and take the necessary action to solve it. The same process is necessary when dealing with your thoughts. Otherwise you let a negative thought reach a catastrophic conclusion, for example,

"This always happens to me," which runs through your head endlessly, blocking rational thinking.

Thoughts repeated for a long time will lead to the formation of automatic positive thoughts (APT) or automatic negative thoughts (ANT), which run deep into the unconscious mind. Because of their automatic nature, they influence our decisions in an automatic way with little or no logical control. Typical repetitions are "I know that something bad will happen. I will fail. This always happens to me. I think I am dying." These thoughts are familiar to many of us. Such thinking may lead us to avoid doing important things, for example travelling or attending courses, or, even more serious, may cause panic attacks.

Therefore, working on having balanced thoughts and building a portfolio of positive thoughts will eliminate unreasonable negative reactions with time.

Think for a moment about having coffee with a friend repeatedly mentioning the long chain of life problems never solved. Do you remember how mentioning these things affected your thinking for the rest of the day? It is common to let our thoughts run away from us and unrealistically let them manifest the feelings they suggest, for example anger. This happens easily when the mind is preoccupied with an uncontrolled or conflicted situation. Of course, it is very positive to help a friend by discussing an ongoing problem and trying to find a solution for it. However, talking for hours over the course of weeks only to complain and blame others for the unwanted situation not only will fail to change anything but also will create ANT for all parties involved.

Uncontrolled ANT will dance in your head all day and night without control and create the danger of having you go off track or be lost at sea, not knowing which direction to sail.

For example, saying "I will never find a job, I always meet the wrong person, or I am always on the wrong side at the wrong time," is familiar to all of us.

Even more serious is that ANTs block constructive thoughts and prevent rational thinking, for example, "Shell I try something different or there must be a reason for that." If unreasonable thoughts are dominating your life, they will always bring disappointing results and deepen your negative self-conditioning. Frequently, you may not be aware that when you feel bad or hopeless or think that everything is going wrong, you condition your mind with negativity. When negative thinking is repeated for a considerable period of time, it will be accepted as fact by the unconscious mind and will influence an automatic, uncontrolled, impulsive reaction.

Therefore, learning to keep a healthy balance between our thoughts according to our experiences is a factor of having a better life. Hypnosis is an excellent tool to reframe such conditioning as ANT. This is another example of the idea that it is not hypnosis we should be worried about but what thoughts we let ourselves accept (both when in hypnosis and when not in hypnosis), be they our own thoughts or those of others.

Twenty-seven

Master Your Thoughts

> Nothing is either good or bad but thinking makes it so.
>
> William Shakespeare (1564–1616)

Now we understand that our actions (whether conscious and unconscious) are the fruits of our thoughts. What we hold for a long time in the unconscious mind will move us in the respective direction. Therefore, it is crucial to learn how to automatically fill our minds with constructive thoughts most of the time. Positive thoughts will be our assets when rainy days come. They are stimulating, they increase enthusiasm and creativity, and they are the fundamental basis for learning effective coping strategies and problem-solving tactics and helping us to achieve our goals.

There are many ways to be in control of our thoughts. Each way is effective, but all of them require practice before we can leverage them to create automatic positive thoughts (APT).

Below, I present simple steps to build positive thoughts:

1. The most important step is to be aware of your thoughts. Being aware of the balance between negative and positive thoughts helps you to recognize your thoughts and control them. One way of knowing the content of your thoughts is to make a list of dominant positive

and negative thoughts you have during the day. Do this for a whole week. See examples in Step 6.
2. Ask yourself, are your thoughts constructive and stimulating you to move in the right direction, or are they putting you under the bus, causing you to feel bad at the end of the day?
3. Ask yourself what the reason is for having these negative thoughts. If you have a problem finding the reason for your negative thinking, read Chapter 46: Assessing Your Present Position to find the answer. After doing that, you should have no reason for continuing to nurture negative thoughts. Instead you could concentrate on a new plan to move forward.
4. Stop intrusive negative thoughts. They are negative intruders preventing you from sailing to your new destiny. You can stop persistent ANTs simply by refusing them.
   Say to yourself, "Stop it right now. I know I need to do something positive."
   If the thoughts are persistent, ask again why you think that way, for example, "Why do I think that I can't do anything well or find the right solution? Is it because others say this, or is it because I made a few mistakes in the past?"
   Repeat this exercise each time you start to have negative thoughts or feel bad.
5. Defend yourself from ANT by saying one of the following things:
   - "OK, maybe others have that opinion, but it doesn't mean that they are right."
   - "If I make mistakes, as everybody does, I can learn from them and do better next time."
   - "What I believe is more important, as I know and trust myself, whereas others don't."
6. After stopping the ANT, immediately change your thinking to make it positive, and use your positive thoughts as suggestions in self-hypnosis.

"I know that I can do better. From now on, nothing and no one will stop me from reaching my goals. I always look for the best solutions to ongoing situations and close the matter in a positive way. I am independent and able to do what I need to do. I am ready to ask for advice and take necessary actions to move forward."

Repeat the foregoing suggestion each time you start to have negative thoughts. You can reinforce positive thoughts by working on them in self-hypnosis.

For an easy start, following is a list of some common negative and positive cognitions. Use this list if you have a problem determining your dominant thoughts. Read the negative thoughts first and ask which of these are familiar to your way of thinking. Then read the positive thoughts and think about them as well. This way you will recognize the dominant thoughts you have every day. For better results, make your own list.

Here are examples of common thoughts we experience every day:

Negative thought	Positive thought
I am a bad person.	I am a loving person.
I don't deserve to be loved.	I do deserve to be loved.
I am not good enough.	I can do whatever I want to do.
I am a failure.	I am always successful.
I am worthless.	I am a valuable human being.
I feel hopeless.	I always look on the bright side.
I always disappoint others.	I am responsible.
I deserve to be punished.	I learn from my mistakes.

You can convert the negative thoughts in the left-hand column into the corresponding positive thoughts in the right-hand column and work on them one by one. For example, "I am useless" may be convert into "I can do whatever I want to do."

Twenty-eight

Affirmations

Build a Portfolio of Constructive Thoughts

Using affirmations is a powerful method for building and maintaining a positive self-image, self-value, and self-esteem. By repeating positive affirmations, you will build up your personal strength. Affirmations are powerful sets of words that serve as self-suggestions to reinforce our beliefs, positive thoughts, and positive behaviour. They have a significant impact on our well-being and decision-making. They are nuggets of verbal cognitive information sent from the conscious to the unconscious mind reminding us of who we are and what we want, for example, "I always trust my intuition" or "I carefully analyse any situation, and because of that I make decisions with confidence." Such positive, constructive self-suggestions repeated over the course of a significant period of time will become automatic, depending on how deeply we believe in the idea and how strong the emotions are behind the suggestion. (See a discussion of the law of suggestion in Part II.)

One person told me, "Affirmations are stupid." Well, if you believe this, then for sure making affirmations will be so and you will stay with the same thoughts you have now. Still, I maintain that it is important to understand the power of suggestion and affirmation, as our thoughts will either keep us on the right track or lead us to crash even in safe waters.

Carefully prepared affirmations are like clean fuel for the mind and will support you when you're lacking energy or motivation. It is of vital importance to use them as soon as negative thoughts or feelings start to fill your body and mind.

Practising affirmations systematically will lead to positive thoughts and beliefs replacing negative thoughts and beliefs. Make a list of your own affirmations illustrating what kind of person you want to be.

If you find that you have a few affirmations written on the same line, you can arrange them in groups, for example as a trio, with one leading to the other, to speed up the process of self-improvement and trigger the logic behind it.

For example, "When I am calm, I concentrate better and have better ideas."

"I am confident in everything I do; therefore, I believe that I am able to face any obstacle. And I always finish any projects I start."

If this is your first experience with a self-improvement programme, then this exercise may feel strange to you at first, but there is nothing abnormal about it. You are simply not used to having an inner conversation with yourself or a positive attitude towards yourself. It may be hard at first, but it is the way to win and grow. This will be the basis for when you start using inner dialogue with your unconscious mind later, when doubts creep in and try to stop you from reaching your goals.

Write down your affirmations and repeat them every day: "From now on, I believe that I am attractive and a great human being. I do whatever I need to do with enthusiasm and to the best of my ability. I am able to systematically make positive changes in my life, as every day brings a new achievement."

Practise affirmations every day. Make them shorter or longer according to your comfort level, and repeat them throughout the day silently to yourself to recharge your confidence. It is recommended that at the beginning of your work, you repeat them, preferably aloud, twice a day for three weeks at least. Build the most important affirmations and make your own portfolio of them to read or repeat in your mind systematically.

You can do this on your way to work, before bedtime, etc. Spending only a few minutes every day performing positive affirmations will bring rewards to many facets of your life. After three weeks, you should be more comfortable with affirmations and sense the first automatic changes in your thinking and behaviour. Affirmations serve as good hypnotic suggestions for when you are working on self-hypnosis.

At the beginning, it will be more beneficial to choose one affirmation per session. Practising self-hypnosis will significantly speed up the process of replacing negative thinking with positive thinking. It will make a huge difference in how you think and in your ability to do what you want to do.

Millions of people use these simple exercises successfully to learn positive thinking and increase self-belief and self-esteem.

Following is an example of how to work on affirmations:

- Write and rewrite the affirmation: "I am a friendly and loyal person."
- Think about the meaning: "Because of that, I have friends I can rely on."
- Visualize it. See yourself with a friend having fun together.
- Have deep positive feelings behind it. Feel the pleasure from that meeting.

Repeating positive desires is a powerful strategy to feel better about yourself.

It is better to work on the most urgent issues first. In time you can work on trios.

Below, I present examples of essential cognitions that will help you keep a healthy balance in your Trio Mind:

- "Every day I show my appreciation for being part of the universe."
- "Every day I remind myself that I am a unique and valuable human being."

- "I am grateful for my ability to learn. I feel healthier and wiser every day."
- "I have a lot of energy to be active, be creative, and enjoy life."
- "I trust myself and my unconscious mind without limitation."
- "My memory is improving constantly by exercising my mind."
- "I am in control of my beliefs and thoughts all the time."
- "I respect myself, others, and the rest of the world."
- "I am responsible for all my actions."
- "I believe that I am capable, and I do deserve to be successful in whatever I do."

When these thoughts become more automatic, they come to your conscious mind as automatic "flash images" from the unconscious mind. You can visualize them as well, as they need to be reinforced regularly (see more in Chapter 51, on visualization). It is important to be consistent and practise them until they stay in your mind most of the time.

The most important thing to remember is that only you have the power to decide what you will do, feel, and think, not others.

Twenty-nine

Power of Emotions

> Whenever yours feeling conflicts with your wishes, feeling will be the victor.
>
> Neville Goddard (1905–1972)

Emotions play an important role in our life as they express our past and present experiences. The feelings inside us are the decisive factors of our actions and choices. On the other hand, if uncontrolled, our emotions can damage our self-belief and lead to irrational thinking and behaviour. Simply speaking, emotions can either cause us to fly or burn our wings. Only by knowing their purpose can we benefit from them without being betray. Therefore, I would like to present the most common emotions we experience and discuss how they affect out choices.

We need to remember that each of our emotions has its own role in our life, depending on the situation we are facing. As with thoughts, determining which the right emotions are will depend on the situation. For example, it is normal to experience feelings of anger, sadness, hopelessness, or fear when facing unfortunate or life-threatening situations. These feelings stimulate us to take appropriate action when we need to protect ourselves or survive. "I had the feeling …" is frequently heard from people who follow their feelings when making a serious decision. Successful people frequently rely on their intuition. We all know as well that when something good happens to us, we feel happy and have the energy and motivation to explore our experiences further. Everything seems to be beautiful, and we believe that anything is possible, without limits.

However, all emotions should be in balance and in proportion to the situation. It is not reasonable to remain "stuck in love" with an abuser or a manipulator, saying, "But I love him [or her]." It is not good to live with anger for years over something that happened in the past or no longer exists, thereby destroying your own life and the lives of those around you. In fact, both of these emotions are out of proportion and may be very damaging in the long term.

Long-term unreasonable feelings can be recognized as chronic negative emotions, causing the Trio Mind to remain in a negative mood. If our Trio Mind is constantly filled with negativity, our actions will reflect this. Chronic negative emotions are like an electric shock in our heads and will flow into our minds uncontrolled, causing irrational thinking and impulsive actions.

Therefore, it is important to learn how to control your emotions in any situation. We know now that it is up to us how we feel. We can let emotion control our lives, or we can take over and be in control of our emotions. Keeping a healthy balance in the Trio Mind can put us in a better position to assess any situation, analyse it, and make better responses. By staying calm, we can see more choices, make more rational decisions, and have better plans for the future. Once mastered, this process will drastically change our life and the lives of those around us.

However, to be able to control our emotions, we must remind ourselves of the real meaning of different emotions and what consequences they may bring when we follow them day by day. We think that we know what our emotions are, but are we living by them every day, just believing that we are in control? It is surprising how often we let our emotions take control of our decision-making process, which puts us in a more difficult situation. We know the refrains: "I can't stand this." "I hate you." "I know I shouldn't have done that, but I was so angry."

So let's go through a variety of emotions to gain a better understanding of them in order to eliminate them or be in better control of them.

When working on emotions in self-hypnosis, you can start with a positive suggestion such as, "From now on I control my feelings. They don't control me." Also, you will notice that in the following chapters I sometimes offer a suggestion or therapeutic suggestion after discussing a particular phenomenon or technique. You may use these suggestions when you engage in self-hypnosis or affirmation-based thinking.

Thirty

Negative Emotions

> Holding on to anger is like grasping a hot coal with the intent of throwing it at someone else; you are the one getting burned.
>
> Gautama Buddha (563–483 BC)

I would suggest reading the above quotation once more. As I mentioned before, all feelings have a purpose and are useful tools that can be used in different situations.

It is normal that experiencing physical and emotional pain from an illness, suffering from abuse, grieving, feeling hopeless, or being subjected to unfair treatment quickly leads to frustration, anxiety, fear, stress, anger, hate, revenge, jealousy, or depression. However, if these feelings preoccupy your mind all the time, they may damage your life in every respect. It is important, too, not to suppress your emotions or ignore them. If they are persistent for a long time, they may not vanish by themselves. Chronic negative emotions change brain function and, when uncontrolled, have a devastating effect on one's personal and family life and affect the whole society.

We know that the captain's moods can get the whole crew on their toes in the most hopeless of situations or else make the ship seem like the worse place on earth. Therefore, we need to really understand and accept that long-term negative beliefs, attitudes, and emotions will keep us in a negative mood and cause us to repeatedly take negative action. Like a boomerang, negative or reckless actions towards others will return to us, hurting us even more.

Furthermore, uncontrolled negative feelings, growing like weeds in a garden, cause the mind to get stuck in obsession and irrational responses. These feelings prevent us from being constructive and reasonable and stop us from enjoying life. Simply put, they block positive thoughts and actions.

Our actions governed by negative emotions will push us to the brink of destruction and cause even more pain and more negative reactions. When our mind is preoccupied with negative thoughts, our behaviour reflects this negative attitude towards ourselves and the rest of the world.

Anger, Hate, Revenge, and Bullying

We all are aware that anger and hate are extremely damaging not only to the person experiencing them but also to those closely associated, or to entirely innocent people. Entertaining anger and hatred is like dancing with death, with no winning side.

Therefore, it is not OK to live with anger all the time, and it is not OK to put petrol on the fire when we're feeling angry to create even more tragedy. If someone hurts us, after having our first reaction of anger, we can then think of how to prevent a similar situation from developing in future.

Many of us take our anger out on an employee, spouse, or child. We all should try to stop doing this, as there is no excuse for someone losing their temper because they were angry! For example, it is OK to be angry if someone overslept and failed to give you a lift to an important interview. Despite this disappointment, it would be foolish to smash that person's car in revenge. It would not give you the job and would likely put you in a difficult situation with the police. It would be wiser in future to be more independent or more careful about whom you ask for help.

Another example of uncontrolled anger creating devastating consequences involves a dispute over who had the right of way between two young drivers at a London roundabout. The angry driver attacked the other driver, a young man, with a knife and killed him in front of his girlfriend without saying one word! Recently, a bus driver was caught on camera purposely hitting a cyclist in his way because the cyclist annoyed him! Uncontrolled anger has ended young lives and sent people to prison for years. And whole families suffer because of one person's anger!

Anger can destroy whole cities, triggered by unwanted sports results or political or economic factors. At many sports events, including the Olympics, people have tragically died instead of having the fun they paid for in hopes of witnessing examples of the real human spirit.

Vancouver, Paris, and London are just a few examples of cities that have experienced destruction after big sports events. A small group of irrational drunk people started the demolition and took the rest of the disappointed fans with them to foolishly burn cars and buildings—and sometimes their own property—in this madness.

The result of this is always the same: death, casualties, devastated families, and many destroyed homes. Innocent people lose their health and careers. Many youngsters are expelled from their universities because of stupidly following the riot just for fun. Those responsible go to jail sooner or later, their families are heartbroken, and no one benefits from it in the end. There are no winners—only losers!

Where has common sense gone?

Anger for any known or unknown (to the unconscious mind) reason is dangerous and leads to irrational behaviour, for example bullying. Bullying is a growing problem around the world. It can occur at home, at school, or in the workplace. Many teenagers who are the victims of bullying live with catastrophic thoughts and false beliefs, feeling hopeless. Unfortunately the number of suicidal actions growth because of that.

We must set things straight. It is not normal to derive pleasure from hurting others. It is not funny to make a joke at another's expense. It is not normal to destroy someone else's dignity for fun, as we see more frequently on the Internet. Whoever it is, such behaviour needs professional help. To protect bullies is to enable them to do it again, which puts another innocent person in danger!

It is not OK to take a passive part in bullying either. Watching a bully act on the Internet or at school is taking an active part in it. If someone takes pleasure in seeing someone else hurt or killed, this is a red flag to seek help. To enjoy watching the gang rape of a helpless teenager is even worse than the act itself.

There always will be people who find fun in others' pain, but the rest of us together can make huge changes and stop this madness. It is time to make sure our children understand how bad bullying is. We must confront this growing trend by having open discussions if we want to protect our children.

Hate and revenge will lead to more damage on both sides in an unending cycle. Unfortunately, the shocking consequences of anger and irrational actions can be seen every day in homes, on the street, at work, and in public places. Domestic violence, road rage, and drunken behaviour are a nightmare for many children and adults. Living with the desire for revenge will bring more pain and vengeful actions, and the cycle continues. The same pattern of destruction is seen behind closed doors in many families, classrooms, and neighbourhoods. The consequences are the same, and it hurts the same as, or even worse than, the unfortunate events, because the pain comes from someone close. The outcome of revenge, hate, and anger is a pain. Similarly, pain leads to anger, hate, and revenge—nothing else. Someone must break the cycle and shake hands for the sake of all, especially the children.

Anger must be treated or controlled, depending on its origin, but it must never be ignored.

Therapeutic suggestion: "Relaxing deeply now, I understand that only by staying calm I can be in better control of any situation and act more rationally. By relaxing my mind and body on a regular basis and working on my self-beliefs and self-value, every day I feel more confident that I can control my emotions. From now on I control my feelings; they don't control me."

Thirty-one

Other Destructive Emotions

> The mind act like an enemy for those who don't control it.
>
> Bhagavad Gita

Jealousy

Jealousy is another negative feeling that may lead to serious destruction. Depending on the scale of the situation, it may destroy the life of the jealous person and the lives of the other parties. If a person has a hard time because someone else is having a good time or has something new or better, it shows that the person's thinking is irrational and their energy is directed in the wrong way. Jealousy can be about anything and anyone. In several cases it may lead to destruction of the whole family.

Jealousy indicates weakness, a poor self-image, low self-esteem, and lack of confidence. Jealousy in a relationship is common and can paralyse both parties. It may lead to physical harm and mental torture. Jealous people can spend entire days trying to discover what someone else is doing and control their life.

When suspicious thoughts and behaviour preoccupy our mind, this obsessive pattern will stop us from doing what we are supposed to do. This way we create the unhealthy path leading to neglect of our responsibilities to ourselves and to those who depend on us.

Whatever the situation, it is more rewarding to concentrate on one's own life and make it more fruitful and independent. This way there will be no reason to worry about what others are doing. Those who are in control of their own lives concentrate on their improvements and goals and will have no reason to fear or accept others' dishonesty or suspicions.

If someone believes that they have been cheated on, controlling the other person will not change anything. If others do not respect us or are dishonest, then we need to seriously review those relationships. Professional assistance may be helpful, but in some cases the relationship should be ended to prevent more damage. Sometimes separation may be the best neutral position, allowing us to see the accurate picture and buy time to find the right solution to the problem.

There is always the possibility of starting a new, more prosperous life. What others do is their decision, and in some cases there is nothing we can do about it. However, we always can make changes to our own lives, and this will be enough to be on the right side. In many cases making even small changes stimulates the thinking of the other person and may lead to better results.

The same rules apply when someone is obsessed with jealousy over tangible and intangible things. If someone has a problem accepting that the neighbour has a new garden table, it reflects that the person has an unbalanced state of mind. A reasonable, friendly person would say, "Well, they worked hard for it, and I am pleased for them." Instead of grinding your teeth and suffering from insomnia, it would be better to congratulate the neighbours for their choice and accept an invitation for a cup of coffee on a Sunday afternoon. When sipping coffee, you may be surprised to hear that a local garden centre has special offers on tables from which you could benefit as well.

Those who are victims of jealousy should seek help as well and learn how to protect themselves and any other people who are affected. Learning how to control our emotions and responses to life situations will make us stronger and help us find resources for how to react better in similar circumstances.

When we are confident about ourselves, there is no reason to worry about others' behaviour. Being self-confident will help you to make your decisions and choices in a much more controlled manner.

Suggestion: "I feel good when someone else has a reason to be happy. Others' happiness and well-being increases my energy and motivation to be active and creative and share these good feelings with others."

Anxiety and Phobias

Anxiety, phobias, and worries are our enemies and can destroy our physical and mental health, as well as damage and paralyse our life's momentum. Anxiety is an unrealistic fear in the absence of real danger. This feeling stays with a person most of the time, damaging the body and mind functions. Those affected suffer from panic attacks, have difficulty breathing, and are often bombarded with catastrophic thoughts that something bad will happen. Uncontrolled anxiety leads to health problems such as heart disease and affects circulation and the immune system because of the hormonal imbalance it creates. With anxiety, a person's thinking becomes irrational and causes actions which disturb normal living patterns. Withdrawal from daily duties or overprotection is characteristic, and depression may follow. It is like the person has a "broken switch" and is unable to stop these emotions from boiling over. When rapid and irregular breathing happens, the immediate action should be to breathe into a paper bag (to increase the level of carbon dioxide), and later start to breathe slowly and start to use the suggestion "Each time I feel tense, immediately I say to myself, 'Relax now,' and immediately I relax and am in control." Breathe in slowly, counting to three or four, and breathe out, counting to five or six. Say, "Relax now. There is no reason to feel like this." Repeat the process three times. Phobia is an irrational fear of something that is presenting no danger, for example a spider. Constant worries about anything can stop us from living to the fullest today and planning for the future. Taking precautions is a responsible action, but out of proportion concern, or fears may preoccupy a person's mind. Above all, it will prevent a person from living a normal life.

A therapeutic and posthypnotic suggestion to use is this:

> "Relaxing very deeply now, I can relax every muscle in my body and calm my mind. Being in control of my breathing, in and out, increases the pleasant feeling of relaxation from the top of my head down to my feet. This proves to me that I can control my feelings. By controlling my feelings, I can control any situation in a calm and mature way. And each time I feel anxiety or fear where there is no danger present, immediately I can calm my mind and body by taking a deep breath, holding it while counting to three, and exhaling while saying to myself, "Relax now." Immediately I will start to feel relaxed, as I am relaxing now, and this feeling will stay with me long after I end this session of trance."

Grieving

Grieving is a very painful and complicated experience that occurs when we lose a loved one. It is a very individualized process, meaning that everyone will go through this difficult time in their own way, according to their own needs and involvement. Each case is very sensitive and unique. Many factors will influence the level of sorrow and pain we feel. We are more prepared mentally to say goodbye to our elderly family members and less prepared for the loss of a young person or child and for sudden tragic events.

However, if the grieving period is considerably prolonged without signs of a gradual return to normal activities, the person may need help to make rational sense of what happened and learn how to cope effectively with the pain. During prolonged grieving, a person might neglect other members of the family who are grieving as well and need support at this time. In other cases, the grieving person's life can be terribly affected, leading to more problems such as job loss, drinking, and drug abuse. The person's confidence and self-esteem may be profoundly affected, and depression could keep the person in a dark tunnel.

Explore the Memory of the Lost Loved One

Every six months, a very nice couple would come to our surgery for a check-up. The love and admiration between them was touching and grabbed everyone's attention. However, suddenly they stopped coming. After eighteen months, the woman came to the office alone. We heard that her husband had died, and she had a difficult time accepting the loss. She was a very intelligent woman in her sixties. Each time she came, she shared with us how lost she felt. We all saw the signs of depression. She withdrew herself from her social life, her family was worried, and she was in distress. However, she liked to tell me stories about her husband, about their relationship, and about his unforgettable action during World War II, especially during the London invasion. One day, I asked her why she did not write about all these fantastic stories, even if it were just for her family. The reaction was immediate. She stood up and said, "Why didn't I think of that?"Within a short time, she presented her stories in a local community hall, recovered from depression, started her social life, and was helping others to recover from their own grief.

Having positive memories of the person we are grieving for helps us to recover from chronic sadness and hopelessness. We can use the happy moments of our life together to move on with positive energy. Memories are forever, and we can share them with others. Sharing positive memories may be a gift to other family members so they can cherish facets of the deceased person's personality and values they may not have been aware of. Grandchildren may have a book about Grandma or Grandpa's achievements which they may be proud of and may want to follow their example.

As we have learned, hypnotherapy and working on the unconscious mind will help us to come to our senses regarding our loss. We can find better strategies to deal with any situation, including the loss of a loved one. We all have rainy days, but we should never stop living. Life is too precious, and every day should be appreciated to the fullest. The time will come when we can accept what we cannot change and let go for others' benefits.

Therapeutic suggestion: "Relaxing very deeply now, I find it easier to understand that there may be situations over which I have no control, but I can accept these and cherish the good memories I have. Good memories are my assets, giving me a lot of courage and optimism. I can make good use of my memories by sharing them with family and friends. I can write my memories down so that anyone can benefit from them."

Guilt

The feeling of guilt is one of the most damaging emotions if it stays with us for a long time. Guilt will keep us in a dark cell like a prisoner. We may blame ourselves for something we did not do or for things we did and feel sorry for. For example, a mother may blames herself for her child's death, but the illness was totally out of her control as it was incurable. Sometimes we feel responsible for some unpleasant event, but our guilty feeling is out of proportion. In other cases, we may feel guilty for our inexcusable actions, even when the matter is closed and the penalty has been paid.

Long-lasting guilt will destroy our confidence and self-esteem and strip us of any plans. What happened in the past is something we cannot change, but we can learn how to prevent such events in future. Whatever it was, we must be free from feeling guilty and learn how to forgive ourselves and others. Even if we are responsible for some misfortune, there is no point in punishing ourselves for the rest of our lives. Everyone, including criminals, has a right to start a new life when they have served their sentence. Letting go in many cases is the best remedy to heal wounds in the family, to heal enmity between friends, and to move on. Living with guilt for a long time is destructive and shows our weakness and irrational thinking. Asking for help is always a wise move.

Therapeutic suggestion: “Relaxing very deeply now, I see clearly that what happened in the past should stay in the past, but by learning from my mistakes and being honest with myself and others, I can move forward. I already paid for my mistakes, and now I need to concentrate on restoring my trustworthiness and building a positive future for myself and others. I believe that I can start to rebuild and find success. I am willing to ask for advice and look for resources in my unconscious mind to make the right move to reach my goals.”

Thirty-two

There Is a Better Way – Positive Emotions

> The law of attraction or the law of love … they are one and the same.
>
> Charles Haanel (1866–1949)

We now understand that false beliefs, chronic negative thoughts, and long-term negative emotions lead to irrational choices and actions, which bring about more negative results.

It is time now to turn away from all these negative factors of Trio Mind and turn towards constructive and positive approaches. Calmness and wisdom are icebreakers. Positive emotions have been proven to be of great value. They helps us to have a safer and more successful journey. Good feelings have a positive effect on our physiology and mental health. Our decisions and actions will change according to how we feel at the time and what emotional assets we have from the past. Positive emotions facilitate healing and increase our energy and motivation to act and to explore the world.

Positivity is the best gift we can share with others to help them to stay on the positive side. Good feelings act as magic, affecting all three parts of the Trio Mind, bringing peace of mind and a feeling of satisfaction at the end of the day.

So, instead of ignoring positive feelings straightaway, we should try them out first. It would be foolish not to. People pray in their own way in order to be free from negative emotions and receive the gift of love and respect.

I would like to present a clear picture of what happens to the body and mind when we feel positive about ourselves and the rest of the world. Changing into more positive attitude towards life could be the turning point to experience safer, more enjoyable sailing.

Love

When we are in love, or when we love the world we live in, it gives us an enormous feeling of happiness which is evident in everything we do. It is like having wings and flying, and we want to share this great feeling with others. The whole world looks beautiful, and everything seems to be so easy. We believe that we can buy the whole world and that the sky is the limit for our enthusiasm and expectations. Our energy is at its highest level, our thinking is much more active, and we have a desire to enjoy life even more. We are willing to forgive others easily, and our mind explores ideas. Nothing can stop us from taking more action.

Planning the future, communicating with others, and problem-solving seem to be much simpler when we are in love. When the fruits of our efforts are harvested, the happiness, passion, and enthusiasm is overwhelming and increases our gratitude for everything we have and are able to share.

Feeling love and being loved gives us a greater sense of our humanity and a deep feeling of serenity. Love is also a great asset to have when going through difficult times, when all bridges are falling down. We can more easily adjust to and accept life events with sincere appreciation for what we still have. Respecting everyone and everything around us brings us love and respect from others in most cases. The literature on love is more popular today than it was in the past. Poems and song lyrics express the need for love for everyone, everywhere. We need to receive and give love in order to survive and stay physically and mentally healthy.

Therefore, it is important to remember that especially during our rusty days, everyone needs loving words to make their day brighter. Children need to be reassured often that they are loved unconditionally. When children grow up with love, they feel safe and develop a positive curiosity about life. It is proven that children without love have serious psychological problems. They may be shy and may withdraw from their usual activities. They may have problems with communication and in relationships. Often they blame themselves for not being loved, as they believe that they are bad and do not deserve better. Others deprived of love frequently become angry, aggressive, and dangerous to others.

By having a loving attitude towards everything that Mother Nature gives us, we grow spiritually and experience the deepest meaning of life: serenity and creativity.

Unfortunately, many of us believe that they never experienced the feeling of love, thinking for example, "I can't love anyone, including myself." It becomes worse when they pass this belief to their children and keep the cycle going. Others may lose the feeling of love when some tragedy happens, such as illness, personal tragedy or trauma, or being betrayed. In such cases, cloudy thoughts start to occupy the mind and may trigger the process of long-term negative conditioning, leaving the person miserable or angry for years.

The truth is that life without love is meaningless and blocks our creativity and enthusiasm to go for something constructive. It also causes us to minimize the importance of supporting others. Frequently those who have never experienced love are lacking in remorse and can be dangerous to others.

The fact is that we can change our attitude and beliefs about love in either direction.

By using our mind's potential, it is possible to open ourselves and fill our minds with feelings of unconditional love. Psychological therapy, especially with hypnosis, will cause a significant change in attitude towards life in a short time. The benefits of living with love will be discovered and brought to the surface or regained. It is never too late to start to live with an admiration of the beauty of the nature, seeing the beautiful sky, the snow, or trees, and share your feelings with the people around you, as love spreads rapidly. You have a choice: you can have fun and live with love, feeling good about what you have around you, and boosting your belief and energy to build a better life with each passing day, or you can just complain about everything and be miserable all day.

Suggestion to practise: "I love everything around me, all the people, children, animals, and plants and the mystical ways in which the world works. Feeling loved and giving love makes me feel good and increases my energy and enthusiasm to reach my goals."

Passion

Passion is another powerful feeling. We all need to feel satisfaction from our lives. If we do something with passion, the final product will be excellent.

The greatest artworks were created with passion, which is one of the crucial elements in goal achievement that is common to all geniuses. Whatever we desire, if we are passionate about it, we send to the unconscious mind a better picture of what we want, supported with deep feeling about it. In turn, we receive guidance and resources from the unconscious to accomplish what we wish to do.

Top performers always show passion in what they do. Successful people live with passion every day, and there is no place in their lives for thoughts such as "I won't bother with that." There is truth in the popular saying "Good things come to those who are patient."

I would like to present two contrasting behaviours: perfectionism and excellence.

We can hate everything about us and around us, or we can love it. It is our choice. Living with passion not only makes us feel great but also may change someone else's life.

Suggestion: "Whatever I do, passion is the engine for my achievements. Passion brings the best results and the greatest feeling of satisfaction."

Love it or Hate it.

A certain highly skilled engineer was always reliable in everything he did. Everything was done on time and according to a high standard. He was always very logical and judgemental. Despite his perfectionism, there was something cold about him both at work and at home. He saw anything that he was doing was an obligation, including spending time with his family. This attitude was reflected in his personal life and his business life. He always felt unhappy despite having a good career and financial stability. He had problems relaxing, and when asked why he was so restless, he said, "I have to finish the job as soon as possible as I hate to do this."

In contrast, a young woman was employed to help an elderly woman by cleaning her house. Each time she arrived, she was cheerful, joking or singing. She did her job quickly and always did more than was expected. When she started cleaning, it was like magic. She cleaned from ceiling to floor, inch by inch, without missing a bit. When she finished, everything was shiny and fresh, with everyone saying, "Ah!"

Contrary to the man, she loved what she was doing and did everything with passion. She was a happy person, even on rainy days.

Enjoyment

The feeling of joy is one to be remembered forever. Joy is a powerful emotion which can put us on a new life track. The feeling of joy can help us recover from illness, increase the functioning of our immune system, and prevent many psychological conditions such as depression. Joy will increase energy, enthusiasm, and creativity. Happy memories are very powerful resources that help us maintain a positive Trio Mind and help us get through tough times. The human mind has the incredible ability to recall emotions and pleasant moments of the past at any time and in any situation. These things are much-needed resources when our days are filled with heavy clouds and hopelessness. Therefore, the more good memories we have, the better the resources we have to deal with daily tasks.

It is important to give children a lot of enjoyment to ensure their good physical and mental health. Spending time with a child playing games, exploring new activities, or simply doing something together increases their confidence and creates memories, which can serve as the foundation for their whole life. There is a big difference between taking a child to the playground and playing with that child while at the playground. Positive feelings are automatically collected in a child's wisdom box and will be valuable resources for the darker days.

Summertime Memory.

One of the clearest memories I have from my childhood is the time I spent with my uncle during one of my summer holidays. He lived in the countryside where social life was limited to a dance on Sundays and a trip to the market every Monday. The rest of the time, it was hard farmer's work and contact with a nature.

During lunchtime, my uncle used to sit on the bench at the side of his house and watch his pigeons. I always joined him there. He told me stories about each pigeon, and we had a lot of fun observing them. There was nothing around us, just the hard-working farmers full of love, passion, and gratitude for nature and life. I enjoyed every minute of it. More than half a century later, I still vividly remember the sunny day, the breeze on my cheeks, the sounds of the pigeons. I still feel the unspoken love radiating from the man who was appreciating every day and everything he had, enjoying it to the fullest. He shared his passion and joy without words, and it has stayed with me forever.

Enjoyment is of paramount importance to all of us. We can experience joy from having a good time with family or dinner with friends, or engaging in hobbies. Comedy is a powerful healing tool for both children and adults. Some people have the ability to enjoy everything they do because they are able to create pleasure or fun from any situation. For example, some people clean the house while listening to favourite music and exercising at the same time. It was reported on a TV programme one day that in one US hospital, the nurses would dance and sing while doing their duties in order to lose weight, as they did not have time to work out at a gym. They lost weight and had a lot of fun. The patients enjoyed it as well, and the atmosphere on the ward was fantastic.

When we have fun and feel good, these feelings improve our immune system and our body functions. Our mind puts all our worries to the side for the moment. This may be enough to restore the balance between body and mind and boost our energy and enthusiasm to do something constructive or see clearly the solution to a present problem. We all know that when we feel happy, the grass is greener, and we are much more tolerant and easy-going with others. It is easier to see the solution to any problem. We enjoy sharing this good feeling with strangers, and we compliment others.

Suggestions to practise: "I enjoy everything I need to do." "I enjoy spending time with my family and children." "I enjoy learning new things." "I enjoy new challenges."

Gratitude

One day, my nurse shared with me what happened on her way home the previous evening. She was six months pregnant, and at the end of a hard day, she just wanted to put her feet up at home as soon as possible. Unfortunately, the London Underground was closed because of an accident, so she decided to walk three miles home. On her way, the weather became cold and very rainy. Two hours later, she finally reached home, frustrated, tired, and looking for sympathy from her husband. He said to her, "I am glad you are at home, and I am so grateful that you had the courage, the energy, and two healthy legs to get back home safely." At first I found it shocking to hear that, but his statement stayed in my mind, and the more I thought about it, the deeper the sense of gratitude I found.

Gratitude is a powerful, essential, valuable feeling that gives us the satisfaction of being a great human being, appreciating every day of our life and everything we have. This feeling helps build a sense of belonging and causes us to feel a part of the whole universe. Moreover, it is a powerful tool in removing negative thoughts and feelings from our mind. It opens the door to more opportunities, as opposed to being blocked by destructive thoughts such as "I never win, I am a loser."

Gratitude gives us a deeper sense that we are living as we are able to see, hear, and feel the greatness of the world. We can enjoy the beauty of our planet, the beauty of our home, and the potential of our body and mind. We are happy with what we have, and we wait for opportunities patiently, believing that if not today, then maybe tomorrow we will reach what we are looking for. This in turn enriches our experiences and our resources for future situations.

If we go through our daily routines with enthusiasm, excitement, satisfaction, and hope, at the end of the day we will sleep like a baby. With a sense of gratitude, we will be able to be more efficient and better deal with any obstacles. We can find good things in any situation and enjoy them.

Optimism

A worried mother said to her teenage daughter, "Dear, we have only ten dollars for the whole week. I don't know how we will manage before I start my new job." The teenager replied, "It's OK, Mummy. It's your ten dollars. We can do with it whatever we want."

Their spirits rose immediately, and they decided to cook their favourite dishes from scratch. After buying the food, they had change left over for a chocolate bar. The afternoon was one to remember.

Small things, such as a few kind words, can make an enormous change in any situation, for ourselves, for those around us, and even for a stranger. It is up to us how we approach our life experiences. We can complain, cry, and blame others for our misfortune, or we can stay calm and do what would be most appropriate in that situation and then be proud that we were able to behave that way.

When we are busy and bombarded with daily tasks, it is easy to take everything for granted. When this happens, all our assets immediately lose their real value. This happens naturally because we stop seeing, enjoying, and appreciating life. You might take for granted someone who is very close to you, or your favourite car, or most disastrous of all, your health and good spirits.

Gratitude and respect for others increases our enthusiasm and makes us feel great as a human being. Those who know this feeling simply don't want to lose it. Whatever happens in our life, finding the positives and appreciating what we have is a crucial tool to survive. It helps us find the energy to go forward during stormy weather.

Those living with gratitude can see the bright side and find a way to reach their desired goal. Those who fail to be grateful may find themselves trapped in ongoing frustration, feeling that the grass is always greener on the other side—far from their grasp.

Suggestion: "I am grateful that I can learn, walk, create, develop my abilities, etc."

Thirty-three

Stay Calm and in Control of Your Feelings

A change of feelings is a change of destiny.

Neville Goddard (1905–1972)

At any time, our feelings should reflect what we are experiencing. However, prolonged negative emotions for any reason are roadblocks to rebuilding a positive attitude and moving on. Therefore, to keep a healthy balance we must know how to control our emotions at all times. Staying calm and in control of our feelings is one of the three factors in securing our creativity, making right decisions, and having success in whatever we do. Being in control of our emotions will open the channel to look for more effective coping and problem-solving strategies to deal with any stressful situation.

The fact is that if we don't control our emotions, they will control us. Frequently we hear, "How can I control my emotions given my stressful life and the demands on my time?" Let's look at another fact: losing control over emotions causes millions to see out harmful medications, street drugs, and alcohol and/or lands people in prison for breaking the law, which only creates a new problem in their personal and professional life. Over the long term, drug or alcohol use will reduce brain function and impair rational thinking. So now you have a choice: to stay with damaging emotions or to stand up and start to control them.

I will begin this chapter with a presentation of few rapid, very effective psychological exercises to control emotions in any situation, when you need to feel calm and in control at once. These are psychological techniques which can be use prior to a stressful situation such as an exam or interview. They can be practised during self-hypnosis as well to reinforce the positive effect.

It has been clinically proven that feelings can controlled by many methods.

First we need to recognize the ongoing feeling—"What makes me feel like that?" For example, an exam, travelling, or an interview may cause an unpleasant feeling. The next step is to deal with that emotion effectively. This can be done by stopping or at least interrupting the unpleasant feeling.

> Exercise 1: Stopping the negative feeling in order to stay calm and in control
>
> Step a) Recognize the feeling, for example nervousness before an exam or interview.
>
> Step b) Say to yourself, "Stop the feeling right now. I am well prepared for it. I stay calm and in control."
>
> Repeat as often as necessary.

When such confrontational action is taken, the intuitional feeling should disappear. It is logical that such a feeling acts as your friend (intuition), indicating that something isn't right and needs your attention. Your response to it is, "OK, I have received the message and will take care."

> Exercise 2: Disturbing the negative feeling
>
> Each time you start to feel anxious, take a deep breath and hold it. When exhaling, count backwards from five to one.

This simple exercise will disturb the process of negative conditioning. You can practise it on a daily basis to feel better immediately and eliminate the unpleasant feeling that is preventing you from doing what you want to do. This brings an immediate calming feeling and can be used in any situation when your stress level is elevated such as exams and public speaking.

Breathing Exercises

Breathing exercises, which have been well known for centuries, are simple but very powerful techniques to help you control your feelings quickly. The mind responds to breathing exercises easily, especially if they are supported by positive thoughts.

They relax and improve the function of all the organs in the body, increasing blood circulation and the supply of oxygen to the brain. Relaxing your mind improves the harmony between the conscious and unconscious mind and helps us sort out our experiences, thoughts, and feelings.

Optimal results can be expected by trying all these exercises and choosing the one which is best for you. Some are longer, others are quicker, and each may be more beneficial in a certain situation.

Exercise 1: Deep Breathing Exercise (1 minute)

You can close your eyes if you wish, to increase your concentration.

Breathe in, counting from one to four.

Hold your breath to the count of three; breathe out, counting from one to six or seven.

When breathing in, imagine that you are inhaling calmness and relaxation.

When breathing out, imagine that you are releasing the tension from your body.

You may choose to see different colours; when inhaling relaxation see (e.g. blue).

When exhaling tension see (e.g. black).

You can reinforce this by silently saying "relax" each time you breathe out.

Breathe in, hold your breath, let it go, and relax.

Repeat three to five times.

This exercise is practical when you are facing stressful situations and you want to relax quickly. But it takes practice. With time, you will become more familiar with making a quick shift in your mind. With increased creativity, you can make modifications to this simple but effective exercise.

Another method is to reinforce this breathing technique to relax by using a physical gesture or a suggestion.

Exercise 2: Fist and Breathing Exercise

Make a fist with your hand when breathing in and counting from one to four.

Breathe out while counting from one to six.

Release your fist and say to yourself, "Calm and relaxed."

Repeat this three to five times.

You can repeat the whole exercise a few times a day when you are tired or stressed.

In the next chapter you will learn how to control chronic negative emotions.

Thirty-four

Controlling Chronic Negative Emotions

Controlling stubborn negative emotions is essential if you wish to be free to do what you need to do or what you want to do. If you suffer from ongoing feelings of anger, disappointment, and so forth, you can start to work on this problem with these simple exercises.

If a negative feeling persist for a long time, especially when there is no need to feel like that, it is a sign that those feelings are chronic negative emotions (CNE). Learning to be aware of the unconscious signals is a skill itself and the most precious one. Practising self-hypnosis will help you differentiate intuitional feelings from CNEs. If these simple exercises do not help, you should seek professional help. You may suffer from a more serious condition needing urgent attention. For example, feeling hopeless, feeling sad, or losing control over your behaviour is a clear indication that a deeper evaluation of the problem is required, along with immediate proper treatment.

Otherwise, to be more in control of your daily emotions, you can use the exercises in the previous chapter or follow the ones below. Knowing all of them will help you to choose the one which is the most effective for you.

Step 1: Always recognize the intuitional emotions (anger, sadness, anxiety).

"I feel angry each time my partner doesn't keep his [or her] promises. I feel betrayed.

I am furious when others don't do what they should do. In such circumstances, I feel like I am losing control. When I think about an exam, I have butterflies in my stomach. I failed the last exam I sat for."

Step 2: Stop the persistent negative emotions;

"Stop this feeling right now! From now on, I control my feelings. They do not control me." Repeat this as many times as necessary.

The two foregoing exercises are similar to the methods described in the previous chapter for use in urgent situations. These are effective in a variety of other situations when you feel tense.

Below are other useful exercises which will help you to control your emotions even more effectively. They are useful when you experience persistent anxiety or stress during the day and are disturbed to the point that you do not finish your tasks. Practise these exercises with or without hypnotic trance in a safe place.

Exercise 1: Scale and Breathing (10 minutes)

Close your eyes to increase your level of relaxation and visualization ability.

Now imagine a scale in front of you that reads your emotional level. On the scale, zero represents the state of maximum relaxation and ten represents the highest level of stress.

- Read your present tension level.
- Now take a deep breath, counting from one to four.
- When breathing out, counting from one to six, reduce the level of stress by two or three points.
- Say to yourself, "Relax deeper, and decreasing the tension by two points."
- Stay in this relaxed state of mind for as long as you wish. When finished, open your eyes and enjoy the feeling of calmness and freshness of mind. Repeat three times.

Reaching the level of four or five is ideal for staying calm and active. Reducing your stress level to two or three, you should be feel deeply relaxed. Gradually you can work at reaching a deeper state of relaxation if you wish.

Once you become familiar with this exercise, you can make your own decision about how much you want to reduce your tension by using this exercise. It is better to reduce pressure gradually by one to two points first, until you reach a comfortable and relaxed state.

It may help to make a note in order to have a record of your feelings at the beginning and the end of the exercise. Take time to learn it. Practice makes perfect. By becoming more familiar with how your body and mind can cooperate for your benefit, you will be in control of your feelings to the point that you feel comfortable in any situation.

Exercise 2: Redirecting the Emotion

During the day you may redirect your feelings by being preoccupied with a constructive activity, reading something interesting, watching a comedy, or practising relaxation techniques. During the night you may recall a good memory and concentrate on it for a while. Then apply the following suggestion, either with or without in self-hypnosis: "And now I have a good, deep sleep until the morning hours. I will wake up refreshed, ready to start my day and tackle my daily duties with enthusiasm."

Exercise 3: Analyse Your Negative Emotions

Ask yourself what you can do to change the stubborn feeling. "Maybe I need to start to believe that I can be successful. Perhaps I need to communicate better with people. Or maybe I need to stop worrying and getting angry all the time."

Exercise 4: Challenge Your Negative Feelings

Say, "I am a mature person and can control myself. I am in control of my feelings. They do not control me."

Exercise 5: Accept What You Can't Change with Dignity

Even when all bridges are falling down, we still have a choice how we feel about it.

There is a classic scene from the movie "Zorba" showing the failure of a huge project on the first attempt. After the initial shock, all the contractors link arms and start dancing.

Frequently, staying with negative feelings connects us with failure, or other unpleasant experiences. This may keep us in the unpleasant past and prevent us from starting again.

In fact, many times the greatest achievement comes after a deep fall, if you have the ability to let go and start again. If you can't make changes to an ongoing situation, you can at least put your mind in a constructive mood to keep yourself going the right direction. Such ability may be a survival tool in many difficult or hopeless situations.

Exercise 6: Make the Unlikeable Likeable

There will be some cases where you can't make any changes and must learn to accept it, at least for the time being. This is a better solution than feeling angry. If you must do something that you really do not like, it would be more rewarding to start to like it. For example, if you hate ironing, you can start to like it. Do it while watching your favourite sport or concert. You can find a way to feel satisfaction in everything you "must" do, or you can stay in a miserable mood with pitiful results in most cases.

Exercise 7: Refuse to Stay in a Negative Frame of Mind

Ask yourself, "Do I want to be the person who has this negative feelings all the time, for example being grumpy, unhappy, angry, or unsatisfied?"

Reminding yourself who you really are will help you to make the right choice to calm down and solve the ongoing situation in a mature way, instead of behaving as a dissatisfied person. Whatever the situation is, staying negative will lead to many problems. On the other hand, by staying calm, you show your wisdom and dignity. Choose what mood you want to go with for the day. Chronic frustration is very negative emotion, usually leading to poor performance. Your mind will follow your emotions and attitude, so it will either feel guilty or angry or feel satisfied and proud of your accomplishments.

Exercise 8: Convert the Destructive Feeling to a Constructive One

This is an excellent tool to stay calm in any situation. Repeating this exercise daily, with self-hypnosis or without, will change how you think and automatically will adjust your feelings in any situation. It may be a starting point to gain control of your negative emotions as anger, sadness. Say to yourself the opposite, constructive self - suggestion. Examples are as follows:

- "I am calm and in control."
- "I control my feelings; they do not control me."
- "Every day I control my feelings better than the day before."
- "I own my feelings, and I can control them."

Anyone who is willing to learn can convert negative emotions and thoughts into positive thinking and action.

Exercise 9: Classic Relaxation Technique (5–10 minutes)

This can be used as an induction method to experience trance.

Sit down comfortably in a safe and quiet place and breathe slowly in and out.

When you breathe out, say to yourself, "Relax."

Take in a second breath, and when you breathe out, say, "Relax deeper."

Take the third breath in. When you breathe out, say, "Relax even deeper."

Take a fourth breath in, and when you breathe out, say, "Relax deeper and deeper."

Take a fifth breath in. When you breathe out, say, "Relax the whole body now."

You can reinforce this exercise by visualizing the tension (which you may perceive as black) leaving your body.

This breathing exercise, together with suggestions for relaxation and staying calm, is a powerful tool to use in any stressful situation. Once it is mastered, you need anything else to remain calm and relaxed anytime you so desire. Your unconscious mind will respond to your command.

Exercise 10: Classic Progressive Relaxation

Another useful method to relax the body and the mind is to suggest to yourself while breathing in that you relax muscles, or whole parts of your body, from the top of your head to the bottom of your feet. This is also a good induction method to initiate light trance.

Sitting comfortably with your eyes closed, say to yourself: "Relax the muscles in my head and shoulders now. Relax the muscles of my chest and abdomen now. Relax my pelvic, hip, and thigh muscles now. Relax the muscles of my calves, feet, and toes now."

Stay in this relaxed state for five to ten minutes, then open your eyes, feeling refreshed and ready to take on your normal activities.

If you think that the foregoing exercises are too simple to be of help, you are wrong. In fact, these exercises are what you need to do to be in control of your emotions. Starting to control your thoughts and beliefs will automatically change a negative Trio Mind to a positive one and put you on the road to success.

Other simple techniques to control emotions include repeating to yourself, "I am in control of my feelings. They don't control me" (this should become a habit, and it will work automatically with time if exercised properly); remembering to take regular fifteen-minute breaks every forty-five minutes during the day; listening to your favourite music; watching a comedy; and doing simple exercises. These techniques are never out of date and keep the balance between body and mind. They work! They will prevent an accumulation of negative feelings and thoughts as well. This way you can open the door for more positive thoughts about yourself, which will allow you to be more creative and successful in everything you do.

Thirty-five

Anchors

Reinforce Positive Thinking and Emotions

Each affirmation or suggestion to stay positive and feel good can be reinforced by anchoring it with specific cues. This way you can experience the same feeling in the future when needed simply by repeating the anchoring cue to yourself.

For example, to feel more relaxed anytime you wish, make a fist and, when releasing it, say to yourself, "Relax now." Immediately the feeling of relaxation will spread through your body and mind.

This is a powerful technique to add to your portfolio of positive emotions and experiences. We know that emotions are associated with experiences and vice versa. In this chapter, you will learn how to benefit from this natural process of body and mind.

Building a bank of positive emotions will be an asset available to you when you are feeling down. For example, each time I look at a very old picture of my grandma's house, it brings back wonderful memories of my childhood, and automatically good feelings fill my mind.

Past feelings and memories (good and bad alike) can be recalled automatically by trigger cues. In my case it is a picture that serves as a trigger cue, but for you it may be a specific smell, tactile sensation, or sound. We can use this ability of the mind to pair positive memories with any of the senses, for example touching a necklace to bring forth a feeling of contentment.

So why do we need anchors? Any past experiences are stored in the mind and can be used for future purposes. We can learn from the bad experiences and store the positive ones as an inner resource for future use. By pairing (anchoring) positive emotions and memories with a physical sensation (touch, sound, or smell), we can build our own portfolio of positive feelings. For example, the sensation of being very confident during final exams may be retrieved for use in future interviews.

All positive feelings can be recalled, reinforced, and anchored by visualization exercises. By learning this skill, we can build our treasure box of good feelings. Each time we feel good about ourselves, for example when we achieve something or feel happy for others upon receiving great news, we add this feeling to our treasure box.

Exercise 1

Choose a trigger cue to make a physical bond with your feelings. It could be flicking the wrist, making a fist, or putting two fingers together. Other commonly used trigger cues are touching the ear or saying significant words such as "great, relax, calm, or yes." Anything will do.

You can use two of these techniques at the same time, such as touching a chain and saying "yes." Each time you experience good feelings, hold the trigger cue for fifteen to twenty seconds to make a strong connection between the feeling and the trigger cue.

Repeat this five times or until you are able to feel the good feeling.

In stressful situations, repeatedly using the trigger cue will automatically allow you to bring forth the desired anchored positive feelings. With time and practice, your anchors will be reinforced and more strongly recognized.

You can build a chain of positive emotions by using the same trigger cue with all positive emotions when you feel them. If you prefer, you can make separate anchors for different feelings, such as confidence, calmness, or positive tension for the purpose of performance.

Each time you anchor something, imagine that you are putting another medal into your treasure box. This method is used in sports, by celebrities, and in many daily activities by millions of people around the world who wish to stay calm and in control and reinforce positive beliefs about themselves. The simpler the cue is, the better association it will have. You can use your imagination to find which cues suit you best. You can use this technique anytime you need to feel calm, relaxed, and confident.

An example of anchoring is as follows: A tennis player may want to stay calm but would like to feel the necessary degree of tension and increased concentration to hit the ball in the right direction. He or she practises visualizing the ball moving in the right direction. When the shot is successful, the good feeling of achievement may be anchored by making a fist with one hand or squeezing the racket hand. Many athletes use a fist with their opponent as a friendly gesture, but they also create the association with an emotional state of mind when this technique is successful. It goes like this:

Positive feeling → gesture → anchor → gesture → positive feeling

Anchoring can be significantly reinforced during hypnosis. This is a powerful process that does not require your conscious involvement. The positive feeling and thinking is automatically recalled each time by making the anchoring gesture. Hypnotherapy is such a powerful tool to restore balance to the function of the mind because it is done directly in the unconscious mind. It will help you to find the cause of your feelings and to reframe and correct them. In addition, you will learn how to approach life events in a calmer way with better control over your thoughts and emotions.

Self-hypnosis is an excellent vehicle for many psychological techniques intended to repair the "emotional switch". Most of us need only to pay more attention to our present feelings and thoughts, analyse them, and become willing to accept that there is a need for change. You can control your feelings by natural means in any situation, be it your personal life, your professional life, or when you are performing. You do not need medication, alcohol, or drugs to stay calm and feel great about yourself. More than this, practising self-hypnosis can eliminate the need for medication, which means you also get rid of the side effects.

Now that we are more able to be open to new prospects and stay calm in any situation, we come to the most important part of securing a successful life: having confidence.

Self-hypnosis is an excellent tool to stay in control of your mood and your thoughts because it anchors them directly in the unconscious mind. You can be calm and in control in any situation. Enjoy it. If these simple but effective psychological exercises do not work for you can listen to the hypnotic relaxation programmes from my website, which will allow you to relax within a very short amount of time. If you still have a problem relaxing your mind and body, see a doctor to eliminate a more serious cause of the condition.

Thirty-six

Power of Belief

False beliefs can steal your freedom.

What we learn during our childhood and later creates our beliefs. Based on what we belief, we let our minds fill with different thoughts and feelings. Our beliefs, thoughts, and feelings influence each other, and our decisions are fundamental to our health and our achievement of goals.

When we can keep a healthy balance between our beliefs, thoughts, and emotions, the body and mind are in harmony. However, after a long span of dramatic experiences and disappointments, we may need to correct to our feelings, responses, and beliefs. Like after a heavy storm, we need to stabilize the ship before we may resume sailing.

Let's discuss beliefs in more detail now. Beliefs are shaped by the information we receive from parents, society, and the environment, beginning on the first day of our lives. We learn and shape our beliefs by using all our senses: what we see, hear, feel, taste, smell, and touch. Gradually we make distinctions between what suits us and what does not, what is hot and what is cold, what is good and what is bad, and what is pleasant and what is unbearable. With time we learn how to effectively face similar situations, which gradually establishes our personality and beliefs. Naturally we create specific beliefs and thinking and behavioural patterns according to our experiences and how we understand them.

However, we continually adjust our beliefs and thoughts with each new experience and each new bit of knowledge. This is a part of our development, coping, and survival mechanisms. In addition, established expectations from family, schoolteachers, schoolmates, society, and friends have a significant influence on how we understand the meaning of our experiences. If we grow up in a sound, positive environment, it is more likely that we will model these beliefs and thinking patterns in general. Similarly, growing up in community with negative, destructive beliefs might have a strong influence on our thinking and behaviour. Depending on how mentally strong we are, we may be more or less susceptible to illogical ideas from outside. For example, we might easily accept bad ideas when we are desperate for some gain, or we may reject the positive suggestion that we look at the real picture of our present unhealthy situation.

Sometimes beliefs may be based on false, misunderstood, or contradicted information. A deeper problem arises when such beliefs are well established, not corrected by our self-assessment or by others who are close to us.

Classic examples of false beliefs of the past (which indicate an unwillingness to accept new ideas) are that arranged marriages are good, that the earth is flat, that the moon is out of reach for humankind, that all cancers are incurable, that hypnosis steals the mind, and that the number thirteen and black cats bring bad luck.

If people had persisted with these beliefs, then the chances would have been minimized of discovering the New World, looking for a happy marriage, and doing more extensive research to find a cure for cancer. Also, no one would travel on the thirteen of the month and black cats would never find a loving home.

I would like to present the true story of a grandmother's stubborn beliefs and the consequences on her grandchild.

False Belief

At a tennis academy in London, a grandmother originally from Romania used to play tennis with her granddaughter. Each time the girl "failed", her grandma lost her temper. In the presence of many other players, she shouted, "You are useless," and threw tennis balls at the child. Her aggression went on and on, causing the little girl to cry on the bench, cowering like a scared kitten. The scene was so aggressive that court officials had to stop the public abuse and ask the woman to leave the court. The grandmother's explanation was that the child's parents were athletes who believed that the use of punishment and aggression was the way to train a child to be a champion. Indeed, in the past it was a common belief that heavy punishment paved the way to success.

This is an example of being rigid in one's beliefs, refusing to consider any new concepts. In this case, science and facts have proven that the opposite is true. We now know that patience, creativity, persistence, and praise is a much more powerful tool to improve human performance. The result of this rigidity was severe damage to the child's self-esteem—and it destroyed her enjoyment of playing tennis.

Everything is always changing, and what we have believed up to now may not be true tomorrow. If we are not open to new information, we might sail in the wrong direction, until we recognize that our old beliefs are no longer working for us. We saw in Chapter 23, where I discussed the "community in a coma", how easy it is to be stuck in beliefs which feel comfortable to us but which actually keep us in an uncomfortable position for years. It is common to ignore positive ideas when we are in denial and falsely believe that everything is OK or else live with anger and revenge, destroying everything and everyone around us, instead of looking to solve the dispute positively for both sides.

The saddest example of a person's stubborn beliefs is the true story of a mother and daughter who did not talk to each other for two years after a row about a dress. Each believed that the other should call first! One day the daughter was killed in a car accident, leaving her mother with a deep feeling of guilt for having been so stubborn in her irrational belief.

Frequently, people will stop a positive suggestion to open themselves up to all opportunities by giving a "but" response, thereby forgoing a solution to the primary problem.

The filter that censors suggestions for change can be affected by many psychological conditions such as low confidence, fear, hopelessness, desperation, and lack of trust. Beliefs may be misshapen by confusion, lack of knowledge, immaturity, low self-value, physical and mental weakness, or deep negative emotions.

Confusion is common when the information we receive contradicts other information or when there is no comparison with other experiences, with one person saying one thing and another person saying another thing. Long-lasting confusion may lead to widespread ineffectiveness in our actions. In some cases, this may result in a poor self-concept and diminish our willingness to search for additional independent information. Several instances of confusion may lead us to become aggressive or withdrawal. In either case, the probability that we will make the right decision and succeed is low.

People frequently allow themselves to be victims, irrationally believing any suggestion from outside without carefully analysing it. The best example of this behaviour is jumping from one diet to another with limited, if any, effect. Many diets even have illogical and unhealthy names to start with, such as the chocolate diet or the laxative diet, but are still accepted by those who are desperate to lose weight, instead of learning a healthy lifestyle.

Another example is that global research has proven that medical hypnosis is beneficial and is used safely by the largest academic centres. Despite this, many people still believe that hypnosis is dangerous, and even more are likely to refuse such therapy because of their fear. Sometimes a person may be easily persuaded to accept unprofessional therapy because a friend believes that it is best.

Another example of having weak beliefs is repeatedly believing the promises of people who never keep them. Many of us fail to recognize manipulators, irrationally believing that they are providing us with the opportunity of a lifetime. Often we witness people make illogical decisions that others have advised them against. For example, some people send money to total strangers they meet on the Internet who promise their love without even having first seen the alleged object of their affection.

We must admit that logic is conspicuously absent in all these cases and that people who behave this way are not in good partnership with their intuition. Simply put, people make such decisions when they are desperate and/or when their thoughts and emotions are out of control. Therefore, if you are really looking for a better quality of life, it is important to be more flexible and open-minded with your beliefs.

Fortunately, the fact is that beliefs are not permanent; they may be changed by any number of different factors at any time. Change is natural, and it is the constant that gives momentum to of our existence and the universe. We are different today from what we were yesterday. So is our thinking and beliefs, which change with age, education, and new experiences. Having a willingness to look for new information will allow us to update and increase our knowledge. Scientists, politicians, legal authorities, and even religious institutions review past and present assumptions and rules and update them according to the new discoveries life brings. All successful people show a deep belief in what they do.

We must do the same if we want to be on the right side of things. It is possible to review and clarify your beliefs. This way you can learn to look at the big picture, instead of being stubborn with what you believed before, without even trying to consider things from a different point of view. In any dispute, by being open to discussion you are already a winner, as you have a chance to prove to yourself that you are either right or wrong. Both are positive, as finding real facts will open the door to necessary change.

In cases of uncertainty, it is better to put ourselves on hold, cool down so we can see the real picture, and take time to gather more information. Sticking to rules is necessary, but sometimes rules are rusty and we need to follow our logic and intuition instead. To any rule there may be exceptions. Some rules may be time-worn and no longer effective. These rules should be changed if we want better results next time.

Irrationally accepting or rejecting others' opinions may minimize your options or lead to problems in future. Therefore, it is important to constantly work on improving your values, logic, and beliefs so that you can be in a more comfortable position to make choices. It is a complex matter to feel confident in any situation. However, starting by being open-minded and willing to build a strong personality will help you to assess any situation before making a decision.

Now you can add to the list of who you are the following positive statements:

- "I keep my senses alert and my mind open to new ideas.
- "I analyse all ideas before accepting or rejecting them."
- "I take some time before making the final decision."

I will guide you through useful psychological techniques that will help you to assess any situation in a rational and logical way. Learning to trust your unconscious mind's resources (intuitions) will increase your assertiveness. Logic should be your GPS at all times, and intuition should be your best friend. Once you make up our mind about something, your mind will go in that direction as if towards a magnet in order to reach that image and ignore other suggestions along the way.

Thirty-seven

Mr Can't or Mr Can

> The most damaging Trio Mind state is to have a bad self-image.

In this chapter, we will go more in depth into the specific type of negative conditioning leading to the expression of self-beliefs such as "I am worthless and Bad things come to me, "which may preoccupy your mind and destroy your self-value and abilities.

The level of confidence we have reflects our beliefs about our values and our ability to fit in with the rest of the world. Depending on what our beliefs are, we may feel good about ourselves and easily take appropriate actions to fulfil our life desires, or we may stay behind the door, believing that we are not good enough to be on the other side.

The fact is that the stronger the positive beliefs we have about ourselves, the more fruitful resources we have to survive and achieve what we need or want. In contrast, when we let negative thoughts and feelings about ourselves storm our head for a long time, we open ourselves up to self-destructive behaviour, assuming that we are not valuable human beings, that we can't do better, or that we deserve an uncomfortable life.

Beliefs such as "I can't, I hate myself, I am useless," sadly keep many people trapped in their false beliefs, which were developed when they were children or perhaps later.

Mr Can't or Mr Can

Mr Can was living with his family in a small cave on an island. Unfortunately, the cave was flooded each time a storm struck, and he worked very hard to remediate the damage. The harder he tried to repair the cave, the worse it became. One day after a heavy rain, he felt frustrated and shouted, "I can't cope with it any longer." Feeling hopeless, he started to believe that he couldn't do anything more. Finally his family left him, and neighbours started to call him Mr Can't. He used to sit down on a fallen tree and wonder what had happened to his life. The emotional pain was difficult to bear, but he didn't know what else to do. He thought that if only the rain would stop, then trees would be shorter, allowing him to reach the fruits, and snakes would stop squeezing into his cave. Then his life would be much better.

One day, feeling tired, the man closed his eyes. He sat wondering and letting his mind to float from one image to another. After a few minutes, he saw a picture of a new, dry home. He imagined himself reunited with his family, being successful, and being a respected member of the community again. When he opened his eyes, surprisingly he started to feel better, and he said to himself, "I need to find a safe home. I deserve it, and I can do it." His energy increased, and he felt the urge to search for a home straightaway. He didn't know what he was looking for, but the vision of a new, safe home was clear in his mind.

A short time after this experience, the man fell into a grove, and when trying to get up, he saw an opening to a big cave higher on the hill, blocked by stones and old trees. He had the feeling that it was the place to build his dream home. He started to clean the cave and then drew a simple plan on the ground. Soon curious neighbours came to help him finish his project. His family came back.

As his enthusiasm and confidence grew, believing that he could do much more, people started to call him Mr Can again. Every evening he sat on a fallen tree, wondering, connecting with his inner self, and feeling grateful that he was Mr Can again.

The story of Mr Can shows how easy it is to become trapped in stubborn negative thoughts and believe that misfortune is a permanent partner in our lives. Being exposed to a repetitive negative statement from outsiders or ourselves, especially when our self-defence mechanisms are poor, may damage our mental strength and body function. Negative beliefs and thoughts may trap us in the feeling of being useless and hopeless. Unfortunately, such a pattern of thinking is a back door to many illnesses, depression, addiction, aggressiveness, and even suicidal thoughts.

Constant negative self-judgement, or negative suggestion from someone else such as "You are ugly, fat, and useless," may create a false belief that "I am ugly." This, in turn, may lead a person to develop a negative self-image and low self-esteem for years, reducing his or her creativity and performance. This negative self-image leads to even more negative thoughts, inducing sleeplessness, only to arise the next day feeling worse about ourselves and worrying about everything. Moreover, when we believe that we can't do something, we block many channels for incoming information and creativity that otherwise would allow us to accomplish even the simplest tasks.

The consequences of having a poor self-image are that the legs are hobbled, the tongue is tied, and one's attempts to meet people or do something in life ends with the mere intention, not with action. We can have many dreams and ideas about what we would like to do, but with such low belief in ourselves, the chance that we will achieve those dreams is low, in direct proportion to our confidence.

People with low confidence are uncomfortable about asking questions for fear of sounding stupid, and they are reluctant to express ideas as well. Because of this they miss many opportunities, even when they see them. Thoughts such as, "No, that probably is not a good idea," will stop them from taking action and going for their goals as a confident person would do. Having little confidence is like being in a prison cell with the reality of who we really are blocked.

Low confidence → negative criticism → poor motivation → poor performance

One common reason for low confidence is a sudden change in personal or family circumstances, bringing doubts about the future. Frequently, low self-confidence develops as a result of a traumatic experience, such as physical, mental, or sexual abuse or the death of a family member. Lack of love and security, bullying, and critical judgement are common factors leading to low confidence. Fear of being rejected may strip us of dignity and freedom. Fear of being exposed to laughter may paralyse us and our natural talents and bring with it the danger of withdrawal on an unconscious level, leading to decreased creativity, a passive lifestyle, and difficulty making decisions. Such cases are frequently seen after an experience of trauma or abuse.

Low self-confidence can develop because of stressful experiences when we can't clarify our thoughts or we don't understand what is going on in our life. Feeling hopeless, sometimes we accept what is on offer from someone else or give into the selfish demands of manipulators for the sake of peace or to be on the safe side.

High-level performers such as artists, writers, and athletes frequently experience loss of confidence just before accomplishing a task. Top athletes often show a drop in confidence when something goes drastically wrong in practice just before a competition. They may start to have doubts about their ability, despite past successes. The final result will be poorer performance because they are afraid to make changes, even if they are very uncomfortable with the current situation.

Sometimes we may feel confident around people we know but very uneasy in the presence of new people. We can be comfortable with ourselves, our abilities, and our responsibilities in our comfort zone, but we may have problems expressing our personal feelings or presenting our capabilities to others outside that zone. This may happen when we put too much pressure on ourselves with irrational expectations and then just can't cope with it, feeling like losers.

Lack of skills and poor organization may lead to life disappointments and cause us to make repeated wrong choices, damaging our self-esteem or self-image. Fear of failure may be the result of unsuccessful past experiences which cause us to believe that we always fail. Whatever the reason for feeling bad about ourselves or inadequate, such thinking prevents us from creating and building our independence.

In the next chapter, I discuss the common things that damage children's confidence in order to raise awareness of this issue and show how we can prevent this problem.

Thirty-eight

Children's Confidence

> Give a child love so he or she may know what love is, and pass it to others.

There is no doubt that the building blocks of confidence develop during the early years in the light of experiences at home and school. Initially a child's mind is free of negative thoughts, but with experience and learning from mistakes, the child's mind starts to build beliefs and associated feelings. Because children's ability to judge is in its first stages of development, they need constant guidance and repeated explanations of how to do things, instead of irrational punishment for making mistakes. Children experiment with everything, but the experiments may go a different way than adults expect.

We all are exposed to good and bad experiences, but with sound guidance, we learn to understand the difference the two. However, when we are exposed to stressful or confusing situations most of the time, we may be not strong enough mentally to assess those experiences properly. Sadly, this can happen during childhood when a child faces problematic situations which may not seem to be dramatic to an adult and therefore which may be easily undetected. Unfortunately, many things that damage children's confidence are frequently ignored by adults who believe that things can't be that bad. But they can be, as I will go on to illustrate.

A common mistake adults make is when they expect a child to do something, assuming that the child must know how to do it, but in fact the child does not know how to do it, even though her parent showed her how to do it before. The child still may not understand why it is so important to do as her parent told her, or else it could slip her mind to do the task. Therefore, before punishing a child, adults should take the time to make sure that the child fully understands what is expected and why.

Children can be terribly affected by false beliefs, for example that they are unworthy, when they are exposed to constant criticism or a lack of love. Thousands of teenagers are abused at home or outside the home, or bullied on the Internet with tragic consequences, because they are not able to make rational judgements and believe that something must be wrong with them. Too many teenagers commit suicide because they are too fragile to face constant physical or mental abuse.

Another problematic situation may develop when a child is expected to behave well but adults (parents) do the opposite, or do "adult stuff", including breaking common laws and refusing to show basic manners. In such a case, the child is likely to be confused as to what is right and what is wrong.

Everyone Is Saying Something Different

In school, say a child learns about discipline and organization and how to attend to his surroundings. The issues of respect, honesty, and friendship are discussed every day. At home the situation is different. Violence, shouting, cheating, and lack of respect for family members is a daily scenario. Drinking and drug use is a regular occurrence. No one cares about anything, there is a mess everywhere, and no one has any self-discipline. There is no time for nice words or playing together. The adults call neighbours bad names and wish upon them things no one would like to experience. At school, the teacher expects to see her student in clean clothes, but at home, the boy's daddy is shouting with a beer in his hand, "I have no time or money for that rubbish."

In this common scenario, the child wants to follow the teacher's rules because they make sense, but at home, the teacher's ideas are ignored and everyone shows no respect for what was discussed in school. The dilemma begins: the child is terrified that friends will find out the true story and starts to hide the real situation by not inviting friends home.

The situation gets worse when there is a different atmosphere in a friend's home. The question is repeated in the child's mind, "Why is my home so different from other kids' homes?"

Negative emotions may start to develop quickly, for example anger and shyness. However, in most cases, children will not tell anyone how they feel! They may feel ashamed, or afraid they will be punished, or that no one will care. The confused child may have a tendency to behave badly, just not knowing what to do. At the same time, the child still loves his parents and wants to be loved and feel secure. But no one understands. The school expects something that is impossible from the child, and at home no one understands and the situation is too difficult to cope with. The child is confused, feels hopeless, and knows that whatever he does, there is no way to win.

In the long term, the child may avoid both the teacher and his parents, as they are no longer role models for the child. The only thing the child can do is to wonder why everyone is telling him different things and how to fit himself into everyone's expectations. Wondering about this confusing situation but without any tools to change it, the child may show changes in attitude, behaviour, thinking patterns, and beliefs, and these patterns may end up persisting for a long time. The child may withdraw from the irritating environment and become more difficult to communicate with. Likely the child will learn to manipulate so as to gain attention in all scenarios, which definitely reframes the dilemma.

Whatever that child does, there is a high probability that he will be vulnerable in this confused state of mind. There is a danger that he will become an easy target for people with bad intentions. Lying and creating stories to cover up the truth is common in a child raised in this type of environment. The child's attention may be focused on finding friends who care. That is what matters now—not what people do but that they care.

Feeling disappointed and not having the proper tools to deal with new experiences, the child is just one step away from desperately seeking for any remedy that will cause him to feel better. A rapidly growing number of children around the globe rely on drugs, alcohol, or prescription medications because they have been neglected and are unable to cope with daily demands. Self-medicating by using drugs or alcohol leads to even more irrational thinking. The absence of basic moral values and responsibilities frequently leads to irreparable damage in a child, and the whole family suffers. Shaken confidence is in fact a common reason for failure, uncontrolled behaviour, getting in trouble, and abuse of alcohol or other drugs. This is an extreme example, but unfortunately it is a real and frequent one.

Sometimes, unrealistic expectations or limits set by parents, teachers, or religious authorities have an enormous impact on how a child feels about herself.

Therefore, it is important to teach children how to protect themselves and be more selective about which suggestions from outsiders they listen to. They need help from adults on how to build strong self-beliefs, self-concept, self-value, and self-esteem all the time and in all situations.

So, what we can do to feel more confident and make sure that our children grow up with positive feelings about themselves?

To prevent the negative conditioning of children with irrational and harmful suggestions from outsiders or from us, we need to understand how confidence develop.

Our ego represents our natural desires and our need to survive and be lovable. We feel good when we do the right thing and when we are able to give to others. We build our self-image, self-value, and self-esteem according to our life experiences and how we understand them at the time they are occurring.

Repeating positive instructions about what to do and why in a calm manner will improve a child's efficiency and confidence. However, this should be done in a friendly and controlled way—the adult parent should always be the parent. Parents and teacher must be calm and patient until the student is able to accomplish a task successfully. This is the most important strategy to teach a child. It builds trust with the teacher and, at the same time, builds the child's self-image and self-esteem.

I am not saying that we are bad parents or teachers. Sometimes we need to remind ourselves that our children build their beliefs based on what they see or hear and that they will interpret this information according to their mental ability at the time. Simply put, they are watching us like they would watch a big brother, so we all should keep this in our minds at all times.

Sleeping Bunny

One day I was saying goodnight to my eight-year-old grandson Ben, who always insists that he loves me more than I love him. Another grandson, James, age six, pretended that he was in a deep sleep during that conversation. When Ben and I finished our love competition, offering millions of stars to each other, suddenly James woke up and said, "Nana, I love you even more than Ben does."

Children watch, listen, and observe and are very sensitive. They may either show how they feel or not. Too many young people suffer from long-term negative self-conditioning, which is one of the primary reasons for their making of wrong choices in future.

Children need constant reassurance that they are special. They need a safe and cosy home. Even the smallest, poorest home can be filled with unconditional love, care, and security. Such an atmosphere provides the right conditions for a child to be healthy, grow in confidence, and develop his or her full talent and potential. If there is harmony, respect, and love in a family, the child will show constant progress in school and other activities. This in turn will help the child develop enthusiasm and creativity year after year.

Fortunately, with new experiences and a steady, positive environment, children have the ability to regain confidence and start to believe that they are as good as others. This might happen when a good friend or teacher reassures them of their abilities or because they learn more about themselves and start to believe in the potential of the body and mind, leading them to believe that they can do what they want and need to do.

Recent research done at University College London shows that the performance of autistic children significantly improves in presence of calm and comprehensive guidance from parents and teachers. Based on my observations, I strongly believe that even small positive changes at home or school are enough to trigger the child's improvement or recovery within a short time.

Thirty-nine

Open the Rusty Gate and Sail on Open Seas

> Do not waste one moment in regrets, for to think feelingly of the mistakes of the past is to re-infect yourself.
>
> Neville Goddard (1905–1972)

Release the chain of heavy past experiences. Let it go.

The material in this chapter is very deeply rooted in my heart as I worked for years with patients affected by addiction, abuse, or neglect. Every day I saw broken families, victims of addiction, crying mothers, or angry spouses. I saw children scared, confused, and ashamed of their controlling or addicted parents. We know that many victims of abuse live in denial or show overconfidence. Unfortunately, the fact is that they are living with fear behind closed doors, chained to the past and having difficulty moving forward with their lives. Unfortunately, this happens everywhere, in rich and poor homes alike.

We all agree as well that no one has the right to abuse anyone else verbally, mentally, physically, or sexually, but the fact is that many children (and adults) experience this type of abuse every day. Abused children are likely to develop deep psychological scars. This also happens when they witness abuse or fights between their parents. They do not understand what is happening. They believe that they do not deserve a better life or that what is occurring is their fault. Frequently victims are ashamed to share their experiences with others, are confused, and gradually start to feel hopeless.

Other traumatic experiences affecting a child's confidence include misfortunes such as death of loved one, parents who have mental or physical health problems, poverty, and natural disaster.

Whatever the reason for misshapen confidence, it may be difficult for the child to make the right start on her life journey. The good news is that regardless of what happened to you during your childhood or in later life, there is a better life waiting for you. The only thing you need to do is to let yourself to believe that you can live, and deserve to have, a normal, happy, rewarding life. Moreover, you can learn better ways to protect yourself than hiding in fear behind a closed door or living with anger and resentment every day.

However, if you are the victim of abuse, it is important that you take the first step and talk to a trustworthy person to stop suffering in silence. Ask a doctor or a friend to help you. It is irrational and wrong to accept the excuse from someone that "I was drunk or angry and do not remember what happened," or "I did that because you made me do it." No one has the right to make any child's or adult's life unbearable and painful. Parents, grandparents, and teachers must wake up to these facts and be more sensitive to the common problem of abuse. No one should suffer in silence.

The good news is that many abuse victims can recover fully from the past and build a new life from scratch. Learning the primary psychological strategies to find peace of mind can bring you to a turning point in your life and increase your motivation to start a new, rewarding life. Using these techniques in self-hypnosis will not only speed up the process of recovery but also will relax your body and mind. However, if you suffer from serious posttraumatic stress, the best thing is to seek professional help.

The beauty of natural laws is that they work for all of us in the same way, without exception. The most inspiring examples of this are the magnificent achievements of those who in the past believed their lives were limited by their disabilities. The Paralympic Games give people with disabilities the opportunity to develop the hidden potential of their bodies and minds.

If you are a victim of abuse or other past misfortunes, it is important for you to believe that you too can be a winner. Remember, winners never give up, and their determination will bring positive results sooner or later.

The most significant fact is that from now on, you can have an independent adult life. It is up to you what you will choose and how you will build your future. Even if you made some mistakes in the past, it is in the past. Now you can start, and you deserve to start, a new life where you are the confident commander of your ship. The future is open for all, and it is important to start right now.

However, it is also important to understand that carrying the heavy baggage of the past into the future is like creating a barrier which prevents you from reaching the open sea. It is important to be free from all unfinished emotional business before you can set out on a rewarding journey. We all have a choice: we can live with the heavy painful baggage of the past, or we can let it go in order to be free to sail to the destiny of our choice. What happened in the past stays in the past. It wasn't your fault. We can't change the past, but we can start to be in control of our lives if we are willing to be more open-minded to making necessary changes. Now you can learn from your past experiences instead of carrying the unpleasant feelings into the future.

Looking at painful past experiences in a more mature way will better prepare you this time for facing obstacles on the way. Sometimes it takes time, but if you are moving in the right direction, there is something to look forward to.

If our boat is damaged, this does not mean that we must cease sailing altogether. Instead, we can look for a new boat or join with others who may enjoy our company. It may happen that we can sail different route and discover something new on the way before we search for the opportunity to be the commander of our own ship again.

However, know that even the best psychologist will not help you to have an active, enjoyable life if you are reluctant to remove the persistent inner problems and move on. If you want to achieve something better now, you should take the best from the past and start to go with the flow. We all can learn better coping and problem-solving strategies to overcome an obstacle to reaching our new goal. The example in the box shows an example of waking up and changing your life for the better.

Stop Worrying

A thirty-five-year old, a mother of three children, frequently came to our surgery with bruises all over her body. Despite the fact that she feared her abusive husband, she believed that she could not survive without him. She worried how she would find food for the next day.

One day she visited us after more than a year of absence. We hardly recognized her; she simply looked fantastic. We were very curious to find out what happened, and my nurse could not resist asking, "Did you meet a millionaire?"

The woman laughed and responded immediately, "No. I just couldn't take it longer, so one day I stopped worrying. I decided to make my millions and be independent, so I went to a college. Now, I have a job and good supportive friends, and I am in control of my life."

The foregoing example shows that somehow, one day this woman woke up and said to herself, "That's enough." She was a self-motivated person who was experiencing inner growth while living in a passive community. She began refusing to follow the old habitual patterns of her family and friends.

Somehow, one day she was able to see an opportunity to have a better life, and she had the urge to go for it. This shows high motivation and the desire to achieve something special in life. She didn't know how she would do this, but she believed that she *could*. She kept her eyes and ears open, searching for new possibilities and new opportunities to move forward. Somehow, she understood that she needed to break the negative cycle and get out of the trap nets to have a better life. She had the intuition and faith that she could do better in life—and she did.

In fact, we all have a choice. We can stay in an uncomfortable situation, exposed to storms and waiting endlessly for miracles, or we can use all our mind's potential to take the matter in hand and find a way to safe place.

You can be in better control of your life, and you deserve it. Moreover, being free from heavy emotions of the past gives you the opportunity to make better choices in future. Being willing to let go of the heavy baggage of unpleasant experiences, damaging thoughts, and difficult emotions opens the rusty gate leading to the freedom to move in the right direction.

The old belief that "if there is a will, there is a way" is of crucial importance in achieving any goal. Learning to trust your unconscious mind (intuition, inner ego) and having balanced thoughts and emotions are other important factors to having a satisfactory life.

Learning is discovering, and the more we discover about what concerns us, the better and more enjoyable life we will have. Constantly learning and asking "How I can do this better?" is essential to reach goals, fit in better with a society, and build a comfortable life. If we wish to be a scientist, for example, we need to believe that we can and constantly deepen our knowledge. If we want to be the best partner, we must believe that we are a valuable human being who is able to offer protection to others. We must learn how to give our best to the person we have committed ourselves to. If we wish to be financially independent, we need to believe that we deserve to be as successful as others are. If we want to be a top tennis player, we need to believe that we can be who we want to be.

Whatever the reason for feeling bad about yourself, by reading the next chapters you can start to build confidence by knowing how thoughts and emotions govern your life and how you can be in charge of them from now on.

Forty

Tune Your Mind into Believing "I Can"

> Faith is to believe that which you do not yet see, and the reward of this faith is to see what that which you believe.
>
> Saint Augustine of Hippo (354–430)

Anyone can build destructive self-beliefs, just as we all have the inner power to live with positive thoughts and feelings if we put our mind to it. Often, we forget that it is a progressive process to become excellent at something and feel good about ourselves. Moreover, no one can be full of positives all the time or be perfect at everything. Therefore, to succeed at anything, the most important thing is to build a strong personality, strong self-esteem, and a strong self-image and systematically reach goals even the smallest one by one.

Surely when we have low confidence our movements are limited, and our poor self-belief is reflected in our behaviour and communication with others. When we are nervous, we become tongue-tied and everything goes wrong. We all have experiences like spilling coffee, finding it difficult to say no, or being afraid to ask a question or open a door. Exams, interviews, and social contact are difficult, and any public appearance may be accompanied by fear or panic, which minimizes our opportunity to succeed. Frequently, young people tend to avoid asking questions for fear of sounding stupid.

But the truth is that limitations are the fruits of a negative Trio Mind, as no question is ever stupid. Naturally we either know something or don't know the answer. Nobody knows everything. We all are better in some subjects and weaker in others. You may not know something today, but knowing how to find it will make a huge difference in any situation. There is no shame in not knowing, but there is weakness in being ashamed to ask and failing to learn. In any event, pretending that you do know or hiding that you don't know is a sign of low confidence, compared to successful people who always ask questions to find the answers.

Knowing the natural laws better will prevent you from living in constant uncertainty with a fear of the unknown, wherever the situation is—at sea or in the jungle. Only by changing your attitude and looking for better ways to protect yourself from rain you can restore your belief that you can do what you need to do. Even if the first attempt is not successful, it is still one step closer to finding the right solution, until you are in a warm, safe, dry place. Any change brings new opportunity, whereas repeating the same pattern will only bring the old unwanted results, which may become more severe with time. So start to make a change to your self-beliefs and start to feel good about yourself at any-time and anywhere.

As I mentioned before, to survive, grow, and gain satisfaction from life, it is crucial to have a positive vision of who you are and strong beliefs that you can do what you need to do. Confident people know exactly who they are and what they want. They believe that everything is possible and that by learning and persistence they will find what they are looking for. They always expect positive upturns and more opportunities and ideas to overcome obstacles and make things better next time.

The most important thing is to remember that whatever happens on the way, there are always other options to try, but you need to be ready to spot them. Different possibilities will create different outcomes; therefore, the more options you have, the easier it will be to make positive decisions. Having two options causes a dilemma, whereas having one choice is no option at all.

So, what do confident people do? First, they have strong boundaries, which they carefully protect, and at the same time they respect others' boundaries. They are aware of both their strengths and their weaknesses, and they understand that no one is perfect at everything. They do not worry about what others say about them. However, they carefully analyse others' opinions and work on improving themselves. Those who have high self-esteem don't need to rely on others' decisions. They make their own. They trust their intuition and stick to their plans until they accomplish the goal, despite criticism and judgement from others.

Relying on their own judgement, confident people are able to assess new situations (whether positive and negative) in calm manner and respond to them in more rational way. They have the ability to say yes or no with confidence in any situation, and when they take a risk, they always have a plan B. Somehow, they always look on a bright side; for them the half glass is half full, not half empty, as pessimists would say. They simply believe that they can do or have what they are looking for and go for it with strong motivation.

Top athletes win trophies mostly because of their firm belief that they can achieve the goal. Rafael Nodal and Roger Federer, two of the greatest tennis players ever, show passion and determination during each match they play. It is easy to read from their body language that they have a precise goal and strong determination and believe that they can succeed and that everything is possible, if not today, then tomorrow. So they keep going. "Real champions always are looking for new ways to win," Rafael said one day after losing a match. This is one of the beauties of sports, having a strong desire to reach goals based on deep self-belief and determination. The Paralympic Games prove that what seems to be impossible becomes possible with the athletes' strong belief that they can be winners.

However, top athletes and other successful people work on their confidence all the time. They constantly exercise their minds with positive images and thoughts and immediately stop stubborn intrusive negative thoughts from filling their minds.

That's the difference between optimists who say "I can" and pessimists who say "I can't." The optimists cherish even the smallest achievement, as each achievement builds one's strength and enthusiasm.

You can do the same regardless of your past experiences. If your confidence is low now, the good news is that it is only the result of a belief, which you can change from "I can't" to "I can," which will provide the wind so you can start to enjoy sailing again and exploring the world to fulfil your dreams.

Remember that if you don't like yourself or respect yourself, then others will adopt that same attitude towards you. Wise people say that others treat us as we allow them to treat us. Now you have a choice: you can hate yourself and see yourself as useless or start to uncover and be proud of all the unique value you have. Sometimes one's potential needs to be released from behind a rusty gate. Learning to think about yourself in positive way, believing that you are as good as others, is a stepping stone to building your confidence By adopting a positive attitude towards yourself, you will start to value yourself and recognize your endless potential to reach goal after goal and feel great about your achievements.

It is never too late to learn better approaches to life experiences and uncover your unique value without fear of what others will think about you. Positive beliefs are very powerful mental processes that engender constructive thinking about oneself and one's abilities.

When we are confident, we learn more quickly because we are more open to asking for more information and seeking more options. We are more flexible to open discussion on any issue and have a better chance to resolve any matter to the satisfaction of all parties involved. Feeling confident, our coping abilities are more efficient in any situation and our creativity increases, along with our performance.

When we start to make decisions that produced positive outcomes, our self-belief increases, as well as enthusiasm to do more. Satisfaction from our achievements, even the smallest achievement, will turn the engine of increased motivation and energy and improved performance, which in turn will build our confidence even more. By building a strong personality, we will be better prepared to face everyday events in a controlled way.

To stay on your desired track, you need to be equipped with a "filter" to select the most relevant information for you, not for others' benefit. Only by approaching things this way can you build sound skills and come to rely on your judgement.

Forty-one

Steps to Build Confidence

> Build a positive self-image to say confidently, "Yes I can."

In this chapter, you will learn some techniques to improve your self-belief. Systematically building a positive self-image and strong self-esteem will give you the confidence to go for what you want to achieve in life without limits. There are many ways to improve confidence. Reading this whole book first will give you a much broader picture of what it means to feel confident and will teach you how to feel good about yourself and your abilities in any situation.

Following is a summary of all previously discussed exercises which should improve your self-belief in a short period of time:

1. Confidence can be increased systematically by consciously recognizing and eliminating automatic negative thoughts (ANT) and bad feelings about ourselves. Negative thoughts and emotions should be confronted, stopped, and replaced by more constructive ones, as was presented in the discussion about replacing negative thoughts. By stopping automatic negative thoughts about yourself, you will stop the irrational self-criticism which diminishes your ability to succeed. Everyone can do it. Try it!

Exercise

Stop automatic negative thoughts and feelings about yourself.

For example, each time you have negative thoughts, "I can't do this," say to yourself: "Stop this feeling right now. From now on, I am calm and feeling good about myself, and I believe that I can do whatever I need to do."

2. Make a list of your past achievements. After stopping the negative thoughts and feelings about yourself, immediately start to think about one of your successes from the past, or an imaginary one. We all have many achievements to be proud of, some of which may be forgotten or unrecognized. You can start by recalling even the smallest achievements at home, school, or work. If your impulse is to say, "I have nothing to be proud of," I can assure you that you are wrong. Even I know that you were strong enough to survive so far, and given that you are reading this book, you are smart enough to use your brain to learn new approaches to life. Maybe you remember being good runner while in school, a wonderful storyteller, a good friend, or a good organizer. Everything you've done and have is an asset—you did it, not someone else, and all this reflects the unique you. Even a small accomplishment is an achievement. You can cherish it and put it in your treasure box to remind you that you can do things, or you can dump it—the decision is yours. Stop reading and think about it for a few minutes. Repeat the following exercise as often as you can during the day:

Exercise

Make a list of your assets and achievements. Here are some examples:

- "I am a good organizer."
- "I believe that I can learn anything that I need to learn."
- "I am responsible person. I finish any task I commit to."
- "I am a good friend."

3. When relaxing, recall happy moments from the past, and with your eyes closed, memorize and visualize the scene to make it more vivid. By recalling your happy moments and feelings, you may recharge your positive feelings at any time. Maybe you had good holiday with your grandpa, or met a good friend, or won a competition, or had a happy birthday. Happy memories are like rechargeable batteries. You can use them to build up your present personal strengths and feelings, especially when doubts start to enter your mind.

   Exercise

   Recall as many good memories as you possibly can and make a list of them. Keep this list in your bedroom so you can recall these pleasant memories each time you start to feel negative about yourself.

4. Build a portfolio of achievements and memories.

   Exercise

   Choose ten of the most significant achievements and memories from the past and present and anchor them, one by one. Choose one to work on at a time, for example feeling great upon hearing that no one could wrap a present as well as you do. Remember, any strengths you have can be converted into something practical. For example, many companies make millions on packaging!

Now, close your eyes and recall the memory associated with that experience (e.g. a party). See the scenario as vividly as you can, with colours and with people saying how beautiful your package was wrapped. Recall their voices and every word they said. Now, anchor the feeling with a trigger cue, for example putting your thumb and index finger together for twenty seconds and saying to yourself, "Great! Feeling good!"

Repeat this five times.

Work on your other assets one by one.

5. Recognize your weak points. Everyone has weak points they are not proud of. However, knowing them makes a difference in how you feel about it. We all make mistakes and have dislikes, but being aware of them helps us to learn from them and make changes.

   Two women were walking together after leaving their children at school. One was short, the other very tall. When the short woman complained that her life was affected by her height, the tall one responded, "I've always dreamed of being small. Men never open the door for a tall woman." The short one never complained again about her height.

   We all have weaknesses, and we can work on them to feel better about them. We can change them, or if this is impossible, we can accept them and find how we can use them in a more positive way.

   The quotation "Nothing is good or bad, but thinking makes it so" states a fact. By changing how we think and feel about our dislikes, we will find better approaches to dealing with them.

Exercise

Make a list of your weakest points. Make this list according to your own beliefs. Included on this list might be your lack of responsibility, your lack of loyalty, the fact that you have to rely on others, your shyness, or the fact that you are always late to appointments. See the real picture of how you feel about yourself and write about it. If this hurts badly, don't worry. You are on the right path to making improvements in how you feel about yourself.

6. Change negative habits into positive assets.

   Exercise

   Take each negative from your list and ask yourself why you do not like it. Write down your reason(s). Now, find three ways to change it. If you have a problem finding a solution, leave it be for a time and say to yourself, "I need to find the solution by [specify the date or time]." Work on each issue separately, and enjoy the process, as it is a great achievement to eliminate one of your weaknesses. Be patient as you are on the right path to changing your thinking, feelings, and confidence. Moreover, this is a very important step to break the barrier of low self-image and self-esteem.

   If you still have a problem finding a solution after having put it aside for a while, accept this fact for a time. Put it on a separate list of goals to work on later.

(See more about this in the following chapters). With practice, an idea will come to you sooner or later, as working on your weaknesses consistently will activate your Trio Mind to search for resources.

Say for example that your list includes "I hate my body." Start to look at the parts of your body you are proud of. It may be that you can expose your long slim neck more, or maybe your eyes are so unique that everyone mentions them. People do not say that you have terrible body simply because they do not see that. What they see is your unique eyes.

Another solution might be to seek sound advice from a respectable and accountable friend or professional on how to improve your fitness, practise better nutrition, change your hairstyle, or change your clothing style. Even if the first action does not solve the problem completely, it is better than doing nothing about it and living with negative feelings about it. Good things come to those who are patient, so keep going forward. Don't take step back by doing nothing. But do it in a calm and confident way.

7. Make goals related to your unresolved weak points so you can work on them more intensively.

If there is something that you cannot change, you can convert it into a positive asset if you think about it carefully. Say for example that you do not like your loud voice, but it could be a great voice for announcing at sports events. Have you ever thought about that before? Everything exists for a reason—we need just find it.

Remember, each time that you successfully change something negative into something you like, put it into your treasure box as a great asset and anchor.

Following are some examples of negatives converted into positives:

Negative	Positive
"I hate cleaning."	"I have a passion for reorganizing my house."
"I am messy."	"I am well organized."
"I never have friends."	"I am friendly."
"I hate my body."	"I am happy with my body."
"My voice is terrible."	"I have a strong voice."

When you go through this process, your list of negatives will decrease one by one and the positives will increase. Building confidence takes time, but the reward is that your life will change considerably. When you successfully convert negative thoughts or feelings about yourself into positive ones, treat this as a great achievement and praise yourself.

8. Anchor all good feelings each time you feel them, and add each to your treasure box of positive assets.
9. Make your new-found good feelings your own affirmations to recharge your confidence. They are specific to your needs. Repeat them frequently, until they become automatic in your mind. On top of that, follow the example of affirmation, below, to boost your confidence.
   Write and repeat your affirmations every day, for example: "From now on, I believe that I am attractive and a great human being. I do whatever I need to do with enthusiasm and to the best of my ability. I can systematically make positive changes in my life, as every day brings new opportunities and achievements. I anchor my good feelings and memories to add to my treasure box every day." Soon you will notice a difference in how you feel about yourself and the choices you make.

Spending only a few minutes each day repeating positive affirmations will bring rewards in many areas of your life. Repeating them throughout the day will a make huge difference in your thought pattern and how you feel about yourself and your ability to do what you want to do.

All the foregoing exercises are used successfully by millions of people to learn positive thinking, to maintain positive thoughts, to increase self-belief and self-esteem, and to stay calm in any situation. Only you change how you feel about yourself. No one else can do it.

Following is a list of some positive thoughts. You need to maintain a healthy balance in your Trio Mind if you wish to feel good about yourself.

"Every day I show my appreciation for being part of the universe."

"Every day I remind myself that I am a unique and valuable human being."

"I am grateful for my ability to learn. I feel healthier and happier every day."

"I have a lot of energy to be active and creative and to enjoy life."

"I trust myself and my unconscious mind without limit."

"I fill my mind with positive thoughts and emotions all the time."

"I respect myself, others, and the rest of the world."

"My memory is improving constantly because I am exercising my mind."

"I am in control of my beliefs and thoughts all the time."

"I am in control of my emotions. I am calm and relaxed in any situation."

"I am responsible for all my thoughts, feelings, and actions."

10. Every day, work on your affirmations and anchor them to build a positive image about yourself and your abilities and achievements. From now on, make a list every evening of the things you achieved throughout the day, even the smallest achievement, for example being five minutes early to a meeting or sorting a pile of files that previously you hadn't had time for.
    Now make a goal for tomorrow, e.g. to reorganize your office.
11. Build your positive social network to improve your confidence. Try to spend time with people who impress you with their values and who see your value and support you on your path. Gradually build a network of friends with similar interests who are goal minded.
12. Listen to self-improvement programmes to boost your self-belief. Good psychological programmes will help you understand that you have value just like anyone else. This is a fact. Being willing to master the fundamental values such as self-discipline, responsibility, respect, love, and gratitude will open many doors so you can find more satisfaction in life and your achievements.

Hypnotherapy will help restore and enhance your confidence. Hypnosis helps to clarify your beliefs directly in the unconscious mind. It allows you to see any situation from a different point of view and makes it easier for you to see the real picture in a dissociated way, free from painful attached feelings. In a hypnotic trance, it is easier to find new resources to solve a problem or make the most rational decision, leaving you with the question "How did I not think about this before?" Hypnotic relaxation programmes have built-in psychological techniques for improving self-image and self-esteem. Confidence-boosting hypnotic programmes are very powerful, creating significant, long-lasting changes in one's feelings and thoughts within a short period time.

By practising self-hypnosis, you will be able to work on all your affirmations to feel better and enjoy greater achievements every day. Listening to your affirmations during hypnosis will initiate automatic positive thoughts and emotions. Read your list of affirmations before entering trance, and work on them in the therapeutic part of your treatment. Reinforce your affirmations with posthypnotic suggestions so they will stay with you long after the trance is terminated.

One particular affirmation you should use is this: "By working on my thoughts, emotions, and beliefs, I feel better and better about myself and my ability to do what I want and need to do to reach my goals. This process will continue long after I end this trance."

Trust yourself and your mind, knowing that you can do what you want to do. No one is better or worse than other people, but those who listen and learn patiently are winners.

Part IV

Find Your Present Position

Forty-two

Sailing in Stormy Seas

> We may not be able to stop a storm, but we can predict it and look for shelter.

Unfortunately, despite our efforts to make the right choices and do our best, life may bring unpleasant outcomes. Today millions of people of all ages are going through difficult experiences, watching hopelessly as all the bridges fall down in their lives. One of the reasons for getting repeatedly unwanted results is losing the track of what is really going on and not seeing the whole picture behind it. Sometimes we don't recognize that we let ourselves be bombarded by so many responsibilities and expectations or that we are trapped in a hopeless situation.

Frequently we see people reacting impulsively to life events, making repeated bad choices and facing heavy consequences for it. When this happens, many, in desperation, start looking for drugs or alcohol to feel better, instead of looking for the right solution to the ongoing situation.

Given today's demands, it is harder for young people to fit into a rapidly changing world. The pressure on them to conform increases every year. High expectations in schools, workplaces, sports clubs, and so forth are difficult for everyone. On the top of this, many face a difficult situation at home or already have heavy baggage to carry with them.

There is no doubt that leaving school and home for the first time is an exciting experience for teens, but at the same time it is one full of unexpected obstacles. They face serious decisions, and according to their choices, their lives will be successful, average, or miserable from the start.

Disappointments will come in many unexpected ways. Some doors will be open with a welcoming smile; others will be shut without an explanation of why. Sometimes, those who smile at the first meeting turn out to be manipulators, and those who looked unfriendly at first turn out to be most sincere and concerned about your future. There may be moments when young people feel alone with no one to share their feelings with, or there may be too many "advisers" around, complicating the situation even more.

With roiling hormones, young people frequently rush to a decision without thinking what may be at the other end of the tunnel. Temptations are always around, and for people with only a little experience, it is easy to take the bait. Drugs and alcohol are served free in many places. New researches show that when people use drugs and/or alcohol before the age of twenty-five, it may affects their brain function forever and increases their chances of becoming heavy addicts. Many teens show poor judgement, ignoring the message that taking drugs is voluntarily putting yourself on a support machine that will block your creativity and rational thinking, which are crucial to succeed. The fact is that even one dose of any drug, including marihuana, can leave a young person battling with addiction for years or cause death.

Even when they see a red flag, many young people might feel too optimistic to see the present danger, believing that it will be OK if they use drugs. But sometimes this may not be the case and they might have to go through hard lessons, being hurt or disappointed by others' responses to their expectations.

Any careless decisions could take us off course to reaching our goals. Such an uncontrolled manoeuvre may be very expensive and trap a person in a hopeless situation. Many young people face closed doors in the present because they reacted impulsively or irrationally in the past.

Many young people pay for their careless choices until the end of their lives! One stupid mistake can put anyone at the bottom of the ladder, even if previously they were on the top rung—it is true and often experienced.

On the other hand, many lack the ability to recognize that doing nothing all day long, or drinking and partying every day, is irrational and will not take them to their desired destiny either. Others believe that they are smart and therefore can cheat, only to be caught up sooner or later, most likely burning all bridges behind them. Young people may not fully recognize that being a registered crime offender will lock many of the doors to success.

These are just few examples of ways to self-create blockades to success. It may be difficult to clear your name after being charged with antisocial behaviour, abuse, or some other crime. When such a thing happens, it comes as a shock to the young person to be expelled from a good college or lose a good job because of his or her irrational thinking or behaviour. Too many young people put themselves in difficult interpersonal situations or damage their health or career before they even start out. That's the fact, whether we like it or not.

This pattern of behaviour and bad decisions is not only characteristic of young people. The foregoing examples apply to people at any age; however, different periods of life bring specific needs to pay attention to. At middle age, when we should expect to be settled down, unfortunately there are not always red roses in our path. Many of us face large problems in our professional, personal, or financial lives. Disappointment, confusion, hopelessness, depression, and addictions are common, as are suicide attempts.

All our hopes and efforts to give the best to our families may be destroyed as a result of our wrong choices or misfortune. Suddenly we see that all our bridges are falling down and we are facing more and more obstacles in our way.

Problems in relationships may come to the surface after years of happy or unhappy marriage. A spouse may have another friend who understands better, and we might be left alone with financial problems or without a course of where to sail. Many face divorce, which is devastating for the whole family.

At middle age, one's children are going to college, leaving the nest empty behind them, and suddenly parents may start to feel hurt. Being dismissed from routine home duties may bring about a feeling of being left behind, as we were too busy in the previous years to think about ourselves. Children may start to show disrespect for many reasons and follow their own points of view. Friends may be preoccupied with their own problems or slowly disappear from our lives for many different reasons. We may reach a point where there is no one we can turn to who will understand. Frequently, such situations are paired with problems in workplace and a feeling of insecurity. Soon we begin to lose sleep.

However, it is a bigger problem to pretend that everything is OK when we are walking in uncomfortable shoes. With time, we may start to blame everyone and everything for increasing our discomfort, instead of looking for the true picture behind the problem.

Dissatisfaction with professional life is another painful fact to cope with when expectations are not fulfilled. Fear of the future and financial problems may preoccupy our minds all day and night. In the worst-case scenario, being under stress for a long time without seeing a solution to it makes it easy for us to start to look for sympathy or an escape from our duties.

Many seek an escape route despite knowing that an irresponsible social life will lead to greater financial crisis and a broken family. It is like the sensor of logic is switched off, leaving us with more negative thoughts every day, such as "I do not care anymore," and "Why even bother? I've had enough of this," and "No one will find out."

At this age, hormonal changes lead to changes in body and moods. Depression is common, with suicidal thoughts. Obsession with sex or desperation for a partner leads to irrational beliefs to meet the love of one's life, only to wake up alone again with a broken heart or an empty bank account.

Fear of entering the more mature half of life blocks logic as well, which leads to even more irrational behaviour. Obsession with losing their youthful looks pushes many people to spend a lot of money on beauty products, unnecessary surgeries, and other absurd artificial extensions of youth.

We face different problems during the golden years of life, which bring about significant changes. Retirement may be welcomed by some who feel tired after their many long years of work, whereas others would be very happy to continue with their professional life because they enjoy what they do. Worries about finances may be significant. Many lose their partners or live far away from loved ones. Health problems may be a daily concern, and visits to doctors become more frequent than ever. Independence may decrease bit by bit every day. Many of us at this stage of life start to have depressive thoughts, which in turn leads to even faster deterioration of health.

All these daily obstacles lead to secondary problems such as poor sleep and poor nutrition, which affect performance and health even more. Some are confused about what to do. Others show frustration or feel hopeless and hide in depression—all conditions damaging health and happiness with life.

Whatever the reason for lasting unwanted results and life disappointments, the fact remains that frequently we are afraid of seeing the true picture behind it. When consequences of bad choices come to the surface, we say, "I knew I shouldn't have done it, but ..." In many cases this "but" proves to be very costly for a long time, but we do the same thing again, refusing to look at the true picture and listen to good advice. Every day we see many "all-knowing" and "always right" people of all ages who do not recognize that they turn to a self-destructive, negative Trio Mind, chronically experiencing negative thinking, feelings and behaviour, which reduces creativity and the opportunity to succeed.

Forty-three

Denial—Dishonesty with Yourself

> You might see yourself as weak or strong, or you may choose not to see yourself at all.

Feeling better about yourself and your ability to make better choices in life, you can now move onto the next step to improving your life by asking yourself, "Am I honest with myself?" We need to ask this question repeatedly to be sure that we are not living amid conditions that lead to the blocking of rational thinking. To live in denial is to pretend that everything is OK even when all bridges are falling down, bringing suffering, anxiety, breakdown, and hopelessness.

In fact, denial is a survival tool in some drastic situations. It is a self-protective mechanism, like a safe shelter when we are trapped in a no-way-out situation. Many men and women have survived life-threatening situations by being able to create an imaginary scenario, for example something that brings hope or the idea that they have a safe home.

However, the negative side of denial surfaces when someone willingly accepts an unpleasant situation as a comfort zone, believing that it must be as it is. Long-time denial is accompanied by the fear that any attempt to make a change will make the situation even worse. Despite daily suffering, many people refuse to see the real picture of the situation. They avoid the subject even if the frustration and fear never ends. They show a negative attitude towards spotting and accepting any opportunity for change, and they repeatedly make ineffective choices. The truth is that taking no action when facing a difficult situation does not solve the problem.

Sometimes life might seem to be unfair, and it is not easy to recognize that some problems are self-induced and can be changed. This may be the result of low self-value or self-esteem, an absence of coping mechanisms and problem-solving ideas, or refusing to take red flags seriously. This may happen when a person persistently believes, "It will not happen to me" or "This situation is not so bad."

Sometimes we are too busy to recognize that we are staying in an uncomfortable position with an unsatisfying job or unhealthy relationship and creating chaos in our personal and professional life. Constantly thinking in terms of "but" and "if only" keeps us out of reality, until we wake up, change this negative self-conditioning, and stop letting ourselves be victims of misfortune.

Another significant thing that keeps us away from a successful life and smooth sailing is any form of poison to our body and mind. Abusing addictive substances leads to serious side effects or to addiction, with the devastating result of lost control over our lives. We all have unique knowledge or experiences relating to addiction. Some of us believe that we can control our drug or alcohol use, but life shows us a different picture. Every day we witness people trapped in the arms of addiction. We need to be honest and admit that this condition is self-induced and is epidemic now around the globe.

So the question is why millions of people are willing to give up their freedom and become prisoners of addictive or toxic substances.

Even more bizarre is the belief that something will not affect us—but it does. If we continue this epidemic poisoning of ourselves, and if we continue tolerating this sort of behaviour, the next generation will be even more affected by addiction. Statistic show that 80 per cent of the population of the United States is in some way affected by addiction, either personally, by living with addicts in the family, or by working with addicts in the public sector.

Global warming and territorial boundaries will be of secondary concern compared to addiction, and it will be difficult to find people anywhere who think rationally and engage in sound decision-making. Every day millions of people seek painkillers and tranquillizers to get through the day and sleeping pills to sleep at night. It seems that we are unable to function without taking some chemical! Dependence on drugs, alcohol, and prescription medication is a huge problem at any age and around the globe. So is our ignorance of it.

The facts are that any form of addiction takes a person hostage and leads to irrational thinking and self-destructive behaviour. Even worse is that many think that it is the normal thing to do to use drugs or alcohol and that everyone does it!

Denial is one of the most damaging symptoms of any addiction. Addicts live in denial that they have no problem, and they avoid those who tell them that they do have a problem. Denial is characteristic of people on either side of addition, be it the addict himself or the family trying to hide the problem from the outside world, in fear of more serious consequences of their loved one's addiction. As addiction is a serious problem around the world, even more severe is the ignorance and denial of this fact at home, in schools, at work, and by authorities. No one can deny that addiction (either to drugs or alcohol) is the primary cause of health problems, personal unhappiness, divorce, career failure, financial difficulties, and accidents. It affects the addict's life and damages the lives of all people living with or associated with the addict, at home, in the workplace, and within society. This means it affects all of us. In Canada alone, one in four highway deaths is caused by a driver under the influence of drugs or alcohol.

The real problem starts when children are affected by an addict's constant bad decisions and her denial that her family's life is perfect, but in fact the child is withdrawing from life more and more in fear of abuse or neglect. Children in this sort of situation are hopeless and do not understand what is happening. It is easy to damage our relationship and everything else we have with them and later blame others for our misfortune, or let ourselves down with depression or anger.

Hoping that miracles changes will come tomorrow will not solve the problem either. We must acknowledge that there is no worse home for a child than the one where he lives with his irrationally thinking mother or aggressive father in denial that everything is out of order, where every day brings new suffering.

Sometimes we deny that we allow ourselves to be victims of manipulators, or we have a tendency to believe that a certain person loves us when all facts prove the opposite. We tend to respond impulsively to events, wasting a lot of energy going in the wrong direction, which brings poor results, but still being reluctant to make any change. Sometimes we hide in depression or live with growing anger. All these responses lead to more irrational choices or to no decisions at all—either way leading us into darkness.

The facts about our actions speak for themselves. They correspond with natural law, resulting in the same consequences each time. Cheating damages one's personal, family, social, and business relationships. Neglecting duties pulls a business down and leaves others suffering because of someone's ignorance, saying, "It will be OK" or "Someone else will do something about it." Abuse is always abuse, and there is no excuse for it. The same is true of manipulation.

Second to ignorance, another reason we put ourselves in difficult situations is because we are out of control, preoccupied with our selfish demands. When we let ourselves lose the balance between the healthy functioning of body and mind, confusion arises and emotions dance in our heads without any control. The consequences can be severe, such as facing criminal charges, having a nervous breakdown, or foolishly losing tangible and intangible assets.

Professional dissatisfaction can be difficult to admit to. The affected person feels uncomfortable and ashamed to admit that they need help to sort things out, because they believe that they failed at something. When rainy days come, it may be a difficult and painful experience. In such moments, some people simply break down or take the first available remedy to make themselves feel a little bit better for a short time, only to make another irrational choice with even more serious consequences.

Despite our best efforts, sometimes in unfamiliar stressful situations we simply do not know what to do to solve the problem. We try many different approaches, but none of them work. The problem we have may be the result of an irresponsible family member, an illness, a professional incident, or a financial difficulty. The list is virtually endless. There are many times in our lives when we are afraid to see the truth of our present situation. We hope that the uncomfortable situation will vanish by itself.

Sometimes we live with secrets because we are ashamed to admit that we need help to get out of an unmanageable situation. Other examples of things that lead to denial are family problems which are kept behind closed doors, physical and mental abuse, neglect, financial problems, and personal misfortune. Many of us are frightened to see the real picture because we believe that we did something wrong or are useless. The fear keeps us isolated, ties our tongue, and allows us to suffer in silence.

We choose to pretend that everything is OK or believe that something will change. In most cases the change may never come and the situation may start to deteriorate. Unfortunately, if the affected person lives with denial for too long a time, it will become very difficult to prevent further damage.

Good advice from family or friends is rejected automatically as this triggers our weak point of hiding a secret. However, keeping these emotions to ourselves will not change anything. Living in denial can freeze our life with severe consequences to our mental and physical health and seriously affect the life of the whole family. To put the broken pieces back together may be difficult and will take a long time.

The questions are, how we can prevent such a situation, and why some are able to make better choices than others?

This is a complex issue and involves our beliefs, thinking patterns, and emotions. Becoming aware of the blocks that keep you from moving on is the first step to allowing yourself to move on and take your first steps away from the hopeless situation and towards a more rewarding life.

So if you think that you are able to relate to some of the foregoing situations, stop for a moment and think about it. It may be a turning point in your life, a time for brave action. In the next chapters, you will find answers on how to get out of the stormy weather and find a more enjoyable life and smoother sailing. Using simple psychological techniques and reinforcing them in self-hypnosis will bring about positive changes within a short time.

Forty-four

Being Honest with Yourself and Others

Only by playing your cards right can you be winner.

Honesty is the basic foundation for all kinds of relationships and successes. To successfully reach goals, we need to follow a number of moral and ethical values to have a good relationship with ourselves and others. As strange it sounds, even the biggest achievements will not bring satisfaction if we are not welcome at any port because of our attitude: "I don't care," "Why bother?" "These things only happen to me," etc. Therefore, it is important to work on our human values and maintain balance within the Trio Mind. To be in good relationship to ourselves, we must invest time. It is an art in and of itself. But we all can master it, and it may be a milestone for any kind of relationship or personal achievement.

Being dishonest with yourself and others is like living in the shadow of fear, knowing that the truth will come to the surface one day. In the long term, dishonesty may seriously damage your personal life, your family life, and your dignity.

Dishonesty towards others strips many people of trust and causes them to lose the support of other people close to them. The consequences of dishonesty may be hard to repair, and regaining trust may take a long time, if it ever happens at all. For those saying "No one will know," one day all ports may be closed, leaving them behind rusty gates, alone on the stormy sea. Regardless of previous achievements, the dishonesty will be recognized sooner or later and may bring long-term isolation.

In contrast, honesty with ourselves and others opens many doors to new opportunities and lightens the path to increasing confidence and peace of mind. Being honest brings trust, which is the foundation for any kind of relationship and goal achievement. If you used to succumb to the temptation to do what you should not do, improving your self-value is the best way to protect yourself from making bad choices again.

Therefore, the questions "Who am I?" and "What I can do about it?" should always be on your mind, especially when you are going through turbulence in your life. It is important to look carefully at what went wrong and honestly take full responsibility for it, in line with your honest beliefs and moral and ethical values. You might say, for example, "Maybe I should think how to be better prepared for exams," "Maybe I should learn to control my finances," or "Perhaps I should learn how to control my emotions." Many of us are frightened or feel ashamed to recognize our irrational behaviours, but facts never disappear. On the other hand, no one deserves to be cheated, and no one has the right to cheat others. In the long term, the cheater is the loser and will be treated as one.

The good news is that dishonesty is a weakness that can be changed.

You can start to work on honesty by asking yourself the following questions:

- Am I honest with myself and others?
- If not, then why I am being dishonest, knowing that it is not right and will turn against me?

Then you can say, "Now that I see the facts, I can make positive changes."

Make it a goal to improve your honesty with yourself and others, and be amazed how many of your shortcomings disappear, one by one. Then you can make the following affirmations:

- "I am honest with myself and others. Because of that, I feel great about myself."
- "Only by being honest can I take responsibility for my decisions.
- Because of that, I have earned the respect and trust of others."
- "Honesty is my GPS for making choices.
- "Because of this, I know that I do my best."

Motivations for honesty include feeling good about yourself, being a trustworthy person, and having friends.

Forty-five

Waking Up from the Comfort Zone

> Being willing to see the true picture allows you to erase what is bad from your past.

The rule is simple: to make the right start, we need to do things right. The same rule applies to any aspect of our life, whether it is improving our personality, performance, business, or relationships. Our lifespan consists of different phases, and each needs the right start if it is to be successful. Making the right plan is important at any age, whether you are just starting out in your adult life, at middle age, or approaching the golden years.

I would like to begin this chapter by offering you the reassurance that regardless of your present situation, you are a valuable human being building the future of the world. We all have something to offer, and we each have a unique talent. The fact is that despite what happened in the past, we always can start again! Always there will be mistakes to learn from. However the fewer silly mistakes we make, the higher and faster we climb the ladder. Unfortunately, many repeat the same bad choices over and over again without recognizing that it is not what life brings to them but what they choose to bring into their life that matters.

Starting out with a clear vision of who you are and what you want to achieve in your life will keep you on course to discover joy and attain your desired destiny. Above all, this will help you stay away from any unhealthy temptations along the way. Each of us has our own life, and we all should be the captain of our own ship. Some would like to sail across the Pacific Ocean; others, along the Costa Blanca shore. You may wish to build the biggest bridge in the world, or be a perfect mother, friend, or write a book. Whatever desires and ambitions you have are great—as long as you know what you want and know how to focus your effort to bring about a successful final result. This is the way to find satisfaction at the end of the day. Which ports you wish to visit or anchor in should be your decision along.

When you are entering adult life, the bigger the picture of your destiny you have, the better it will be for you, your family, and the rest of the world. I believe that we all should feel free to have our dreams and build on them in our shipyard without limitations. However, to make our dreams come true, we need to convert each dream into a realistic goal. To achieve the goals, we need to be willing to take the necessary actions and make the necessary sacrifices, as all great achievers do. It is important to gradually build our personality, increase our respect for ourselves and others, trust own judgement, and sharpen all our senses to make the right decisions.

Sailors know where they want to sail and prepare themselves for the voyage months or years in advance. Then they enjoy the ocean winds, knowing how to face them. They know the signs of danger and follow the weather forecast instead of assuming that things will be OK. Increasing skills and learning to follow your intuition will come with experience, but guessing may end your journey at an iceberg.

From now on, we will discuss the main features of securing the way to do things right whatever you starting point is. We will start by preparing a list of goals to achieve and the factors needed to make changes.

Let's start with building a clear image of who you are now and how you feel about it.

You can do this at any time you wish in a fully awake state of mind. When you become more familiar with self-hypnosis, you can work on this question during trance, when sitting in a safe place and in a comfortable position.

First, ask "Who am I, and who do I want to be?" You should regularly repeat this question in your mind. Visualize yourself as you wish you were, including how you look and what you do. Write it down, read it, think about it, and put it on the wall in your bedroom so you will see it every morning and evening. You can change the images, reshape them, and erase them at any time. It is OK to make changes because you are searching for the real picture of yourself. After two to three weeks of practising this, your vision of who you really are should be clear. Working on this in trance will help to speed up the process, and your true desires will start to come to the surface automatically. This way you will draw high boundaries, along with knowing your personality and interests, just by focusing on the image of yourself as you wish to be in your private life, family life, professional life, and social life. This is the perfect tool to help you make decisions and reject any contradictive suggestions, temptations, demands, or abuse from others.

Examples are as follows:

- "I want to be a successful baseball player."
- "I want to be a writer, or something else."
- "I want to be a good friend [or brother, or son, or something else]."
- "I want to be a kind and respectful person."

Second, take action now. Only if you are willing to take even the smallest step out of your comfort zone will you start sailing in the direction of your choice and enjoy what you do. Wasted days bring restless nights and more ineffective days. Wasting your time with losers and with those who are going nowhere will bring about disappointment sooner or later. Whatever your situation is, the best formula for moving in the right direction is to take the first step today and then take a little bit bigger step the following day.

I like the saying that the journey to Rome starts with the first step, and regardless which road you choose, if you are persistent, one day you will enjoy the best coffee in Rome. It is not important how big your goal is, but it is crucial to finish one task with satisfaction and say to yourself, "Yes, I did it." The common mistake is to think, "I will do it tomorrow." Tomorrow always will be tomorrow, but we live only today. If you are facing some problem already, know that with the beauty of your mind you can make a small, positive change right now, regardless of the origin of the problem. You can take the first step even if it just sorting your desk, sending long-delayed letters, visiting the library, or writing the question "Who am I, and who do I want to be from now on?"

Third, know that truly successful people obey the law, uphold cultural and moral values, and respect their opponents and themselves. Because of this, they increase their chances of having what they want. They don't break the law because they know that uncalculated risk may lead to devastating results. They simply can't afford to break the law, and they would feel bad about themselves doing so. This is why they are excellent in everything they do. They are successful because they make smart choices and are good, trustworthy negotiators. They only take calculated risks, meaning that if something goes wrong, they are still in a comfortable position and have a backup plan to recover.

The secret to making the right decision lies in how strong our personality is, how confident we are, and what ambitions we have. Be smart, prepare yourself for a good start, and enjoy sailing to the port of your choice. If you are not fully satisfied with your life so far, it is time to take the tiller and stay in control for the future by taking full responsibility for your actions. What chances you have for a better life depend on how badly you want to change your present life. Change must come from you. You need to take action and be willing to learn whatever is necessary if you want to be successful. Continuing the same old patterns will keep you in the same position, feeling worse and more hopeless every day.

Taking the first step to making changes will automatically change you thinking. For example, if you are dependent on others, you may start to think about taking some courses or connecting with people from a different environment. This would be an opportunity to build a new positive social network and expose yourself to new ideas. It would be like turning the corner to find new energy and motivation to take care of yourself in the right way. If you have had bad experiences in the past, no one can change this fact. But instead of staying in an uncomfortable position, it is better to let things go and make a right start to a new life. Learning from your experiences, good and bad, is an asset that will prevent you and others from undergoing similar experiences.

It is proven that successful people show the highest level of activity and creativity when under pressure or after some misfortune. They always take action and try to do something different next time. They never say that they failed. They trust their intuition, believing that one day the right door will be open again. They are willing to move out of their comfort zone to find new opportunities and surround themselves with people going in the right direction to achieve their goals.

Regardless of your age or financial situation, finding new interests or hobbies is another way to start living with passion. There are many activities you can enjoy, from learning to play tennis to painting, or discovering the history of your neighbourhood and helping local people. With new energy and enthusiasm, you have a better chance to learn and grow from past irrational behaviour and start being honest with yourself and others.

Whichever direction you want to sail in, now is the time to master a few elementary skills. In the next chapters, you will analyse particular movements one by one and add them all to your everyday routine.

Forty-six

Assessing Your Present Position

To every action, there is an equal and opposite reaction.

Isaac Newton (1643–1727)

All the previously mentioned conditions—living passively, living in denial, or living in delusion—are connected to each other and have one thing in common: they all are products of repeatedly making wrong decisions, and long-term irrational thinking.

If you recognize that you do one of these things, don't feel bad about it, because you can make the decision right now to change it. We all have different experiences, expectations, and stories to tell. We all can be confused from time to time as we are bombarded with an enormous amount of contradicting information from different sources. The media, including TV and the Internet, put pressure on all of us, and we are faced with more demands in our professional and social lives. These constant high expectations can easily cause our minds to become heavily burdened. Living with "I have to," or "I can't cope," or "I am afraid of tomorrow" increases the stress, and then making a decision may not be so simple.

On top of that, bad things happen to all of us from time to time, and there is nothing we can do about it. Nature has its own laws. Tsunamis and earthquakes will happen, as they have happened in the past. Incurable illness or addiction may take away everything we have without mercy. We may be trapped in uncomfortable situations at times but we shouldn't endlessly blame ourselves for this, as in most cases it is the result of many events put together. On the other hand, it is in the past, and now we have the opportunity to change it. Making mistakes is as well a normal part of the process of experimenting, learning, and growing up.

However, problematic situations develop when we stop learning from our experiences. Whatever difficult situation you are facing now, only by knowing exactly what is happening you can stop it and begin to move in the direction of your choice. Even if you created the problem, it is better to accept that you had no control over some of the events at that particular time, despite your best intentions. What you can do is learn how to be in better control of your life, instead of wasting energy and time by complaining, "This always happens to me."

Learning to deal with life events in a more efficient way is the starting point for a better future. We all can improve our ability to think, better protect ourselves from damaging influences from outside, and look for safer and more enjoyable sailing. You can learn to approach any challenging situation in a more controlled way and make better choices in a calm way.

It is difficult to find the best definition for success, but there are some conditions which help us secure success. These are as follows:

- Having a clear positive picture of who you are.
- Being independent to do what you want to do.
- Having a vision of what you want to achieve.
- Believing that you can do it.
- Having the satisfaction of your own achievements.
- Being respected and respecting family members and society, even when they have a different opinion.

Mark those conditions which already apply to you, and be honest with yourself. This will help you to admit whether your present situation is what you want or whether you want to open a new chapter of your life by moving onto the right path. When something goes wrong, it should be an alarm bell urging you to look at the true facts and ask yourself, "Is it right?"

There is no need to blame others. We need only look at our reactions to the situation: "What is my part in the situation, and how I can change it?" Others may or may not be willing to make changes, and there is nothing we can do about this. But we can change our own reaction and responses to it.

Be smart enough to recognize where you are now. Write it down on paper to stimulate your mind. Ask the question over and over again. Once you do this, the fear of the unknown will start to fade away.

The following are examples of things you might write:

- "I recognize that I am in abusive relationship, and it must stop."
- "I acknowledge that my business is on the decline. I need new assessment."
- "I constantly have a problem going through interviews. I need to find out why."

By becoming more familiar with simple psychological exercises and by learning to use self-hypnosis, you will be wide awake and stop living with your secrets and fears. Instead, you can start to build your own strengths on solid ground to make a fresh start. New ideas will start to flow, and immediately you will be more open-minded to new opportunities. Above all, you will learn how to prepare yourself for sailing to the port of your choice.

Forty-seven

Seeing the True Picture

> I am standing by the shore of a swiftly flowing river and hear the cry of a drowning man. I jump into the water. I lay him out on the bank. I hear another cry for help. I jump into the cold water … Nearly exhaustion … it occurs to me that I am too busy jumping in, that I have no time to see a hole in the bridge that is causing people to fall in. What do you do, you do want to make the most sense—you repair the bridge?
>
> Irwin Zola, Upstream

Once we admit that our current situation is unacceptable, we automatically create an opportunity to change it. It is the most difficult but most essential step to take if we wish to find a turning point in our life. The second step is to recognize the main reasons we are in such a position. When we know precisely what makes us uncomfortable, we will know what we need to change to improve the situation. This is as certain as two plus two making four, and it is the way to open the door to get out of an uncomfortable situation.

We all have habits and comfort zones, and as long they do not disturb our plans or damage our life, we are fine. Discomfort starts when we fall out of balance, and the problem begins when we lose control over our destiny and let ignorance or lack of knowledge influence our decisions.

When all bridges are falling down around us, we need to be honest with ourselves, maybe for the first time, and see exactly what is happening in our lives and why. For every problematic situation, there is a reason for it, and without understanding what creates the situation, we remain trapped and may feel hopeless.

Ask yourself the following question and write down your answer: "What are the primary causes of my present situation?" Think about this very carefully.

The purpose of that question is to find the accurate picture of the troubling situation without blaming others or yourself for it. When you are aware of what keeps you in this situation, you will be in a better position to end the seemingly endless cycle of "misfortune," and free yourself from it.

Thinking about your situation without fear will increase the clarity of the picture of what really went wrong. You may have recognized that you are living in denial or are passively waiting, thinking that tomorrow all your problems will be solved. You may be afraid of change or be too stubborn to admit that you made the wrong decision. Perhaps you blame others or something else for your situation. Unreasonable thinking—"If only others would change" or "If only I had this,"—is the most common reason for being stuck in an uncomfortable position. We all desire a better life, but too often we have a tendency to rely on others to deliver what we want. Frequently we are met with the unrealistic expectations of our spouse, children, friends, or boss or the authorities. Others may never change to suit us, and there always will be those who expect too much from us. Others may gain satisfaction from keeping us in the same position, whether we like it or not.

Making a list of anything you are not happy with in your life and why it will prevent you from living in darkness any longer.

Example 1. "I fail exams because I feel useless. I need to improve my confidence."

Example 2. "The harder I try, the worse things are. I need a new approach."

Example 3. "My communication skills are bad. I need to clearly express what I want."

Example 4. "I tried to lose weight, but I never made a rational plan for it."

Once we take the first step, it opens a new pattern of thinking about how to make changes to an unwanted situation. Even a small change will turn the tide, then other changes will soon follow.

For example, facing an abusive partner calmly, instead angrily, may change his or her responses. Thinking "I will find a job" instead of "I can't find a job" increases the chance of a successful outcome. In business, being willing to call experts and ask for their advice may save the company.

Willingness to Change

An enthusiastic Italian family had run a successful restaurant in South London for years, but recently the business was on the decline. The harder they tried, the worse it was. To avoid having to close up shop, a young member of the family asked for professional help. The experienced business manager came with a bag full of ideas, but the owner was very reluctant to accept them. He firmly believed that he knew better, as the business was good before. He blamed the economy, high taxes, and other factors for the downturn. In addition, the owner was emotionally attached to the past success and was reluctant to let go of the old way of doing things. However, after long discussions and many protests, new ideas were put into practice for a trial period. Within a few months, the business reached record profits.

The experienced business person saw the whole picture from the outside. She recognized that the recipes were perfect, but she felt that a fresh approach was needed to catch the eyes of passing people. The owners did not see the need for change until someone made them aware of the problem they were facing and the real cause of it.

Working with self-hypnosis gives us an excellent opportunity to see our present situation more clearly without judgement or other unpleasant emotions such as shame, guilt, and anger. As long we are willing to be open-minded and increase our skills, we are on the winning side and can open the door to find new ideas.

According to famous the physicist Albert Einstein, there are no failures, only experiences from which we can learn how to do better next time. What seems to be difficult to change to the conscious mind (for example working too hard with poor results) may be achievable in a relaxed way or by drawing on unconscious processes.

Changing to simple thinking, for example, "The old way doesn't work. I need to do something different this time," may bring positive change. You can start by ceasing to view a false picture of yourself. For example, seeing yourself as a failure will cause your unconscious to work for you in a creative way in an effort to move you out of that uncomfortable position. Becoming willing to unlearn the old habits which created the conflict between the conscious and unconscious mind is the right way to move forward. Therefore, it is important to practise exercises that help you gain control of your thoughts and emotions in all circumstances.

How do you spell
love?
-piglet
You don't spell
it. You feel it.
-pooh

Part V

Goals

Forty-eight

Go for What You Want

Creating a picture of what you want highlights the path leading in the direction you need to go.

Now that you feel better about yourself, your abilities, and your positions, it is time to learn more about the importance of setting goals and the best way to achieve them. We all make plans to some extent, both consciously and unconsciously. We are always thinking what we will do, what we will eat, or whom we are going to meet. But frequently those thoughts are chaotic and superficial, leading to poor end results. The worst thing is when we do not follow our plans. At the end of the day, we know somewhere deep inside that we wasted another day. We could have easily done more and done things better, but still we followed our old habits, thinking, "I don't know, maybe tomorrow."

Achievements are the most influential factors in feeling good about ourselves, and having a habit of setting goals takes us to a higher level of achievement. Unfortunately, only a small percentage of people make goals at all, and an even smaller percentage accomplish them. Sadly, many of us never were told in school or at home how important it is to have goals. Sometimes people have an idea of what they would like to do, but after a short period of euphoria, doubts start to creep in and their energy starts to wane. Then come the old feelings: "I can't do it," or "I am not sure about this idea." Other times people say they have no time to set goals, and they dance to the same tune, going round and round for years, only to become more stressed and disorganized every day. Frequently I have been told that it is confusing to set goals. Some people spend considerable time writing their goals but have ineffective strategies to reach them. Others just give up when the first obstacles appear.

But facts speak for themselves. Not knowing which port to sail to, we sail to an unknown destination, which may not be the place we want it to be. This is like sailing without a navigation system, letting the wind to take us to some unknown destination.

On the other hand, I've heard many times that people do not make plans because they prefer "surprises" in their life. Well, surprises are guaranteed, but they are not always pleasant. Sometimes they are painful and costly and often come at the most inconvenient time, leaving frustration and confusion in their wake.

In fact, many psychological studies show that having goals increasing one's probability of achieving those goals. However, the goals must be precise, supported by strong motivation and determination to reach them.

Writing down your goals is like a being a commander making plans to sail. Once you form a clear picture in your mind of what you want, your unconscious will act as a GPS, showing which direction you need to go in to achieve it. Also, having goals reinforces your self-belief of who you really are and what you want. This in turn automatically increases your energy and motivation and the possibility of achieving personal and professional goals or improving performance and health.

In addition, writing down your desires and dreams is a very powerful technique to discover and shape your real interest, as your mind will start to search for information to clarify the vision of the real you. Your unconscious mind has inner resources and will supply them to you sooner or later when you are looking for answers to your questions and fulfilment of your requests. Having a clear vision of the goal, your mind will keep your focus on that task, gain additional important information, and reject information not connected with your desire.

Moreover, you will be more motivated to have better control over your emotions, thoughts, and decisions. You will be better equipped to deal with obstacles or temptations along the way, and this will make you more confident to say "yes" or "no" to any ongoing situation. With a strong vision of your goal, you will automatically surround yourself with supportive people who share a similar interest, instead of wasting time and energy with people going nowhere. It will be easier to make the right choices, instead of putting off things until tomorrow or not making decisions at all.

Writing down your goals is the most important factor in building success and gaining independence. By following your goals, you find the most significant value of life: the joy of living and of having a challenge, instead of frustration, disappointments, confusion, or relying on others whether you prefer to or not.

Those who are serious about their lives make plans for today, tomorrow, and the near future. Those who make plans for the next day and accomplish them take their evening cup of tea with relief and satisfaction. With the day having been successful, the feeling of accomplishment will increase the level of energy and enthusiasm to go through the next day's tasks with a sense of challenge and joy.

Wise people say that the longest journey starts with the first step. You can take the first step now to reach your goals, one by one.

Below, I present the simplest explanation of how writing down your goals works. In the next chapter, you will find step-by-step instructions for how to do this.

- Write and rewrite your goals until you have a clear picture of what you desire.
- Read your goals aloud or silently to find their real meaning.
- Analyse your goals carefully, asking, "Is this really what I want?"
- Ask, "Why are these goals important to me and those close to me?"
- Picture each goal with your eyes closed for a few minutes. See as many details as you can.

- Have trust, and let your unconscious mind deliver the goal to you.
- Practise this technique at least twice a day, and keep the image in your mind until your goal is accomplished.

I strongly advise that before you write down your goals, you read the next chapter on goals in order to fully understand the importance of the many factors that work towards creating goals. You will find each aspect of goal achievement discussed separately. By reading them, you will have a full set of well-designed personal goals to make a right start on your new journey, whatever your starting point may be. Each chapter illustrates the important issues which, when converted into goals, will improve your well-being and open your horizons to successful and enjoyable sailing.

Forty-nine

When You Don't Know What You Want

Confusion—Shall I Stay, or Shall I Sail?

Another frequent mistake people make is to drift at sea, not knowing where they are going day by day, month by month. This happens because some people have no vision of what they want from life. There may be many reasons for this, such as living passively, living in illusion, or living in denial; lacking basic skills in planning; being confused; and having unawaken ambitions.

There may also be a medical cause associated with this way of living, such as a terminal illness or a psychological condition like posttraumatic stress, a neurological disorder, or depression. These conditions demand professional help and would benefit from medical hypnosis.

Without having some vision of who we are and what we want to do, we live a rather fruitless life. In the long term, we will find it difficult to set any goals, and our lifeboat may be anchored behind rusty gates. When we are under constant stress and fear, confused and preoccupied with negative thoughts and emotions, our creative power may be temporarily blocked. In this condition, it is difficult to find the motivation to do anything.

Fortunately, in most cases it may just be a matter of waking up and sorting out our thoughts and feelings to have a new start. Following are the steps to take to achieve this:

1. Read this book to the end to gain a better awareness of the importance of turning your mind towards positive attitudes, regardless of your past experiences and present beliefs about yourself and your abilities. Carefully work through all the exercises to build stronger beliefs about yourself and your potential. Start to practise the techniques one by one to feel better. This is an educational book and needs to be read many times, especially when you find yourself lost at sea again. Each time, different information may get your attention, so keep going.
   We all have dreams, but only a positive attitude increases our faith that the dream we have can come true. Even the most ambitious dream will fade unless we fully understand that successful sailing is a result of making a commitment, obeying common laws, and trusting our logic and intuition. That is the main difference between successful people and those living in a coma, or dreamers.
2. Concentrate on relaxing your body and mind. You can start by listening to a relaxation hypnotic programmes, which can be downloaded from my website, as this may remove the barriers preventing you from thinking clearly. Relaxation hypnotic programmes are made up of simple psychological approaches to stimulate the mind's processes in order to clarify thoughts and block negative emotions. Feeling calmer will help you to better understand the need for change and will increase your beliefs that you can do what you want. This way you may feel the urge to commit yourself to making the effort to learn new ways of making better choices and gaining satisfaction from all you do. However, it takes time, and the results will depend on your willingness to make even the smallest change and

your commitment to be consistent every day about improving your life.

Keep it simple. One step a day will help you reach your desired destiny one day! Without taking the first step, you will never get there!

3. A useful approach is to start changing all your negative thoughts about yourself into positive ones, as was presented in previous chapters. If your thoughts and feelings are negative, it is likely that you know what you do not want in your life, instead of knowing what you do want.
4. Another useful approach to stimulating your mind to develop new ideas is to imagine or pretend that you are someone else. For example, think about a movie or book you enjoyed whose main character lived a life that you would like to live. Maybe you have a hero or friends you admire and would like to be like.
5. Be honest with yourself. Think of who you would like to be and what you would like to do. You can have it!
6. Make a small search by asking others or yourself, "What do I like to do? What gives me pleasure? Am I happy? If not, why not? What makes me unhappy?"
7. Make a list of everything you do not like about yourself or your life, and change these things into positive one.
8. Make a list of things you would like to do if you had no restrictions. This can give you a clue as to what you want. Use this information to set a goal, and then work towards that goal.

   Examples:

   - "I like to build model cars. Maybe I could be an engineer or make toys."
   - "I like to read children's books. Maybe I could write children's books."
   - "I like to decorate my house. Maybe I could be an interior designer."

- "I like reading different books. Maybe I could take the entrance to UCLA."

Any goal can be fully accomplished when there is a reward for it.

For example, you spend all day on computer creating advertisements but never send them to anyone, and you have no income to live on. This is not an accomplishment. Make a sound goal: "I love to create ads because I am good at it. I am going to do it professionally so it brings me an income of [insert the amount] a year."

In the following chapters, I present fundamentals which will help you find the way to be a respectable commander of your ship and safely reach your desired port. There will be the rocks for you to navigate as you go through every day experiences. These will reinforce your potential to do and have what you want.

Fifty

Structure of Goals

> If you are looking for perfection you will find it, if you are looking for trouble you will find it as well.
>
> Pablo Picasso

Writing a sound goal is a skill in and of itself. Writing your goals will bring final results that are in line with the structure of your goals. If your goals are precisely defined, your unconscious mind will have a clear picture of what you want and will search for it.

Below are important factors to securing well-prepared goals:

1. Start writing your goals with some idea of what you want to have or achieve. Think about it to make a more precise picture of it. List everything you want now and in the future without limitation, believing that nothing is impossible. However, first I suggest starting with goals which are believable and more realistic for you. It is not a sound goal to become a doctor and spend all day on the beach doing nothing, unless you want to be a doctor on duty during beach competitions. With time and experience you will be able to go for more complex goals.

2. Goals may be related to anything you want to achieve, such as the following:

    - Materialistic gains, such as a car, an increase in income, or own business.
    - Personal improvements, such as general health, a stronger personality.
    - Professional improvement related to creativity, obtaining a degree, or being promoted.

3. Goals must be well defined and challenging if they are to be effective. Write down your goals in the present tense as if you have already accomplished them. Add as many details about what you want as possible, such as places and people involved, your feelings, and your sense of satisfaction from your achievement. For example:

    - "I have a successful business in computer programming, employing one hundred people," etc.
    - "I have a hundred-foot catamaran with two engines, four cabins," etc.
    - "I earn a degree in engineering from Imperial College London in 2018."
    - "I win an Olympic gold medal in singles tennis competition in 2020."

4. You can add details to your goal each time you read it. For example, "Now I specialize in creating new tools, so my income has reached $200,000. I am working from home so I can divide my duties between business and childcare."
5. Goals should be positive in nature for you and others; otherwise you may find yourself lonely and lost at sea, with no one to share your achievements with. Cheating or selfishly taking the easiest opportunities to reach what you want and hurting others is not the right way to gain success and have

satisfaction from it. Even when feeling that you have lost an opportunity, you should keep the positive and constructive goal in your mind, as you may be surprised to encounter better options. Frequently we hear, "I missed that opportunity, but now I have an even better proposition."

Example of a sound goal: "My business improves my life and supports my community."

Unfriendly goal: "My business has grown because I have destroyed the competition."

6. Include the precise time of accomplishment: "My book will be published by 23 December 2019."

   It is important to ensure that delivery of the final product comes at the right time for you. This will help you to make decisions, instead of repeatedly thinking, "I am not sure about it." However, do not confuse this with making irrational impulsive decisions, which will be discussed later.
7. Write up to five motivations behind your goal, asking yourself, "What are the benefits of my goal?"

   Motivations are the essential things that push you towards achieving your goals. For example, you motivation might be to recover from a mental or physical fall. Your motivations are the fuel behind your goals, the things that give you the enthusiasm necessary to maintain the persistence needed to keep going. Motivations are critical in reinforcing the signal to the unconscious mind of what you want and how serious you are about obtaining it.

   Some people have told me that they have encountered problems when trying to find a motivation for their goals. Therefore, I present step-by-step examples on this issue.

   Example 1: Your goal is to have your own business. Your motivations might be as follows:

   - financial security for the family
   - the ability to work from home and manage your time between your work life and home life

- the ability to spend holidays with family
- satisfaction and improved confidence that you can be successful
- being independent and the ability to help those in need the community.

Example 2: You want to be the number one tennis player.
"Being the number one tennis player gives me personal satisfaction and leads me to challenge my potential and abilities. I gain great satisfaction from my achievements, which increases my enthusiasm to do more. It gives me the opportunity to promote sports and share my experiences with others."

8. Writing and rewriting goals stimulates the conscious mind to search for what you want to achieve. Rewriting, reading, and analysing each goal will cause you to add more details and make corrections to the first draft of your goal.
9. Analysing your goal is a very important step in that it helps you fully understand the real meaning of the goal. It is important to take time to think about the goal's real meaning. This gives insight into what you really want. Revise your goal until you feel comfortable with it. Check that it includes all the foregoing facets.
10. There is no limit to how many goals you can write, but it is important to work on one goal at a time. After making the initial list of what you want to achieve, select your goals in order from the most important at the least important. You can make groups of goals that support one another.
    For example, "I want to be a champion" can be paired with supporting goals related to things such as improved physical condition, discipline, and diet. Another example is a supporting goal to improve public speaking skills and confidence. Choose the most important goal and start to work on it, along with all the supporting goals.

11. Any long-term goals should be divided into short-term goals (daily, weekly, monthly) which will be reached one by one, like climbing a ladder rung by rung. To be the number one tennis player, the champion, means having a goal to win smaller tournaments first, from provincial tournaments to national tournaments, and up to Grand Slams and Olympic challenges.
12. Avoid goals that contradict each other, for example, "I want to be a dancer" and "I seek to avoid exercise."
13. Other goals on your list should be read systematically. Having more goals will keep the big picture of your long-term plans, and who you are and who you want to be in future, at the forefront of your mind. With time and practice, you may notice that the number of goals grows smaller, but they will be more precise and headed in the same direction. Be wild at the beginning when you write down your goals, as your mind needs a lot of details about what you really want.
14. Repeat your goal twice daily, either aloud or silently. By verbally repeating the goal, you create the picture of what you want in your mind. Repeating your goal with a broad focus helps you to add more details and create the full picture of what you want and why. Working on the conscious mind requires repetition (over an average of twenty-one days), and it takes fifteen to thirty minutes at first, but you will be one step closer to making the right move if you want to achieve something.

Working on your goals while in a hypnotic trance will reduce the time significantly. The results will depend on how big the goal is, how much you believe in yourself, and the level of your determination to achieve the goal.

Below are examples of writing long-term goals.

Example 1 - Goals

"On 15 June 2014, I win the West Coast sailing competition. I start a journey along the Pacific coast from Vancouver to Los Angeles. The expected duration of sailing is one month, reaching the final destination on the fifteenth of July. I am well prepared as a skipper, and I have a well-equipped yacht, experience, and skill. I have a dedicated crew to accomplish my goal. I practise eight hours every day to improve my fitness. By entering into this race, I will provide charitable support for the children's hospital in Vancouver, simultaneously grabbing young people's attention and attracting them to sailing. I will also help create a positive image of British Columbia."

Example 2

Coffee Shop

"I open my own coffee shop in the centre of London on 6 January 2020. It is equipped with modern dark red and black tables and armchairs. I employ ten young people. The coffee shop is family friendly and serves the best-quality healthy organic food and snacks. The profit target is £80,000 for 2019, increasing every year by 10 per cent. I employ my husband as the coffee shop's accountant and my sister as staff manager."

In both examples, you will find sub goals such as organization and recruiting people.

When you are clear that your goal is what you want, move on to the next chapter to learn how to initiate the unconscious mind's processes to reach your goal.

Fifty-one

Visualization and Imagination to Reach Goals

> Logic will take you from A to B, imagination will take you anywhere.
>
> Albert Einstein

Guided visualization is a very powerful tool to achieve any goal. Visualization involves the process of sending the images of what you are seeking to the unconscious mind. Repeated images, especially when supported by strong emotions, will be accepted by the unconscious. When this happens, the unconscious processes will automatically start the search for information connected to accomplishing your goal. When you have a strong repeated image in your mind of what you want, your energy and enthusiasm will increase, improving self-discipline and sharpening all senses to search for the right information.

Visualize your goal as frequently as possible in a waking state of mind and during self-hypnosis. Work on your goal in the therapeutic/goal part of the session, and always support the practice with posthypnotic suggestions, for example, "The change/goal I accepted during the session of trance will stay with me long after the trance has ended." Or if the work is not finished, you can use the following: "As my unconscious mind knows what I want, it will work towards that long after the trance has ended, until the goal is reached on [specify the date]."

Repeating your goal with a broad focus helps you to add more details and create a full picture of what you want, how you want to achieve it, and why. Because it is a powerful automatic process, visualization should be done in a positive and constructive way and performed in as relaxed a state as possible.

You can visualize your desired goal by creating a picture of yourself with the goal already accomplished. You can create a movie of the whole process, from the beginning of writing down the goal to the final moment when the goal is accomplished. Be the main character in this picture, seeing yourself through to the positive end. During visualization, it is important to see details as you would like to see the process leading to the attainment of your goal. Enjoy it and anchor it, for example by making a fist and saying, "Yes, I did it."

Add more details to your picture (colour, things, people, etc.). The clearer the information sent to your unconscious, the more successful the outcome. Feel the pleasure and satisfaction you imagine you will feel once you achieve your goal.

Visualization should be performed at least twice a day for about five to ten minutes at the beginning, but the more you practise, the stronger the image you send to your unconscious mind.

With practice, you may start to learn "flash images", which are a powerful method that takes only a fraction of a second. These images are like a shooting picture of the goal sent to the unconscious mind, reinforcing the search. Flash images can be repeated at anytime and anywhere, even between other activities.

If you are not used to visualization, follow these steps:

1. Choose one goal you want to work on. Read all your motivations for pursuing it, and analyse the goal.
2. Close your eyes and visualize yourself with this goal already accomplished.

Once the image of your goal is accepted by the unconscious mind, it will sensitize and activate all your senses to see, smell, hear, feel, and taste what may be important in achieving your goal without your apparent conscious involvement. This way you are able to feel the temperature, see things or people, hear sounds, and smell the smells around you, both real and imaginary.

Example 1: If you want to go on holiday, close your eyes and visualize the people you want to be there with you as you enjoy yourself. See the place and the surroundings. Feel the air. Hear the sounds and everything else that is part of the fulfilment of your dream. Create the most comfortable place to relax.

Example 2: If you want to be confident and pass an exam, see yourself answering the questions with a smile on your face and with confidence. See how happy you are when handing the finished papers to the examiner. Project it like a movie, all the way up to the moment when you receive the results. See how you open the envelope with the college's logo addressed to you. Read the results indicating that you passed the exam. See the word "Pass" and the signature of the examiner. Finish by seeing yourself being happy, surrounded by people congratulating you for your achievement.

Imagination

Imagination plays a crucial role in reaching our goals and helping us make changes. Imagination is a product of the creativity of the unconscious mind. It can be in the form of resources necessary to accomplish your goal, which will increase the search process by providing a pure new image of what you want.

Example 1: You have a problem with feeling enthusiastic. By creating a scenario in which you are involved in fascinating activities, you automatically improve your feelings and actions.

Example 2: When you are feeling tired, try to imagine that you feel great, strong, and active (you may imagine this entirely or use a recollection of a good feeling from a past experience). This way your body will release the reserve of energy which will allow you to move on.

Example 3: Imagine that healthy energy is coming into your body from the universe, or that the sun's rays are recharging each cell in your body with a calming effect.

We all know the sudden feeling of urgency to do something after watching a programme, movie, or sport event that appeals to us. For example, many want to play tennis after watching the Wimbledon tennis tournament. This is an effective way to increase creativity and belief and trigger the unconscious mind to search in that direction.

Moreover, during imagination and visualization we can find solutions to our problems simply by asking ourselves for advice. For example, what is holding you back, or what can you do to speed up the process to reach your goal? You can make a whole movie in your imagination and see the process of reaching your goal, including the outcome of the goal and the benefits of your achievement. Visualize the goal as frequently as possible if you are serious about achieving it. Repeating your goal with a broad focus helps you to add more details and create the full picture of what you want, how you want to achieve it, and why.

You can use your imagination and visualization to work on any matter, such as to stay calm in any situation or to improve your performance in a sport or an interview. Imagination reflects the power of the mind, and by using it, you can improve your health, coping strategies, and confidence significantly. Hypnotic trance significantly enhances creativity, visualization, and imagination and speeds up your achievements. Visualization during self-hypnosis facilitates the reaching of any goal and can be used during all parts of the hypnosis session to relax your mind and body or to induce trance. It can be for therapeutic purposes as well, as you will practise in the following chapters.

However, never visualize or imagine something negative for yourself, or others. Your unconscious will follow that image. If your visualizations are positive, they will direct you towards your goal. If they are negative, exactly what you think or visualize will occur.

Fifty-two

Determination—Make Your Dream a Reality

> Our doubts are traitors and make us lose the good we oft might win.
>
> William Shakespeare

When you know which port you want to reach and why, the next step is to wait for the right moment to start sailing. Having goals is one thing, but achieving them is another. Many of us make goals with the belief that this time we can accomplish them. However, life proves that our enthusiasm somehow fades within a short time and many of us stay in the same position as before. The best example is a New Year's resolution to stop smoking or drinking and lose weight.

Therefore, part of having a well-constructed goal is also having strong determination to accomplish it.

Determination can be improved by the following:

1. Repeating the image of the accomplished goal. As long as the image is in your mind, nothing should stop you from moving in the right direction. When you stop to repeat the picture too early, the vision of your desire may fade from your memory and the whole process to reach your goal may vanish. This is

the most common reason why many of us are not successful with our goals.

2. Revising your motivations, as lack of motivation is the main factor in not achieving goals.
3. Setting the final date of accomplishment. Setting the final date of accomplishment is crucial to maintaining and improving your determination to go for your goal. This will stimulate the unconscious processes to reach the goal within a certain time frame. Having a final date set for your goal will increase your self-discipline and persistence to reach the goal on time. Otherwise, your search for information and resources may slow down.
4. Trusting the unconscious mind to supply resources in the form of urging you to do something. Experienced people call this intuition; they just follow their gut. For example, if you are working on time management, the first sign that you are progressing towards your goal might be when you see unfiled papers and sort them automatically, compared to your old habit of ignoring them. Or suddenly you will decide to go to the library to find more information in line with your goal, compared to postponing doing this for days or weeks as before. With time and practice, you will notice signs that you are on the right track.

   Act immediately upon the first insight delivered by your unconscious mind. Once you miss the impulse, it may be gone forever. Ignoring unconscious resources will be treated as though you no longer want what you are seeking. Be patient but open-minded enough to notice everything you need to accomplish your goal. When the message comes along, take it and use it.
5. Have strong emotions behind your goals. As I discussed in chapters 29, 30, 31, 33, and 34, on emotion, passion is the fuel for energy, enthusiasm, and determination and has the power to take to you where you want to be.

6. Stop any negative thoughts as soon as they start to dance in your head.
   The biggest barrier preventing us from reaching our goals is doubt. Even the shadow of a doubt may stop the process of searching for relevant information by the unconscious mind. This happens when a goal is not supported by strong beliefs or when your self-esteem is low, making you wonder if you are able to reach your goal. This might happen when you are afraid that others will hold it against you if you achieve your goal. For this reason, there is no point discussing your goals with people who are not familiar with goals, as their disbelief, jokes, or criticism may destroy your faith and enthusiasm. At such times, negative thoughts and feelings of doubt might start to fill your mind, causing the image of your goal to fade and the whole process of searching to be wiped away.
   Therefore, it is important to have the image of your goal in your mind, and never have any doubt, even when you are off course. Systematically clear away any clouds of doubt by using positive affirmations and repeating your goal in words and images: "I always reach my goal."
   Whatever happens, be persistent and hold onto the image of your goals until they are accomplished. The stronger the belief and the deeper the positive feelings you have about the goal, the more vigorous enthusiasm and confidence you will feel to go for it. This in turn will increase your determination and persistence until the goal is accomplished. If the goal is important to you, you will be willing to make sacrifices and cross any obstacles in your way.

Goal-minded people go from one success to another. They always tell you that they need to do something. They are in control of their time, and they always know what to do first. Nothing will stop them from getting closer to their goals. They will say no to anything that might disturb their plans. They control their lives, thoughts, and emotions and make choices that are important to them. They know where they are going and why. They keep going until they reach what they want to achieve. The same will be required of you if you are serious about achieving your goals and have a real desire to be in better control of your life.

Sometimes we need to turn in a different direction before we get back on track, or we need to stop to rebalance the Trio Mind and better prepare for the next part of the journey. Like a sailor who needs to anchor for a while to avoid dangerous situation and then start again when the weather improves, you may need to take some time, follow a zigzag course, and make many attempts before you reach your destination. There is a known saying: "All roads lead to Rome." So, if one way is blocked, try another.

It works like a chain—one factor is enough to move the whole process along. Therefore, it is important to work continuously on your confidence, thoughts, and emotions to avoid any relapse in self-belief. Reaching a goal in many cases requires some sacrifices, patience, and stepping back for a while, but with persistence and trust in your mind's ability, corrections will occur automatically when you face obstacles.

Even when you stop to reconsider the vision of your goal and determine that it is still what you want, you should start again. Your unconscious will recognize your previous intentions and will be ready to engage in the process again.

Following are two modified examples of a long-term goal and its accomplishment:

Example 1—Goal-Minded Jane

Sixteen-year-old Jane started to work with us just after leaving school. One day she told me that her goal was to have a holiday in Mexico within one year. She had never been on a cruise before. For many this might not seem like a big goal, but for Jane it was. Her earnings at the time were basic. She had to pay rent and support herself. It was amazing to see her enthusiasm and careful planning for this life experience. She never complained that she didn't have enough money. Instead, every week she apportioned her money for different purposes. Moreover, she always had enough money to buy gifts for family and friends at Christmas and on birthdays. After two months of carefully organizing her finances, she said that she was a bit short and had to find extra income. After a week, she found a weekend cleaning job in a superstore. Shortly after that, she said that even with this extra income, it would be difficult for her to buy clothes and have spending money for the trip. "I have to find something else. My days are already filled, but I will do something," she said.

Her determination and enthusiasm fascinated me, so I started to think about how to help her. During this time, our secretary was unwell, which meant we needed help in the office. I knew that Jane would be perfect for the job, and her determination impressed everyone. I told her about it, and we all adjusted as she fit into this position. Later that year we received a beautiful card from Mexico, and Jane gave me a small bottle of perfume from Mexico on her return. I still have it in my bathroom. Each time I see the little bottle, it reminds me of Jane's strong desire to achieve what she wanted, the strong emotions behind her goal, and her determination to reach it. It was not magic. Her vision governed not only her own decisions but also those of people around her.

Jane enhanced my faith and determination to do something with enthusiasm as well. We frequently hear that good things come to those who wait. And it is true—to reach any goal we need to focus on it, believe it, and be persistent.

Example 2—Becoming a Formula One Mechanic

The following story is the simplest explanation of a very complex process likely to occur on many levels in the mind when working on a long-term goal.

Imagine that at the age of seventeen, your dream is to be an expert car mechanic and work for the Ferrari team in Formula One racing. You live in a small town where there is no university. There are no races in your town, and the local people have little interest in Formula One. You share your dream with your parents and friends, but instead of supporting you, they joke that you are a dreamer. In fact, you have no idea how to reach your goal, and soon you start to think that you have no chance of achieving it. But somehow you still feel that it is what you want.

This moment is crucial to follow your feelings, not letting negative emotions, negative thoughts, or others' opinions destroy your deep desire. Remember, our thoughts and images are carefully scrutinized by the unconscious mind. Some are accepted and others are rejected according to how they fit into our life, how they fit with our beliefs, and how important they are to us. In your case, at this early stage, your goal may be easily rejected by the unconscious mind, as this image is totally new and you have many doubts about your ability to achieve it. Your thoughts and vision are not crystal clear; they are in the shadows questioning the whole issue: "It is not for me."

When this happens, the best you can do is to immediately ask yourself, "Why not?" and write your goal again and again to make it more believable and realistic.

Write, "I can do it as all other Formula One people. I need to find the right way."

This way you reinforce the image of your desire. The picture becomes persistent, and your feelings behind become stronger than ever. Rewriting your goal, thinking about it, and making plans on how to reach it (even if you have no idea at the moment how to do it) will reinforce the whole process and cause it to move forward. Repeated, strong images will be treated as relevant, and your conscious and unconscious processes will be activated, enlisting all your senses to find the necessary information to take you where you want to be.

The unconscious is not critical or judgemental and does not laugh at what is important to you or what you can or can't do. Your sincere desire and strong belief in your ability is what decides if your unconscious will treat the image as a serious one.

To reach your goals, you need to believe that you have the ability to do so and that you deserve it. You need to stay calm and trust yourself. The stronger the emotions you have about reaching the goal, the stronger the message that is sent to unconscious saying that this is what you want.

The next step in this process is to write the goal again in more detail, based on new information or on your imagination:

"Upon completing engineering studies at UCLA in 2016, I am employed by the Ferrari team in Formula One."

Visualize it. See yourself in the red Ferrari uniform in the Ferrari pit, shaking hands with driver Kimi Räikkönen, giving an interview to a TV reporter, etc. Visualize working there. Make it real as a movie to sensitize your all senses.

For example, one day on your way to the library for a math book, you notice a copy of the "Sports Cars Journal." It had been there for a few months, but you never paid attention to it before. You find a lot of information in there, and your interest increases, along with your determination to stick to your goal. You start to read more on Formula One and find that Imperial College in London is one of the leaders in engineering studies. You think about it with some doubts, as the college is far from your home, but you hope other universities will have similar programmes. Sometime after that, you hear that one of your unpopular chemistry teachers is going to London for a seminar on gas efficiency versus electrical supply run by Imperial College London. You never liked the teacher, and you are not sure what he thinks about you, but still you feel the urge (an unconscious signal) to see him. Finally, when you tell him about your interest, he sets his papers on his desk, takes his glasses from his nose, and says, "I had no idea that you had such an interest. I will bring you all the information from London, and we can talk about it later." Bingo! You jump up and down, your energy is sky-high, and you start to believe that now your goal is real.

Some people would say that this was just coincidence. Goal-oriented people would say that it was the result of well-prepared goals and of unconscious processes searching to find what you asked for. Spiritual people would say that you prayed for it. Whether it comes from God, the universe, or your unconscious, or is the result of the power of the mind, is not important at this stage. I leave that question for you and scientists to answer.

What is important for you to know is that the process of setting goals works and can be beneficial in many aspects of your life, helping you to reach what you want? When working on well-constructed goals, we have instincts about what to do or where to go and we have the deep feeling that we are moving in the right direction. With practice, we know that knocking on one door may open the next one, even if it was locked before. This way, we go on and on until we reach what we want. Talking about your goals to people who also set goals will increase your motivation and determination to keep going. Everyone with a strong desire to do so can achieve their goals.

Each case varies according to how big and complicated the goal is. The average time to reach a goal depends on how strong your belief is, how serious you are about it, and how persistent you are.

However, there always will be obstacles along the way. Therefore, to stay on track, it is important to trust yourself and your unconscious mind at all times. In Part I of this book, we discussed that the path to reaching your goal might have its ups and downs, as is common. Some of these obstacles might be natural life events. But when your feeling is very strong about what you want, and when you believe that you can have what you want, you may send the process in a different direction.

In the case we are considering, your faith is increasing, you have support from your teachers, and your determination is increasing. Having achieved excellent results in school, you are finally accepted by Imperial College London. You make a goal for each month and each year, and everything seems to be perfect. Suddenly your financially supportive father loses his job and you are not able to return to London because he has a large family to support. Your heart is broken, and you have mixed feelings. Even more, so far you have been unsuccessful in finding a job, and your grant application was rejected.

But by staying positive, somehow you keep the image of being Formula One mechanic foremost in your mind. *There must be a way* stays in your mind all the time.

Suddenly you have the feeling that you should visit your favourite uncle, who just came back home after few years of doing contract work in Brazil. You share your disappointment with him. After carefully listening, he says, "Son, I have no children of my own, and I am financially comfortable now. In fact, I would be very happy to support you in London. I cannot see a better way to spend my money."

At this stage your unconscious processes are likely to follow your clear image of yourself in the red Ferrari uniform, talking to the drivers, etc. The process of searching in the right ways to achieve your goal continues as follows:

You are already working on your degree. You have made goals for each year and have stuck with them until they were completed. A few days before graduation, you see a note on the noticeboard that the top Mercedes team for Formula One team is seeking talented new people. You cannot believe your eyes, but you run to the office to put your name forward for the competition.

All your senses are directed towards finding ways to get you there—with little of your conscious attention. For example, upon seeing such a note on the board, most students would ignore it.

A few other students apply, but since you have maintained a strong image of your goal, your interview is impressive. Others were impressive too, but you made it to the short list. The tension increases. Doubts start to creep into your mind again, but you shake hands with your competitors, stay calm, and trust yourself. Your desire to be the top car mechanic becomes stronger and stronger, and your heart pumps harder. You make the image even bigger. Having a sharp vision of your goal, your final interview is very successful as the interviewers are impressed with your academic results and your determination. Finally, you get the job. Your opponent gets the job as well, and now you have a new friend. End

The story of the Formula One is a modification of a real one. I know of many similar true stories that worked in the same way. You might know some too, that in a "hopeless" situation, suddenly something beneficial drops out of the sky.

In this example, the goal is huge, but it is sound and fits well with your environment. You are happy to go to London, your family is even closer to your uncle now, and everyone supports each other. Your family members are proud of your achievements and you are on the winning side, knowing that is only a matter of time before you make the move from Mercedes to Ferrari.

In fact, this example shows the natural processes of a child dreaming of becoming a champion, a medical doctor, or a musician. Wise people say, "Where there is a will, there is a way."

Sometimes it may be necessary to make an adjustment to the first plan, to stop in a different port first or change your course. But by having a final destination in your mind, you will take the ship to that destination sooner or later. You may feel the urge to visit more places along the way to increase your clarity, or add crew members to make a stronger team, or adjust to new conditions. Next chapters will guide you how to make a sound goals on the most important factors leading to satisfactory and successful life.

Fifty-three

Personal Freedom

For any action, there is an equal reaction.

Newton's third law of
thermodynamics

Relationships can cause you to spread your wings to fly or can cut them and drop you to the grand. Whatever our situation, we all are in relationships with members of our family, friends, neighbours, and the society we live in, whether we like it or not. We all know how different relationships can be, ranging from heavenly to hellish. Some of our relationships give us love, peace of mind, security, and a lot of satisfaction. Others may be turbulent, may bring very difficult burdens to bear, or may destroy everything we have.

One of the most common mistakes people make in any relationship is to maintain a false belief, such as:

a) "I have the right to control other people's lives."
b) "Other people are allowed to steal my personal freedom."

Therefore, it is important to know how to have a good relationship with the rest of the world and at the same time to secure our own freedom to do what we want to do. Freedom gives us the opportunity to follow our goals, beliefs, thoughts, and emotions. Above all, it allows us to have an equal voice in the final decision as to which port we will sail to. Freedom secures our personal boundaries and allows us to use our time and resources to find what we are looking for.

Securing and widening our horizons to make room for free thought and action also increases our awareness of the requirement to respect others' need for freedom as well. This in turn will strengthen our personal social network and cause others to have respect for us. Ambitious people are willing to do whatever is necessary to have the freedom to make any decision. But to have a strong voice in order to make any decision, we need to be independent.

Being independent improves the way you feel about yourself and your confidence to freely express your thoughts and desires without fear of others' disapproval. Independence is like a strong base from which to take a necessary action, even when some misfortune falls, for example a broken relationship, illness, or bankruptcy.

By being independent, you can enjoy having a say in any situation, be it financial, professional, or personal, and you will be able to say yes or no with full confidence and satisfaction. Therefore, making it your goal to be independent and have freedom in your life choices will trigger your mind to move in the right direction. You may decide to further your education or get professional help in order to become independent. Even if you have no idea just now how to do it, set the goal anyway to stimulate your unconscious mind to search for the best way to accomplish your goal. Be patient and trust yourself.

Examples of suggestions to attain freedom and independence are as follows:

- "I cherish my freedom to make my own decisions to reach my goals."
- "My independence helps me to explore my interests and creativity."
- "I am free to commit to any relationship I wish to have."

Write down five motives for gaining personal freedom, such as increased confidence, having more choices, being the person you want to be, gaining financial independence, and having opportunities to reach your goals and help others.

However, as much as we need the freedom to go for our desires and gain independence, it is crucial to remember that other parties need freedom too to secure their own life expectations. Next chapters will help to find the way to secure your freedom and full respect of others choices. Make affirmations to remind yourself of this crucial element of securing your way to independence and good relationships with others.

- "I respect others' freedom as much as I do my own."
- "I respect those who trust me and let me feel free to do anything I wish to do."
- "I treat others as I expect to be treated by them."

Practising affirmations such as the foregoing in self-hypnosis will speed up the process of change.

Fifty-four

Responsibility

> The commander's mission is ensure the ship is secure until the end of the journey.

Now that you know how to stay calm and decide when you want to sail, it is time to review the basic laws for having a safe voyage. One of the strongest human values is to take full responsibility for everything we do. Responsibility indicates having the maturity to do the right thing. Responsible people understand and follow both human-made and natural values and laws, shaped carefully by experiences since the beginning of humanity. The question is, are you ready to command your ship with full responsibility for your safety and those on board with you?

Let's check the level of your responsibility right now simply by doing a self-assessment of the decisions you make in the course of your day-to-day activities. Be honest with yourself, knowing that you are on the way to making things better. If any of the following examples are familiar to you, I would advise that you reread the previous chapter carefully to determine your present position and set out on a new path from that starting point.

1. Blaming other people and things for unwanted outcomes
   You must admit that such habitual thinking is not mature. It is true that life brings different experiences, and anyone can be lost during a span of time for many different reasons. We all make mistakes. This is the way to learn to do the right

thing next time in a similar situation. However, we hear on a daily basis that things would be different "if only he would stop doing this", or "if only she would not irritate me", or "if only he would give me money", or "if only she would spend more time with me". We must be honest and admit now that such thinking leads to irrational and irresponsible behaviour. Mature people take responsibility for their own personal freedom, financial situation, health, and relationships and any consequences of their choices.

The right thing to do is to repeat to yourself, "From now on I am responsible for my life, and everything depends on me." Add a confession of the particular failing, for example, "I admit that I did not prepare properly for the exam, and I take full responsibility for that instead of blaming the examiner for my failing grade."

Goal: "From now on I am responsible for my actions and its consequences."

2. Expecting others to care for you

   Responsible people do not believe or expect that others must provide everything for them. Simply put, such thinking is evidence of taking advantage of other people. What others do is their own business and responsibility. They may be willing to help other people to make progress in their goals or keep others company, if they wish.

   The right thing to do is to make a goal and plan to take your life into your hands.

   Goal: "I rely on myself, and I take full responsibility for my health and my future."

3. Breaking any rule or law

   It is not responsible to take narcotics (unless under the advice of a physician) or abuse alcohol, believing that you can take good care of your life and your family when on a high. Statistics show that four people are killed every day because of someone driving under the influence of drugs or alcohol. Despite this, many people drink or use drugs. Others live in denial, turning a blind eye when someone breaks the law! "I know, but I can control it" is the common refrain of the drug or alcohol abuser, "I know, but he [or she] had just a few for fun" is the common irrational response from a loved one. Other common bad behaviours are stealing, emotional or physical abuse, bullying, and covering up one's crime.

The right thing to do is to stop tolerating any type of bad behaviour that may hurt someone else!

Goal: "I will stop accepting bad behaviour and will reward good behaviour."

4. Self-centred behaviour

   We all do things which bring some benefit to us, our family, or society. However, it is egotistical to seek after for your gain at the expense of other people's well-being. For example, it is wrong to leave unfinished business behind you, thereby putting your family members, children, or business partners in a difficult situation. It is not responsible to ignore your duties, always being late or not keeping promises and commitments. It is no excuse to say, "I thought it wouldn't hurt anyone."

   The right thing to do—close unfinished business first without burning bridges.

   Goal: "I always finish tasks and end relationships to the satisfaction to all."

5. Repeating the same mistakes

   Careless and irrational behaviour such as replacing one unfaithful, aggressive partner with another abuser; exchanging a badly managed business for another unprofitable venture; going on a diet but being reluctant to shift to good nutritional food and a healthy lifestyle; or being stubborn and refusing to listen to a more experienced person indicates that one has not learned from previous bad choices. If you do not make changes to how you approach the problematic situation, then you are dancing to the same out-of-tune music.

   The right thing to do: when bridges are falling down, ask yourself why and learn from it.

Goal: "I always analyse any situation and learn from my experiences."

If you see yourself in any of these five situations, then think about it. I will leave it to you to be honest with yourself. You wouldn't want to be on a ship knowing that the commander is drunk, making ridiculous decisions again and again or leaving the decision-making and higher-level duties to the crew. In all the foregoing examples, the logic is missing, as is the responsibility and dignity!

The biggest question is why so many people behave irresponsibly, repeatedly bringing unpleasant, damaging consequences to themselves and those who rely on them. Sometimes life puts us in difficult situations, at which time we need to make the choice to sail in a different direction. The same thing goes for our irrational behaviour—it simply may be the right time to admit that we have not been responsible for our actions and to become willing to make positive changes.

The right thing to do is to admit that your choices do not bring about the expected results, so a drastic change in your thinking is needed. A good commander will not abandon his ship or his crew in any situation. He will take full responsibility for making the best out of any situation.

Analyse your past experiences carefully without buts. If you are not happy with your past choices, talk to friends or ask for professional help. Read this book once more to start thinking in a more rational and constructive way.

The fact is that only you can take full responsibility for your present situation and make the needed changes. Only by acknowledging that all your unsuccessful behaviour is the result of irrational thinking can you put an end to your irresponsible behaviour.

To be a responsible person, you need to see the facts, not merely what you would like to see, and act on them accordingly. Responsibility can be learned and improved upon gradually. If you are honest with yourself and take responsibility for your actions and their consequences in a mature way, you are less likely to repeat your mistakes.

Now you can make the decision to be the commander of your life and do the right things. By taking full responsibility from the beginning to the end of your life journey, you will be rewarded by feeling satisfaction at the end of the day. Whatever happened in the past can't be changed, but you can make positive changes for the future. From now on you can start to rely on your own judgement as to where, how, and when to sail. You can take full responsibility to prepare everything to have an enjoyable life, regardless of your present situation and whatever your goals are.

It is especially important for young people to set out on adult life by taking full responsibility for their actions and decisions. Being responsible proves to you and others that you are reliable, and your loyalty will soon be noticed by others. Taking responsibility for everything you do will speed up the process of reaching your goals.

However, it is important to remember that only those who commit themselves to practising every day, come rain or shine, will have the chance to be on a national football team. Only those who commit themselves to long hours of study will complete their degrees. Only those who wholly commit themselves to being a good parent or partner will feel the pleasure of being such.

That is the reality, and we all need to face it. The fact is that satisfaction comes from our own values and achievements, not others'. So, be smart and realistic. Take responsible action in any situation concerning your health, finances, or relationships.

Having built a reputation for being a responsible person, you will be able to enjoy the company of respectful people, and it will be easier for you to recognize manipulators, cruising around like sharks in the ocean, hoping to catch naive victims.

If you wish to get on the right path, make a commitment to yourself to remove any irresponsible thoughts and replace them with constructive thoughts. Waiting for others to bring changes to your life will not bring the sunshine into your life. Constantly reminding yourself who you are and that you are in control of your life and responsible for your choices will automatically increase your maturity. This will improve your confidence and relationships with others, as they will be the first to notice positive changes in your behaviour.

Wise people say that if you encounter ten closed doors, the eleventh may be open to your surprise. But it is your responsibility to knock until the door opens, if you need help or wish to improve your life. If you are looking for new ideas or a new job, keep knocking and asking yourself, “What can I do better?” Your unconscious listens to your questions. You may be surprised to find the right answers at the most unexpected times. Only by seeking out better opportunities will you be able to ensure the best navigation, make better choices, and gain the respect of others.

Everything in life goes up and down; this is a natural law. But successful people commit themselves to stick to their goals, and they are responsible for all the actions they take along the way. Once you experience the value of being a responsible person, it will bring satisfaction to your life. In turn, it will prove that you are able to accomplish what you want, with full responsibility for your actions, as you are in control of them.

Following is an exercise to improve your responsibility:

Make a list of the ten most important responsibilities you will accept from now on. Even if you have no idea how you will take responsibility for these things, put them on your list of goals and work on them according to the level of urgency. Then surprise yourself with the results.

Following are some goals for taking responsibility:

- “I take full responsibility for controlling my life, my emotions, and my thoughts.”
- “I am responsible for all my actions and their consequences.”
- “From now on, I take responsibility for my health, including eating a healthy diet and living an active lifestyle.”
- “I am responsible for my career. I take courses, etc.”

One motivation to support your goal related to responsibility may be the desire to be a confident, trustworthy, independent, better organized, and caring person. Again, all these suggestions, and those in the rest of the book, can be used as therapeutic suggestions in self-hypnosis.

Fifty-five

Recruit Your Crew

Friends share with you and will die for you.

No one can succeed or feel satisfaction in isolation from the rest of the world. We all need to have supportive, ambitious, positive people around us to develop strong, healthy moral and ethical values and be creative. Therefore, building a supportive social network is of primary importance. Of secondary importance is a having a good relationship not only with those who have a similar vision and level of commitment but also with all people you interact with. It is like recruiting a team to sail with you, and it takes skill to do this right.

Many of us had no choice but to grow up surrounded by people with a negative attitude towards life, people who were not appealing role models. There may be situations where we have no choice of whom we live with for a while, and there may be times when we have no influence on other people's behaviour, like in the case of an addict. Other people may start out living an independent life with a great deal of enthusiasm, but one negative life experience may lead them to find themselves with people who are going nowhere or heading in the wrong direction.

Staying with people who refuse to make positive changes may have a negative influence on your thinking, sharply reshaping your ambitions. In the longer term, your whole social network may be stuck behind rusty gates. The fact is that if you choose to stay with people who flout commonly respected rules, laws, and common sense, you volunteer to become one of them (unless you are helping them to change). Spending time with manipulators and drug and alcohol abusers presents the danger of falling off your life track. Joining them may lead you in the wrong direction on a one-way street to failure. Staying with people of low ambition may strip you of your achievements and leave you in excruciating mental pain, wondering what happened to your life.

However, just like a commander may not like all her crew members or their ideas, she will respect them until reaching the end of the journey. Wise people always learn from others' behaviour, both positive and negative. We can model someone else's inspiring behaviour or observe and learn from the bad behaviour of others to expand our thinking and vision and lead us in the right direction. Building a strong personality and knowing where you want to sail will help you to make the right choice in terms of the people with whom you want to sail. Just follow your common sense to find people with whom you can share your enthusiasm and on whose support you can rely.

The ability to recognize the right people who will help you build your social network is paramount to establishing a strong pathway to success, whatever you position is now. Mature people are smart enough to look for red flags, think twice, and take precautions before committing themselves to anything. You can start behaving this way right now by paying attention to what language people use, including body language, as this could give you an indication of what they have on their minds. Respectable successful people never say, "Why bother?" "I am bored," "I don't care." Instead, they say, "This is what I want, and I will find the way to have it," "I respect your opinion, but…" Learning to look at every person with the intention of finding their positive qualities, not just what you do not like, may attract more valuable people to your social network, not only those you like. Some of these people may be different from you but may be have strong character traits in different areas. Always follow the wisdom of the "Don't judge people by the way they look."

My intention here is to encourage you to build your own ship according to how your desire it to be and recruit the people you want to accompany you on the journey. Finding friends with a wide range, or similar, interests and respecting their moral values and attitudes may be a stepping stone to your success and happiness.

At the same time, be smart and learn from those who have a great deal of experience with navigating and recognizing when icebergs are under the water. Learning from experienced, respectable, successful people who are willing to support your ambitions and share their own experiences is the best move you can make.

Sharing your thoughts with trustworthy people will help too, especially before making serious decisions when planning a family, thinking about a new job, or considering which college to attend. Talking to people helps you to review your thoughts and beliefs or shakes things up a little bit, perhaps giving you second thoughts before committing yourself to something you may regret in the long term. Confident people are not worried about others' opinions; they listen to and analyse what others say before making up their own minds.

The best and most talented athletes, professionals, and other successful people need constant advice, reassurance, and support from their coaches, managers, family, and friends. Those who prove that they know best will assist you in believing that you *can* reach your goals. Manipulators and losers will advise you to take drugs or may say, "Forget it. Let's party." Be clever. Have a party only to celebrate your achievements, not in place of working on your goals.

Make goals to build a sound social network. Some affirmations along these lines are as follows:

- "I surround myself with ambitious people. They stimulate my creativity and interest."
- "I enjoy the company of positive people. They make me feel better about myself."

Fifty-six

Communication

The right word has the power to open a rusty gate.

Have you ever noticed the response you receive to a smile or a nice word you gave to a stranger on the street or at the counter when paying your bill? We all know that the smallest friendly gestures can be icebreakers in any situation. Therefore, it should become our habit in any situation to make such friendly gestures. It costs nothing, but it works like magic and brightens everyone's day.

Communication plays a crucial role in helping you maintain a healthy relationship with everyone you encounter. It is the most important tool to achieving your goals and feeling great afterwards. Whatever the relationship is, be it with family, friends, co-workers, neighbours, or authorities, we all have connections with other people, whether we like them or not. To fit well in these relationships, we must communicate with people effectively.

However, life proves that this is not always a simple thing to do. Every day obstacles trigger negative emotions, insulting words, and unrespectable behaviour. This automatically reduces the chance for successful communications and negotiations between people. The consequences of bad communication may give rise to even more negative reactions, such as anger, vengefulness, and hate. Poor communication is the way to break a deal and to break relationships at home, in business, and in other professional fields. Frequently poor communication leads to misinterpretation of facts and may provoke irrational actions, sometimes destroying the lives of all parties involved.

It is very common to take our closest family members, friends, and co-workers for granted. Frequently we believe that they should *know* that we've had a rough day and that we love them. At the same time, they think that we should be aware when they have had a hard day and the fact that they love us too! The simple deficit of words, or an exchange of mere body language, may trigger doubts, negative thoughts, and negative feelings about the relationship. Assuming that someone else should know what we are thinking and feeling is not the same as telling someone else exactly what is on our mind, or simply asking, "How was your day?" Learning to clearly express our observations, feelings, and concerns to others is crucial to securing any relationship. Therefore, spending time on improving your communications skill may be the best decision you ever make.

Being a good communicator means having the skills to reach an agreement that is satisfactory to all parties. It also means being able to present options for further negotiations when disagreements arise.

Following are the main rules for successful communicators:

1. Express your intentions openly and honestly. Repeat them patiently if necessary.
2. Listen to the viewpoints of the other parties and determine what they expect.
3. Intend to conclude the matter successfully for all parties as soon as possible.
4. Take extra time if negotiations are not successful.
5. Always show trust, respect, and willingness to compromise.

Building trust between negotiating parties is essential to finding a satisfactory solution.

Trust is based on openness. Once trust is broken, it may ruin the relationship and damage further negotiation, leaving all parties devastated. It may lead to broken families, a difficult divorce settlement, a damaged business, lost future opportunities for partnership, or damaged credibility in one's professional life. Being a trustworthy person means being transparent with facts and with everyone at any time. It may be difficult sometimes to admit to our mistakes, but it is always worthwhile in the long term. It is much easier to forgive someone for wrongdoing who honestly regrets it than to forgive those who make empty promises all the time.

Good negotiators show respect and never criticize the other party's opinion. Instead, they seek understanding and try to find a neutral solution. They concentrate on the main issue and seek to find the best solution in the shortest possible time. In the case of an unsolved issue, they leave the matter open for further discussion and never burn bridges behind themselves. They conclude the meeting with a sign of appreciation (shaking hands, nodding the head, smiling with respect). They know that being patient and showing respect to the other party is the only way to keep negotiations open and to conclude successfully.

Good communicators are calm listeners and rational thinkers and are open-minded to new ideas. Entering into communication with a positive attitude and expectations increases the possibility of reaching a conclusion that is satisfactory to both sides. By doing these things, you will find it easier to communicate with anyone in any situation.

Demonstrating a good sense of humour and creating a relaxing atmosphere is the cream to the coffee, as is a sincere gentle comment of admiration or appreciation to the other party. Sometimes a simple polite expression of your appreciation can turn the whole negotiation in a different direction.

Following these simple strategies and those mentioned at the beginning of the book, and reviewing your beliefs and thoughts regularly to make sure they are not rusty, you should find it much easier to find the right words to reach a mutually acceptable agreement in any negotiation and have the satisfaction of having done the right thing.

All these strategies have a high probability of being successful in any arrangement, whether at home, in the office, or by phone, as long as your expectations are expressed calmly and clearly.

Following are examples of goals related to communication and motivations supporting them:

- "I treat everyone with respect. Therefore, I easily communicate with others."
- "I believe that good communication can resolve many disagreements."
- "I clearly express my point of view and listen to others' opinions with respect."
- "By being honest, I increase my chances of building a positive social network."
- "In negotiations, I intend to close the matter in a way that is satisfactory to all parties involved."
- "I always play my cards right and expect the same from the other person."

Fifty-seven

Commitment

Relationships may provide you with rocky support or squash you under a boulder.

If you want to have a sound relationship of any kind and be respected by your companion or competitors, you need to commit yourself to all parties involved. Good relationships are based on unconditional respect for, support of, and commitment to the other person.

However, it takes two to tango. When one party systematically neglects the commitments involved in a relationship, there is no balance of healthy thoughts and emotions in such a relationship.

When one party systematically neglects his or her commitments, leaving the other person to deal with all the obligations, frustration, negatives thought, and unpleasant emotions will develop. Arguments and blaming of each other will only divide everyone involved and lead to deeper damage of the relationship or finally to its break-up. This in turn may lead to endless dysfunctional reactions from both sides on any issue, such as finances, spending time together, attending to home duties, taking care of children, or having a free time. The same rules apply in the workplace, between neighbours, and within any public sector.

To have emotional balance in relationships, we need to constantly work on a mutual exchange of care, respect, security, loyalty, and moral support whenever it is needed. Total commitment from both sides will strengthen the bond day by day.

Even when you do not have the resources to fulfil others' needs, being willing to listen and offer your full support to your partner may melt the largest of icebergs. People who have the skill to secure relationships put forth a lot of effort, make a lot of sacrifices, and pay a lot of attention to maintaining positive relationships with everyone, whether at home, at work, or with society at large. Commitment to the other party is crucial if you want to have the same. Relationships in which everyone supports each other and shares tasks equally, bring about the feeling that everyone is equally important. Feeling respected, people will be more than willing to take equal responsibility.

Making commitments to good friends and family is the best thing we can do. They will be the rock to support us always. They will support us in difficult times and help to prevent us from making mistakes, especially when we go wild from time to time, as we all do. It's OK to be overenthusiastic sometimes, but then you need to cool down and return to your senses as soon as possible, before it is too late.

Learning how to work as a team will bring a lot of fun, stronger bonds, and the great joy of belonging to a great family, friendship, or team. We all need to be reminded that we are loved, respected, and worthwhile. And we need to do the same for others.

It only takes a second to give someone a smile, a little signal that you are aware of that person and think they are special. This is especially for children. It only takes minute to make a call, show your respect, and ask, "Is there anything I can do for you?" regardless of your beliefs and expectations.

Making a full commitment is the best-rewarded art for building healthy relationships with your children, your spouse, your friends, your business partners, or strangers.

Make a goal on commitment:

- "I am unconditionally committed to any relationship."
- "I do understand that any relationship is based on total honesty and care."

- "I treat everyone with respect and expect to be treated the same way."

What motivation might you have for committing to relationships? Well, consider quotations such as "What we give, we receive in the same proportion," or "For every action, there is an equal and opposite reaction" (Newton's third law of motion). Commitment brings respect, trust, and a feeling of belonging.

Just follow it to feel the difference.

Fifty-eight

Family Bonds

> Support people unconditionally in becoming who they want to be, and they will do the same for you.

Although the same rules apply to any relationship, family bonds are very unique and in most cases are filled with unconditional love and support. Unfortunately, life proves that not everyone has this type of family. Every day we witness dysfunctional families, leaving all involved in a devastating position. Therefore, let's look deeper into different family relationships to improve our understanding of them.

A marriage is supposed to be built on love, attraction, trust, and total commitment. However, experience clearly indicates that marriages may be full of surprises, good or bad. Siblings may be constantly fighting, or they may be best friends. Many families are grow apart; others offer the most safe and pleasant place to be. So what is really happening behind closed doors with a family? We see every day that common mistakes include taking the relationship for granted or lacking in the fundamental skills to create good relationships. We need to acknowledge that if one of the components of a health relationship is broken, there is a high probability that the relationship will be damaged, in many cases permanently.

For example, ignoring another person's needs, being disloyal, or engaging in physical and mental abuse will systematically cause painful feelings and disappointment or may lead to isolation, anger, and hate. Jealousy and unrealistic expectations from one partner will severely damage a couple's personal life. Finding it difficult to forgive another's mistakes even after a sincerely apology is a common factor leading to a broken relationship between parents, children, or spouses. Unwillingness to find a compromise and bad communication work together to create many misunderstandings and drama. Disrespecting the other person's time and keeping your partner playing a guessing game is mental abuse.

Another common factor in a problem relationship is the foolish belief that it is smart to hide disloyalty from your partner, whatever it is you are being disloyal about. In fact, this only goes to show the immaturity of the abuser. Saying sorry for breaking trust may not heal wounds quickly, if ever. Even with the best intentions, the pain caused by someone's disrespectful and irrational actions may create distance between the parties that lasts for a long time.

Another crucial mistake in a relationship is to curtail your partner's freedom or let your partner steal your freedom, as we discussed before. It is essential to offer full freedom and support to your partner so they can deliver the best they can in their professional and private life. Otherwise, all kinds of negative thinking, negative emotions, and irrational behaviours will develop on both sides. With time, the gap in respect and communication widens, destroying love, bond, and commitment, leaving no space for positive thinking or emotions. The previous romantic attraction may disappear forever.

On the other hand, staying in an unhealthy relationship destroys creativity and problem-solving strategies. Simply put, a person in an unhealthy relationship is so preoccupied with negative thinking and emotions that it stops him or her from setting personal goals and achieving them.

When having a problem in relationship, ask yourself the following questions:

"What is it that is making me angry?"

"Why am I accepting the cheating, ignorance, abuse, etc.?"

Why am I cheating?"

"Why do I stay away from home most of the time?"

If you have a habit of breaking any of the basic principles of a healthy relationship, ask yourself why. Also ask, "Is this who I want to be? Why I am doing this?"

Without knowing the real causes of the problem, you are not in the position to solve it. When working on a relationship, you have a chance to improve it or terminate it if need be. Being in an unhealthy relationship will affect all aspects of your life and undermine all your goals.

Whatever the circumstances are of your unhealthy relationship, the next step is to ask yourself what can be done to make positive changes.

"Should I consider making any changes to the ongoing pattern?"

"Shall I talk firmly and openly to my partner about my real feelings and needs?"

Talking openly about the situation and taking action to be heard in different ways is the right thing to do. Even the smallest change is a change and opens new doors.

In complex matters, it is better to talk to friends and professionals to improve the situation. You always have a choice. It is your life, and therefore it is your responsibility to make it right.

Constantly working on personal growth and independence will make you more attractive and eliminate many fears, such as of being unwanted or useless. In the unfortunate case that your partner ignores commitments, you will be in a strong position to deal with it in an efficient and calm way. People are more aware now, including children, that violence is not acceptable in any form and that no one has a right to inflict violence upon another. Every day more help is available to children and those living in abusive relationships. Help is also available to abusers, who need professional help to deal with anger and their mental state.

It is impossible to discuss every sort of relationship as every relationship is different and depends on the choices of both parties. But creating goals to gain freedom and be independent will build your personal strength and accountability for your life. The same will be true for those who depend on you. You will be able to see the whole picture of your situation and take appropriate actions to improve your life.

Examples of goals for a better relationship:

- "I am aware that my relationship needs improvement if I am to improve the quality of my life and my whole family's life. I am willing to take all the necessary steps to assess the present situation to find a way to change it."
- "Any good relationship is based on trust, freedom, and commitment from both sides."
- "I protect my personal freedom and respect the needs of my partner."

Fifty-nine

Relationships with Children

> Children need unconditional love, and they love to give the same.

Our relationships with our children are very special and of the utmost importance to both parties. We take care of our children, and it is our duty to guide them every day so as to give them the best start to their independent adult lives. There is no doubt that a child's future depends on what tools they have to go through unfamiliar experiences.

In previous chapters we discussed how a lack of love and positive role models has a negative influence on a child's development. Moreover, if a model of commitment and freedom is missing in a child's life, the full spectrum of negative emotions and low confidence will be the only fruit of the unhealthy home environment. Any unresolved misunderstanding or misinterpretation may cause a long-lasting relationship problem and turbulence in the whole family.

It happens frequently that parents are unaware, or else they ignore, the importance of letting children have a voice in what they want to do with their lives.

So let's keep it simple. The parent's responsibility is to secure the child's freedom to develop his or her own interests. Of course parents better know what the child needs, but first they must be an example to their child in all aspects of life, especially expressing an appreciation for personal freedom and independence. Only when we understand the meaning of personal freedom can we offer others the comfort of making their own choices.

I will repeat: parents must be good role models if they care about their children's future. They must use logic and common sense twenty-four hours a day and have well-established positive thinking and control over their emotions and behaviour. When one's senses are fully open to see, hear, and feel the child's needs and interests, one will respond to them in a calm and rational way. This way one can expect to build stronger bonds with children and have a trusting relationship no matter the stage of their development.

Frequently we show a tendency to forget that whatever the relationship is, we do not own another person's life, including the life of our child, spouse, friend, and co-worker. We can only build a healthy relationship with them. When we show them appreciation every day, they will automatically respond to us in the same way.

Children need the freedom to develop into healthy and responsible young men and women. During childhood, they explore the world with curiosity, and if parents give them space to grow and experiment with various situations, then they will experience best way to learn to make more confident decisions. They will have the opportunity to find out what they like and do not like, and what works for them and what doesn't. Telling the child what they "must" do, including what to play, may supress the child's natural potential. By doing things as a "must", without passion, one day they may say, "That's enough. I do not want to do this anymore."

I Don't Want to Do It

Nine-year-old Sarah admitted to her grandma that she did not want to play tennis any more, which she had successfully played for six years. The family was in shock as they had spent a lot of time and money assisting her in pursuing competitive tennis. They asked her to consider delaying her decision until the end of the season, and then they would discuss all pros and cons.

At the end of the year, Sarah still insisted that she wanted to stop playing tennis, and she chose instead going to gym, dancing, and playing volleyball. When she started these new activities, her enthusiasm rapidly increased, compared to the feeling of boredom she faced on the tennis court. She continued to show happiness and progress in school and sports activities.

In Sarah's case, she was confident enough to express her wishes to her family, who responded in a mature way. It would have been worse if the child had not felt confident enough to be open about her feelings. When such a thing happens, a child may try to skip lessons or start to behave badly. Therefore, it is important to let a child discover his or her interests. Introduce your children to many different activities. Even if the experience comes with some ups and downs, this is the right way to build trust and independence.

Follow Your Passion

Kathryn, aged ten, did not say that she did not want to play tennis, although everyone noticed that she used to dance and sing on the court each time she hit the ball. One day she went secretly to the leader of the school choir, asking if she could join. Professionals from the music industry discovered that she had beautiful voice, and soon it was obvious to everyone that her talent and interest was in music, not tennis. She successfully continued her passion for singing and playing piano and flute at the age of fifteen.

The foregoing example shows how important it is to give a child freedom to find her real talent and passion. If a child has strong support from parents in a loving atmosphere, and if all adult family members model moral values, then the child will build those values automatically.

On the other hand, many young people experience broken family bonds, mostly because of poor communication between family members. Any relationship can be improved if the two sides are willing to sit at the table and talk until a final solution is find. Learning to have a good relationship with family members gives a child a sense of security and leads him to develop into a respectful person. Family members may be annoying sometimes and have different opinions, and this is OK. Parents and other family members may have different opinions, but expressing clearly your point of view shows maturity. And at least your family will not be upset that you didn't share your thoughts with them initially. Above all, you will know up front what they think about what you're saying. If they disagree with you, you will have the opportunity to defend yourself by presenting the rational thought process that led you to make the decision, instead of showing immaturity by saying, "I don't care." Most families do care, and any disagreements are mostly the result of poor communication, stubborn negative emotions and thoughts, and failure to apply the above-mentioned requirements of a good relationship,

By making an effort and following these steps covered in this book so far, you will find a way to communicate better, with respect and mutual understanding.

Making an effort to improve communication and your bonds with your family before cutting all ties with them will reward you in the long term. Being open with your ideas and showing responsibility and respect may change a cold atmosphere within a short period of time.

In any dispute with family, make sure you are open-minded and keep your ties with them strong for as long as possible. At the end of the day, we all need family and friends we can rely on. In most cases they will stand by us whatever happens. Whatever the situation is, never burn your bridges behind you. The bridge you decide not to burn may one day be the only way back.

However, there may be families where there is no care and respect, and there is nothing you can do about it. If there is no option to make peace with your family despite many attempts, accept the situation without blaming yourself and concentrate on building your own social network—your own ship and crew. Stay focused on your goals and keep going with the belief that you can reach what you desire. The positive side of going through life the hard way is that you gain more experience and are a stronger and wiser person who is able to look for people you can rely on in any situation. Take this advantage for your own benefit.

Following are examples of goals to improve a parent–child relationship:

- "My love for my children is unconditional. I give them the guidance and support they need."
- "I commit myself to giving my child my full support, security, and guidance."
- "I respect that my child needs the freedom to learn from what he [or she] sees and feels."
- "I give my children freedom to explore life in proportion to their age and abilities."
- "I listen to what my children say and let them develop their own talents."
- "I introduce my children to a wide variety of activities to develop their abilities."

Sixty

Midlife Crisis

Going Down or Going Up

Middle age is a time to take care of yourself. After many long years of taking care of the family, suddenly you start to feel confused about what is going on in your life. It may feel like all your bridges are falling down. Children leave home for college or to start their independent lives. Spouses may start to behave strangely, have secret "friends", and feel increasing pressure or disappointment in their professional life. On top of that, hormonal changes affect the body, and changes in mood are frequent. Days are filled with disappointment and frustration, and depression is common. Using alcohol or other drugs to escape is a common and family problem that worsens every day, leaving thousands of women and men in a devastating situation.

But there is a better way. You need to acknowledge that you have reached the stage of your life where you need to take better care of your physical and mental health.

By reading this book and following the steps to feel good about yourself and be in a position to do what you want to do, you should find the spark to move forward and start to believe that there is a wonderful life ahead of you. You will start to believe that you can do better, that you are young enough to start a new, independent, rewarding life. You can do what many women and men did at your age. People go to universities and start playing tennis in their sixties.

Have the courage to live the way you want to live. Be an example to others who are lost amid the storms of life. You can change professions and start to have more rewarding relationships. The world is open to you with all its possibilities. Practising and working on your goals in self-hypnosis will speed up the process of planning your new journey.

Senior Life—Misery or Joy?

Cherish family and friends every day. Appreciate every minute.

There is no set age at when one becomes a senior citizen. Many people at seventy, eighty, and ninety years old enjoy life and social events, as well as having a lovely time with their family and grandchildren. Senior sporting events around the world are growing in popularity.

Whatever the situation is, it is possible and essential to find meaning and joy in your life again, as is the case for any other age group. How we feel as senior citizens depends on our beliefs and attitudes towards life. We can choose to sit around all day and be miserable or to take some action according to our capability. We can complain about our age, our pains, and our wrinkles and expect others to take care of us.

Although many seniors need help to some extent, it doesn't mean they have to stop enjoying their lives. Many retired people want to continue some duties to stay active and independent and maintain their social contacts. There are many sports clubs that offer various courses for seniors, such as tennis, swimming, group walking, and social clubs. These present one with the possibility of finding friends and making plans for travelling, creating art, playing cards and doing other fun activities, or being involved in charities. There are writers' clubs and dance classes for seniors. The list is endless.

These days, help is available for transport and other needs at many locations. The age of seniority starts when you make that decision and let your body and mind follow your thoughts. Many people live to their nineties and longer and enjoy life. It is never too late to take care of ourselves and take the best from life.

However, to enjoy your life, it is necessary to stop negative thoughts and start looking for more rewarding activities. For those close to their grandchildren, spending time with them and going with them to dances, schools, or sports clubs is a joy. I hope to be able to continue doing such things for a long time. I was called to see many elderly patients, and I witnessed how much more fun they have in residential homes, compared to being stuck in their own big, empty houses. Some of us are afraid to make changes and leave our own homes. It is OK to continue living in our homes if we are coping and have some activities to do and friends to spend time with. But many seniors can barely afford to cover the cost of maintenance, heating, and nutritious sufficient groceries and therefore stay in very uncomfortable situation. Despite this, still many refuse any opportunity to make improvements. For example, if seniors were to sell the house and sort out their finances with benefits for themselves and their families, it would make life more enjoyable for all.

I saw many new marriages take place in residential homes, but in most cases people there have a lot of fun with their friends doing different activities. They maintain their independence up to the end and choose with whom they want to spend time. Being in a comfortable place will relieve the pressure from the family to find the time to take care of you when they are preoccupied with their own lives.

Group hypnotherapy is used in residential homes and is very popular and constructive in helping to maintain your body and keep up your spirits. In old age, there are still many fruits to be picked, so don't give up. Make the right decision now and keep going. Hypnotherapy and self-hypnosis will help you make positive changes in all these areas and to how you think and what you do.

Sixty-one

Self-Discipline

> I do not want to be a product of my society I want to make a product for my society.
>
> Author unknown

Self-discipline is not a duty; it is a skill which makes life more rewarding and enjoyable.

Whatever we want to have or be, self-discipline is mandatory if we wish to reach our goals. It will keep us on the track to accomplish our goals for each day and make plans for tomorrow. This is the right way to start each day with enthusiasm.

Unfortunately, often it happens that we leave our duties for later or are too lazy to do them. We might have good intentions to make plans, but we find it difficult to take the first step and put our plans into action. Stubborn negative thoughts such as "tomorrow" may keep us in the same position day after day and prevent us from achieving our goals. Many times, we make promises to ourselves and to others to do better, but in many cases we never follow through. One consequence of that behaviour is feeling even guiltier that we have failed to do the right thing.

We know the wise saying: "Tomorrow never comes. We only live today."

To lack in self-discipline is like anchoring your boat with the engine at full power, preventing you from moving forward. Self-discipline can be lowered by many medical conditions, such as hormonal abnormalities, anaemia, diabetes, and obesity, and by mental conditions such as depression, addiction, dissatisfaction with life, low self-esteem, poor self-image, and low confidence. Other reasons for low self-discipline are a lack of interest, a poor sense of responsibility, and limited ambition.

Poor self-discipline brings unpleasant feedback because of uncompleted duties, broken promises, and damaged accountability. In the long term, the poorly disciplined person develops feelings of shame for being unreliable to family, friends, or co-workers, with his or her word no longer taken seriously. Moreover, breaking promises to ourselves may trigger the full spectrum of chronic negative feelings about ourselves. Unfortunately, by falling back on our old negative habit of doing things tomorrow, we condition ourselves even more day by day. Tomorrow may be a busy day, and "squeezing in" yesterday's duties may be impossible, creating an even bigger time deficit and chaos in our life and other people's lives. Being aware of the growing mountain of neglected things will bring about dissatisfaction with ourselves, putting us just one step away from denial and looking to self-medicate.

Ignoring this problem will throw us off the track of reaching our goals. Long-term confusion or hopelessness may haunt us. The worst happens when we start to blame others for our *self-created mess* instead of working on our own lack of self-discipline. We start to feel angry that others do not understand, and we start to live with "*but*" again.

By doing what should be done on time, we start to alter the cycle and activate the positive Trio Mind. Self-discipline ensures that we are on time with everything. Automatically we feel good about ourselves and have stronger motivation to go for our goals. Being relaxed increases our ability to focus on the task at hand, and this in turn will bring the pleasant feeling of being a responsible and trusted person.

Therefore, improving self-discipline will keep us on track. Taking action immediately on our goals will preventing us from blowing things up again.

Even the smallest first accomplishment will give you joy and satisfaction and will begin the cycle of having enthusiasm and determination to go for your next goal. This is what successful people do. They reach one goal, even a small one, feel good about it, and then go for the next one and the next. Each time they have a successful outcome, they have a feeling of joy and a sense of maturity.

Goal → Action → Achievement → Satisfaction → Goal → Action → Positive feeling

Self-discipline increases responsibility and vice versa. It brings personal satisfaction and increased motivation. The good news is that we can improve our self-discipline along with other personal goals.

To improve our self-discipline, it is important to work on creating a positive Trio Mind. Follow the steps below to see a difference in your performance within a short span of time:

1. Whatever you need to do, write a goal for it. Find a motive for completing the goal to increase your energy and enthusiasm. Read your goal and visualize the rewarding result of your efforts (a clean house, finished project, home-made dinner, or degree), which will boost your determination to accomplish it on time.
2. Make a list before you go to bed of all the things you need to do the next day. Visualize them. See yourself going through all the listed duties, enjoying doing them and feeling the satisfaction of the results. It takes only ten minutes to visualize what you want to accomplish tomorrow, and it will bring a surprising result.
3. Start changing your thinking from "I have to do this" to "I can do it with pleasure" in different surroundings. For example, take your computer to a coffee shop to work there, or put on your favourite music when cleaning the house. You may recall good memories when doing something automatic, like putting your clean laundry away. Whatever you need to do, make it a pleasant experience.

4. If you are out of touch and have a long list of neglected things you must do, instead of panicking, call the people who rely on you and ask them for more time. Start with adding one duty per day lasting no more than fifteen to thirty minutes. The next day, add two if possible. Make it a challenge to complete them.

   Start to enjoy life and reward yourself!

   Following are examples of goals to improve self-discipline:

   - "I carefully plan my day and accomplish all necessary tasks."
   - "I am committed to my duties. Nothing will stop me from finishing them on time."
   - "I do whatever I have to do without delay. This way I remain on schedule without stress."
   - "I easily accomplished one more thing today to reduce the number of things to do tomorrow."
   - "I am able to complete my course. This will enable me to secure a good job."

Repeat the affirmations twice daily if you need to and feel the improvement.

All the foregoing are examples of affirmations that will stimulate the unconscious processes to act automatically to accomplish your goals. The most talented athlete will not reach his top performance without a commitment to practise every day no matter what. Students must stick to their daily plans if they want to obtain a degree. They will have an inner sense of responsibility and commitment to do what should be done without "but".

Sixty-two

Time Management

Make the Most of Your Time

Time is our biggest asset, and the worst thing we can do is to waste it. Good time management will save you time and energy, reduces stress, give you the feeling of being in control, and bring you much closer to your goals. Above all, you will start to enjoy everything you do and have more time to relax. Your energy and motivation will increase too.

Good time managers always ask themselves the following question: "How can I complete my tasks better and in a shorter amount of time?"

By writing down goals on management, we open our minds to new possibilities, which give us new options to make changes and feel more confident in a short time. Organize and reorganize your tasks, make sound plans for your social and family life and your hobbies, and above all make free time for yourself.

Anything is possible if you put your mind into it.

Taking small steps first will prepare you to take bigger steps later without stress. When we have a positive attitude, we can be in control of our duties. Only by being organized we can eliminate a significant amount of unnecessary work and stress.

When we live passively day by day or show the tendency to push things for later, causing frustration and stress at home and in the workplace, we find that small duties suddenly become big jobs.

Doing these things in a hurry brings poor results. Simply put, we are not in control of our lives. We are in reverse gear and in danger of being crushed.

The fact is that if we are not organized with the small things, then we are not in control of more serious matters. If you don't like everything that you have to do, then at the end of the day everything will be covered in dark clouds.

Science proves that living with a disorganized schedule and in a stressful and messy environment may lead to tiredness, irritation, difficulty relaxing, decreased creativity, and damaged health. You may start to wonder, "Why do I feel tense or tired?"

A team without a good manager shows poor results. In the long term, disorganization and mess may activate a negative Trio Mind for an individual or break the spirit of the whole team.

Children are more affected by physical and mental chaos as their brain activity is not fully developed yet, and this makes it difficult for them to have a positive perspective on a messy environment. The more organization around a child, the better the child's experimentation process to make some sense of the environment. Therefore, it is important to teach a child management skills from the beginning.

If our day is not organized and everything is done in a hurry at work or at home, tangible and intangible things alike, then our thoughts are like dark waves bombarding our head.

Being well organized improves the quality of life for the whole family or for one's co-workers. Making a schedule of home duties for everyone will create teamwork. For example, knowing when it is time to clean up will help people prepare for it, and children can learn to enjoy being responsible while cleaning up. A child lacking in self-discipline and time management skills may develop problems in school.

Following are some steps for effective time management:

- o Make a schedule of your duties, placing the most urgent ones first. Make a goal of how to better accomplish them in a shorter amount of time.

- o Teach others to be responsible for doing their part.
- o Work on each of these objectives until you feel a significant change in your life.
- o Make a list of routine duties for the day, week, month, and year.
- o Mark daily essentials in red—things to do at work, school, home etc.
- o Mark the occasional events, such as parties, in blue. Make provisional time for these engagements.
- o Mark your free time—breaks, time for yourself, social engagements—in green.
- o Regularly review your schedule for the week, the month, and the year.
- o Work on the list every day for fifteen minutes before bedtime.

Making plans for the next day reduces stress and eliminates the wasting of time, being late, forgetting things, or not doing the most important tasks. By planning, we become more aware of what we must do. Our minds are prepared to accomplish things in a calm way, thereby improving our performance. Complete *"must do"* things straightaway, and adjust your schedule (date, time) for other tasks.

Another important thing to do is to review your duties. Having too many duties on your shoulders over the long term is one of the main reasons for stress, resulting in poor outcomes and illness. Perhaps you are overburdened because of inefficient time management or taking on duties which are not your responsibility. Being occupied this way means you simply do not have enough time to do it all, and you especially don't have time for making positive changes. If such a situation lasts for a long time, it leads to poor performance, nervous breakdown, high blood pressure, circulation and heart problems, overeating, alcohol or drug abuse, family, etc.

If you have duties that could keep you busy twenty-four hours a day, it is a time to say "*stop*" and select your tasks more carefully. Find a way to make improvements. Find extra time by cancelling unnecessary activities and shortening other activities, for example watching TV programmes, calling friends, taking coffee breaks, browsing on the Internet for gossip, and long shopping trips. Sometimes we may speed up our performance if we set a schedule for our duties and stick to it.

When we look at the situation carefully, sometimes we find that we need to make up our mind about what our priorities are and make some changes. For example, we might cook one-dish dinners instead of three-course dinners twice a week, go to the bank once a week instead every day, arrange online banking, and read only important emails. Spread the activities across a longer stretch of time, for example swimming during summer months and going to the gym during winter, instead of doing both all year round, which causes stress and diminishes the real value of being active.

Finally, learn to stop making a mess. Within a short time this will make an enormous change at home and in the office. Learning to do tasks as they should be done straightaway will make the difference. The fact is that making a mess will hit you, no one else, as it is you who will suffer the stress of picking up your files or clothes from the floor. Making it a habit to sort out things at once will automatically give you more time to do other things and will prevent panic when suddenly you have a visitor.

Respect your work and ask others to do the same. By making a mess, it shows you do not respect yourself and that you let others disrespect your efforts as well. Letting others leave a careless mess in the kitchen, on the desk, or on the floor very quickly results in an unpleasant condition and creates an additional task for you.

Well-kept and well-organized places are relaxing and stimulating. And it is one of our responsibilities and part of our personal culture to keep our place in order wherever we are, be it on the street, at home, at work, or in a hotel.

Frequently we hear, "I have no time to do this."

If we are being honest, we see that this is merely denial. You still will have to do the task sooner or later, and deep in your mind will feel guilt. By admitting that you need to make some improvements in time management and self-discipline, you can make steady changes to improve your situation and enjoy a cup of tea at the end of the day. Be the commander of your home, your workplace, and everything you do.

At the top of your list, write your goal to be a good time manager and organizer. It may be the most rewarding achievement of your life. It may take you in a totally new direction. If you have problems doing this, read the book again, or ask for professional help to eliminate the negative thoughts preventing you from having a satisfying life.

Examples of goals are as follows:

- "I take good care of my home. I am better organized every day."
- "I am well organized. I carefully plan my work for next day."
- "I do what I have to do at once and always think of how to do it better."

You are the commander of your ship, your house, and your workplace, and you are responsible for the condition of these places. If you should fail, then who will do it? Practising self-hypnosis will help you to make improvements and changes within a short period of time.

Sixty-three

Confident Problem-Solving Strategies

To any actions there is an equal and opposite reaction.

Newton's third law of physics

As commander of your life, you need to have the ability not only to face any problems in a calm and confident way but also to find the right solution to them. Your decisions will determine how successful you are during your lifespan. Making mistakes is not a failure; in fact, we all make mistakes from time to time. However, not learning from your mistakes is a weakness and is irresponsible behaviour. Learning new strategies to face problems and make better decisions will minimize your mistakes and reduce your frustration and disappointment. Moreover, by being better prepared to face daily events, automatically you will increase your confidence and self-image.

In fact, we all learn how to solve problems from the first day of our life. However, if we have good guidance at school and from our family, we learn more quickly and more effectively. Athletes need a coach. Artists need a mentor to keep them on track and support them when their enthusiasm is lacking. In fact, other people can spot our mistakes easily. Therefore, it is wise to listen to others' opinions before we make a final decision.

From now on, it will be helpful to ask the following three questions, which I like to call the Decision Trio Questions, before making any important decision:

1. "Is it really what I want, or does someone else think so?"
2. "What risks does this decision involve? Can I cope with those risks?"
3. "Do I need extra time to think about it before making a final decision?"

Wise people always take the time to search for more information before making a final decision. There is an old saying: "The best comes to those who wait patiently."

By learning some principles, we can improve our problem-solving ability. By making the right decisions, we come closer to our destiny, instead of turning in the wrong direction.

When facing a problem of any kind, it is important to look at the whole picture and make a proper assessment of the situation before making the final decision about what to do about it.

Following are simple problem-solving strategies:

1. Take full responsibility for the situation. When facing a dilemma, by taking full responsibility for the situation we can see the true picture of the problem. By seeing the real problem, we have a better chance of seeing what needs to be changed.
2. Stay calm and think constructively. Letting your emotions solve the problem will automatically put you on the wrong track. Take time to avoid irrational actions governed by negative emotions such as anger, frustration, and panic.
3. Write some options to change the situation in the examples that follow:

An abusive relationship

a. "Shall I obey my abusive partner's request and not irritate him [or her next time?"
b. "Do I need help from outside?"

In business

a. "Is it about making more cuts because of redundancies?"
b. "Should I think of how to increase profits by offering better products?"

If you chose the (*a*) answers, you do not see the whole picture and the main reason for the problem. The probability is that the abuse will not stop voluntarily. Your partner is a manipulator and must be stopped. Increasing your debt will only increase the deficit and put you in very difficult situation.

4. Any problem must be carefully analysed, reviewed, and reconsidered in the light of past outcomes, without criticism or negative emotions. Look for the facts, not for what suits you better. Convert the problem into a goal. Ask yourself, "How can I do this better?" Set a date and time for positive results.
5. Make a list of many possibilities.
6. Write the pros and cons of each of these separately. Write all the possible consequences you can think of. After making these decisions, ask yourself, "Can I afford it?" and "How it will it change my life if it is the wrong decision?" and "Can I afford to take full responsibility for the outcome if something goes wrong?"
7. Before making a final decision, have a plan B. This way you protect yourself and minimize your eventual disappointment and stress because you know what to do in a what-if situation. This is a calculated risk used by successful people each time they need to make a serious decision.

8. If you are not sure what to do, negotiate to give yourself more time to ask for help.
9. If you have still found no solution, wake up and say, "Stop. I need to find the right solution to make positive changes to this situation. I will start to work on it right now and will continue working on it until I solve it."

Start to analyse the situation once more. "Maybe I need to open the rusty gates to make a move to free myself from this abusive situation and start a new life. Or perhaps I should think about getting into another line of business, going to college, or finding a well-paying job."

Look for as many solutions as possible, not just one—from terminating the relationship, to seeking professional help, to presenting the problem to the whole family. Considering your options may bring to light the right answer for how to face the present situation in a more effective way. In business you could consider closing the business, joining a similar company, changing the product, or seeking advice from successful business people.

However, relying only on your own knowledge is one of the most common reasons for making mistakes when facing a challenging situation that nothing has worked towards solving despite many attempts.

When facing a serious problem, we must be open-minded. Sometimes it is wise to listen to others' advice as well. Ask yourself, "Do I have sufficient experience in this field to make the right decision, or do I need advice from a professional or independent person?" Commonly people assume that they know, but frequently they do not know what they don't know. Compare and analyse other opinions, as many people are willing to help. Gain as much information as you can and analyse it carefully before making a decision.

On the other hand, be careful not to reject or jump on any advice irrationally, especially advice coming from people with little experience in the matter.

Decision-making is commonly based on the right framing of a situation. Framing the problem wrongly will make it difficult for you to find the right solution. For example, if someone owes you money, do not make the mistake of getting frustrated and spending additional time and money seeking revenge. Instead, think of how to recover your loss by negotiating and communicating well, or by helping the person who owes you to find a new income source if he or she has trouble doing so himself or herself.

Another example of action borne of irrational thinking would be to teach an unfaithful partner a lesson by having an affair yourself, only to suffer more mentally by having lowered your values because of your anger.

The right way is to try many tactics, ask for advice, and take your time before committing yourself to anything. Use your logic, and trust your instincts.

Examples of goals on problem-solving strategies:

- "I face any problem in a calm way and look for the whole picture of the situation."
- "I always analyse and seek other opinions before making a serious decision."
- "I trust myself and my intuition to make a final decision."

Money Management

Lending may be fun. Repaying is often frustrating. Without a full understanding that we are responsible for supporting ourselves and those who depend on us, it is difficult to find satisfaction in life. Financial insecurity is one of the main causes of stress leading to nervous breakdown, depression, addiction, and suicidal thoughts. A person who is under this type of stress frequently finds her personal and family life filled with frustration, anger, and abuse. Ultimately it may lead to a family break-up.

Money management is a skill that you need to learn if you are to be efficient and comfortable. Just as a commander has to secure assets such as fuel and food for the whole crew, you need to secure all financial needs for yourself and our family.

First, you need to learn to make a budget based on your total income and your monthly expenses. It is compulsory to know how much you have and how much you need to spend weekly, monthly, and per annum. This will be a starting point to making goals to increase your income, reduce unnecessary spending, plan for future expense, and save according to your needs and ambitions. Financial security is obtained when you are in control of three aspects: income, spending, and saving.

There are two golden rules in money management:

1. Save 5–10 per cent of your total income every month.
2. Increase your income by 5–10 per cent every month.

This does not mean that you need to lower your living standard. It means you need to adjust the amount you spend and save. Make these two rules your goals and stick to them.

"But"—no excuses—you need to save at least 5 per cent if you want to be a responsible person and make changes. Make it your goal to figure out how to earn the additional money, for example by taking a part-time job, working from home, creating something, selling a product, teaching, supplying services, or taking an additional course. Until you reach your goal to increase your income and be more comfortable financially, you need to find a way to live on what you have. It is much cheaper than borrowing money without having an income to repay it. However, making reasonable plans about your future income, and showing these plans to people who can help, may open many closed doors. For example, if you show that you are taking a course, your bank may help you to complete your study and start a new job.

Working together with the whole family makes it easier to plan a goal and stick to it. Money management is for everyone to learn. It is just another skill to secure a steady income. Children should take part in family planning as well. They will better appreciate what they have, increase their ambition to study, and learn to be responsible for earning money for their own families later on. Above all, working as a family will strengthen bonds and trust.

Of course many of us want to have a good profession, a steady job, and good business, but just saying "if only" is not enough. Being honest with yourself and others, making plans to gain the necessary skills to have a better job or business, and asking for help will put you on the way to earning a satisfactory income.

People of different ages take courses in order to find better jobs. Courses are offered in many towns and on the Internet. Many are free. There are always people who need help at home, such as with gardening, taking care of elderly relatives, or walking the dog. When a problem arises, the worst thing you can do is to put your head in the sand and say, "Such work is not for me," or avoid those who are waiting for you to repay them.

If you are facing a financial dilemma, follow all the steps covered in this book and open the rusty gates. In the end, your thinking will be more rational, giving you the opportunity to find the right solution while acknowledging what went wrong. The picture may be not be a pleasant one for you to look at, but it may turn your attitude and thinking in a more rewarding direction, which could lead to a much more pleasant situation in the near future. Without taking steps to make changes, you will stay in the same position.

Making a sound goal for increasing your income is an effective way to move forward as it will stimulate your mind to search for new ideas.

Start to stimulate your brain with the following questions:

- "What is the reason for my present situation?"
- "What can I do right now to improve this situation?"

Follow all the steps of problem-solving discussed in the next chapter.

Again, we need to be honest about our present situation and take full responsibility for it. We must make goals to improve it, and then we must act upon the goals. Taking the first step to see the true picture may be the starting point for a more rewarding life. The beauty of the human mind is that everyone holds this potential.

Following are examples of goals to make improvements in your financial situation:

- "I take all opportunities to learn how to increase my monthly income."
- "I am willing to get the necessary education to secure a steady income."
- "I start my own business."
- "I always make a budget for the week, the month, and the whole year."
- "I check my finances every week to know exactly what the situation is."
- "I keep my eyes open for more opportunities to increase my income by 10 per cent."
- "I will repay all my loans by the end of this year."

Practising self-hypnosis will bring about significant changes in your attitude, thought pattern, responsibility, and commitment to efficiently manage your finances and solve the problems in a calm way. In the next chapters, I discuss the basic characteristics of physical and mental health, necessary to master your actions and achievements. You will find examples of how to make goals to improve your life in these areas.

Sixty-four

Mind and Body Fitness

> The feeling inside us is the deciding factor of whether we are winners or dreamers.

Even with the best skills, if our ship is rotten, we can't sail far. Good physical and mental health is crucial to making progress in life.

Learning to keep a healthy balance between body and mind is another skill we all need to have. First we need to fully understand, that the mind and body need good care and constant maintenance. Neglecting this basic rule will undermine body and mind function sooner or later. We now know that many medical and psychological problems are self-induced, as we see long-term stress leading to unhealthy eating, addictions. Typical examples of actions showing that we take the health of our mind and body for granted are poor nutrition, intoxication, lack of physical activity and mental stimulation, and insufficient rest and sleep. All these conditions lead to secondary medical conditions such as heart problems, damage to the brain and other organs, high blood pressure, obesity, joint pain, and cancer. Ill health keeps us in constant discomfort, burning our energy and causing a mental imbalance. Physical and emotional pain activates negativity in the Trio Mind. Our wishes become unrealistic, and our chances of reaching them fade away.

The good news is that many medical problems can be prevented by making small systematic changes to our lifestyle. There are many well-documented medical cases showing that serious medical conditions can be reversed by changing the negative Trio Mind into a positive Trio Mind and changing old lifestyle patterns.

To put it simply, to have a healthy body and mind, we need nutritious food, regular physical activity, positive stimulation of the brain, regular breaks during the day, and proper sleep at night. If we are deficient in one of these elements, it may trigger a chain of dysfunction.

In this chapter I will start by discussing physical and mental activity.

The majority of us know that being active is the most important thing we can do to stay fit, but how many of us do this the right way and with pleasure?

Our understanding of being active is frequently misshaped by the media and the fitness industry. In our fervour to have a figure like that of many celebrities, we almost forget about the main reason for being active: to secure our well-being. Frequently we lose sight of logic and therefore need to look at the matter of health from a different perspective. It is not the most effective, or the only, lifestyle to spend half the day at an expensive gym because you "must". You may hate it, and at the same time you feel guilty that your family does not have a nutritious dinner on the table because you were gone all day. In turn, associated negative feelings and thoughts lead to more irrational decisions, including a decision to neglect yourself. Even worse is feeling sorry for yourself for a prolonged time, as having negative emotions may deepen your negative mood and automatically decrease your motivation to do something constructive with your life.

The facts indicate that we do not need to spend endless hours in the gym unless we are preparing for a competition or it is something we love to do. Physical activity can and should be natural, pleasurable, and practical, not a pain in the neck.

Recent studies prove that as little as ten minutes of intensive exercise every day is sufficient to keep us in good shape! Moreover, imaginary physical activities are shown to have the same effect as real ones. The fact is that when we spend five minutes of every hour in intensive movement, it will make for a total of one hour (sixty minutes) of intensive exercise of the body each day!

It is proven that the vigorous moving the body at different tempos and the stretching of the body after sitting for some time is very effective in boosting metabolism and energy. Regular breaks every forty-five minutes between physical and mental activities are very effective too.

All this is simple and can easily fit into our daily scheduled duties to stimulate the body's functions throughout the day. When we do something that makes us feel good, our mind will be filled with positive feelings, which is very important in increasing our energy, confidence, and creativity. By doing what you enjoy, you will have better results and increased motivation to stay active.

Being active means to be involved in some activities in your personal and professional life, or in hobbies. You may choose walking, swimming, playing with children in the park, playing tennis socially, or being involved in your community. You might garden or clean the house or office for thirty minutes per day, while dancing to your favourite music or changing your position, instead of sitting for long hours in the office.

One does not need a lot of money to stay healthy. Parks are free, empty fields are everywhere, beaches, forests, and lakes are around for everyone to organize some social activities and challenges. On the other hand, you can leave your car home for a day, stop using lifts and remote controls, or electrical appliances to grind the coffee. Small changes lead to big changes in how we feel about our body and mind. Spend some time with nature to put your thoughts in order. When walking on the beach, you may find this is the most comfortable activity to promote the healing of your body and mind.

Choose what makes you feel best and what you can easily add to your daily duties. Logic and intuition support physical activity, so choose something you enjoy. You can start to use your imagination to create fun times with friends and family and when working. As I presented in Part II, this method is successful. Just imagine yourself active, and your body will move in that direction.

Examples of goals for an active lifestyle:

- "I enjoy various physical activities throughout the day."
- "I take a five-minute break for physical activity every hour."
- "I organize outside activities with family and friends on a regular basis."

Stimulating the Mind

Stimulating the mind is paramount. It will eliminate negative thoughts and increase blood flow automatically, which will increase the function of the brain. Insufficient brain activity leads to a slowing down of natural processes of the body and mind and may cause many medical and psychological disorders, for example loss of memory, psychosis, or depression.

There are many effective methods to boost brain function, such as the following:

1. Favourite music of any kind stimulates mind and body.
2. Personal pictures may bring back good memories.
3. An active social life increases energy, enthusiasm, and general well-being.
4. Painting and dancing or other modern mind therapies stimulate and calm.
5. Reading, writing, doing crossword puzzles, playing chess, solving puzzles, and playing games keep the brain active.
6. Having fun has been known for a long time to be therapeutic too.
7. Watching comedies is used in hospitals to stimulate therapy, especially for children.
8. Meditation, self-hypnosis, and yoga are good tools to keep a healthy balance in the mind.

Below are some examples of goals for brain stimulation.

- "I spend at least ten minutes every day reading to exercise my mind."
- "I improve problem-solving strategies by playing different games."
- "I enjoy puzzles and crosswords to stimulate my brain."
- "I love to play chess to stimulate my mind."
- "By playing games, I improve my concentration and memory."

Calming the Mind and Body

Overloading the mind with long hours of work, domestic and family duties, and worries of financial or personal insecurity puts us under stress, and if such stress is uncontrolled, it will lead to exhaustion and mental disturbance.

The benefits of resting at regular intervals are grossly underestimated. Trying to finish everything in one day means we frequently borrow time from our resting and sleeping hours. Some live on borrowed time for years without holidays or even a short break during the day for a cup of tea. When our brain is tired, our thinking and reasoning changes and making mistakes becomes common. Constant tiredness makes us impatient and irrational, leading to poor performance and relationship problems because of poor communication.

It is interesting is that activities increase energy and calm the mind at the same time.

1. Five minutes at regular intervals throughout the day of doing breathing exercises and repeating affirmations is an effective way to keep calm. Over the course of twelve hours, this gives you sixty minutes of relaxing your brain and every cell in your body, which initiates the healing process, increases your energy, and puts your thoughts in harmony.

2. Having fun listening to music or being engaged in a healthy hobby is an excellent natural brain tranquillizer.

Following are some examples of goals for calming your body and mind:

- "I take a break every forty-five minutes and relax for fifteen minutes."
- "I listen to music or relaxation programmes regularly."
- "I enjoy walking and fishing."
- "I meditate on a regular basis."
- "I use self-hypnosis for ten minutes every day to sort out my thoughts and feelings."
- "By relaxing, I calm my mind and body."

Sixty-five

Sleep Patterns

> The best way to ensure healthy sleep is to have a successful day.

We all have different sleeping patterns. Some people go to bed early. Others go to bed late. What time we start the day often depends on what time we go to sleep. Some need only a few hours of sleep to be very healthy and active during the day, whereas others need to sleep longer.

However, to stay healthy it is essential to have approximately seven to eight hours of sleep every day. The problem starts when we override the demands of our body and mind.

There are many medical and psychological conditions which cause sleep problems. Common among these are chronic illness, pain, and cancer. Frequent psychological reasons for sleep problems are overexertion, trauma, irrational thinking, and negative emotions mostly associated with unfinished daily business. Chronic stress, worries, and physical and emotional pain are well-known factors in a disturbed sleep pattern.

Sleep deprivation (insomnia) is diagnosed when the sleep deficit lasts for a considerable period, there is a change in the sleeping pattern, and the person is exhausted during the day, affecting normal life activity.

Taking the brain for granted and trying to increase its function by using drugs, caffeine, and other stimulants has short-lasting benefits.

The energy level gradually decreases, reducing one's enthusiasm for what one must do and negatively affecting one's daily performance. In the longer term, goals will be delayed or abandoned.

Again, the wonder of chemistry came to the rescue when we started to rely on prescription and over-the-counter medications to induce sleep. Many people believe that a simply pill will solve everyday problems. Millions of sufferers around the world use some form of sleeping pill or tranquillizer.

Unfortunately, as with painkillers and other medications, sleeping pills are very harmful in the long term. Dependence is a serious problem, and the side effects are well known to both patients and medical practitioners. I have seen many young patients on sleeping pills. Research shows us that tranquillizers and sleeping pills have been overprescribed for many years. This must be stopped.

Therefore, recognizing and removing the factors leading to sleep problems is paramount. We must eliminate these factors one by one and restore healthy sleep. Sleeplessness is a serious condition that requires therapy. I strongly advise that if you have suffered from insomnia for some time, see a doctor for assistance, because if left untreated, insomnia will lead to serious damage to your body systems and to psychological disorders including suicidal thoughts, accident proneness, and poor performance. Treatment may be necessary to deal with root of the problem and eliminate any underlying medical or psychological condition. The longer the problem exists, the more difficult it will be to find the way back to a healthy state of being.

However, in less severe cases, or if you don't have medical help, try to follow the well-known remedies to restore a healthy sleeping pattern. We now understand that there are many natural approaches which are more effective to restoring healthy sleep, and these are free of side effects.

Do the following to improve your sleep pattern:

1. List the reasons for why you have poor sleep.
2. Eliminate bad habits and implement a healthier approach to your daily tasks.

3. Make a plan for a new pattern.

    a) Make small changes in your lifestyle to restore a healthy sleeping pattern.
    b) Change negative thoughts into positive ones.
    c) Control your emotions.
    d) Set a goal and work on it in self-hypnosis for few minutes.
    e) Practise affirmations during the day to sleep well.

Here are some examples of setting goals/using affirmations to improve your sleep pattern:

- "I finish my daily business before bedtime and make plans for tomorrow."
- "I always make plans for the next day. This way I sleep well."
- "To avoid stress, I prepare things I need for the next day before going to bed."
- "I keep the same bedtime hours."
- "I ventilate the room before bedtime to increase the change that I will sleep well."
- "I keep my bedroom cool, which encourages better sleep."

Other well-known old-fashioned but effective remedies to improve sleep are as follows:

- Aromatherapy—put a lavender sachet or bar of soap under your pillow.
- Take a warm bath or drink a cup of hot milk for its calming effect
- Drink herbal tea such as chamomile, magnolia, or valerian to reduce stress.

Hypnotherapy, meditation, or yoga will speed up the process of restoring a healthy sleep pattern. The results may last long after therapy. A hypnotic trance will relax your body, and specific hypnotic suggestions can be applied to restore your sleep pattern. Therapy will aim to eliminate the primary causes of the conditions. Patients can learn better time management, stress control, and planning to improve self-discipline and confidence.

A few minutes of self-hypnosis will help you to sleep well all night and wake up at the desired time without an alarm clock, feeling refreshed to start the new day.

Hypnotherapy is an excellent tool to harmonize your daily activities and night-time rest.

Sixty-six

Healthy Nutrition

> If you feed the body wisely, the mind will respond wisely.

There are endless books, programmes, and remedies on food, so confusion is growing about what, when, and how to eat. Therefore, I would like to highlight the simple facts on this subject and discuss how practising self-hypnosis will move you in the right direction.

The third law of motion says that for any action, there is an equal and opposite reaction. Body and mind processes are based on the same law. Depending on the quality of fuel you supply to the body, the mind will respond to it equally.

It couldn't be simpler: good food leads to good health, and bad food leads to poor health.

Whatever you are consuming, it will either nourish each cell in your body or supply the energy needed to maintain healthy function and initiate healing or toxify your cells, affecting their function and leading to various pathological changes.

Here we come to real life, where we observe that the simplest task is the most difficult task to perform. This happens because when we are healthy, the feeling of hunger and pleasure is the trigger for the body's natural automatic self-regulated system telling us that a new supply of food is needed. When the mind–body loop is disturbed, logic vanishes and negative emotions such as anger, sadness, and depression start to govern our choices.

An unhealthy eating pattern in the long term may cause malnourishment, which in turn may lead to serious medical and mental problems. Common conditions affecting millions people around the globe are obesity, bulimia, and anorexia, all of which trap people with a cocktail of negative thoughts and emotions. Irrational thinking and looking for a remedy to feel better presents the danger of developing an "emotional hunger" and overeating or engaging in other difficult-to-control behaviour.

These conditions are made up of a combination of physical and psychological factors and need to be treated by professionals.

The good news is that there is a lot of room for everyone to make positive changes to their lifestyle and eating pattern in order to improve health. To maintain or implement a healthy eating pattern, you need to understand the fundamentals of food and body metabolism. Knowing better how this system works will help you to make the necessary adjustments to eat healthy.

Following are common reasons for an unhealthy eating pattern:

Firstly, in the past sixty years, the food industry has put an enormous variety of different foods on the shelf, which constantly catch our eyes. We are buying and eating much more than fifty years ago. Global trading brings new products and foods from the other side of the world. The food industry is booming, bringing an enormous variety of ready-to-eat food which is easy for working families to prepare. Lifestyles are changing, and to put it simply, many of us can afford to buy not just essential food but also more snacks and treats. Parties and dining out are more popular and affordable. The fridge in most homes is fully packed all year long, compared to in the past, when such a thing was only common just before Christmas. Simply put, we are tempted to eat more, and it is easy to do so.

Secondly, chemicals are added to foods. "Too good to be true" proves to be right again. Soon it was discovered that these beautifully packaged processed foods have many dark sides. Heavily processed food contains a staggering number of ingredients to improve shelf storage, colour, and taste, which at the same time significantly changes rate of metabolism and nutritional value. Chemicals added to food include preservatives, hormones, antibiotics, and cleaning products. Some plastic containers release toxic substances which have been proven to have a negative effect on metabolism as well. Fillers discreetly added to processed food and drinks improve texture and taste but are serious factors in our unknowing consumption of countless calories, resulting in weight gain. Misleading phrases on labels, such as "all-natural," and "healthy," trap millions of people into buying unhealthy products.

The accumulation of all these substances over the long term affects our health and leads to various dysfunctions of the digestive system, including stomach, liver, gallbladder, and bowel problems including cancer. Intoxication of the organs, including brain inflammation, heartburn, and constipation, are common. Low energy and apathy resulting from the poor nutritional quality of many foods leads to poor performance in private and professional life, bringing additional stress and worry.

Thirdly, the roots of careless or emotional overeating may be created in the early years of life, or may be the result of family issues, addiction, rejection, and/or emotional or physical abuse. Overweight teens and young people may become very sensitive to physical changes in the body and experience a loss of positive self-image and self-esteem. Feeling hopeless about it (as they do not have the knowledge to assess what is happening), they become resistant to positive suggestions about what to do and are rebellious and frequently live with anger. They have a problem finding a solution to the ongoing dilemma by themselves and tend to live in denial and reject any logical approach to change. Low confidence reduces their coping and problem-solving skills even more.

Fourthly, the media, society, and judgemental and influential family members create additional pressure on young people to look like celebrities, which only continues the cycle. Bullying and constant abusive comments from others further damage confidence even more. People affected by an eating disorder lose control over their thoughts and emotions. They know that there is something wrong but are too weak to take the right actions and make successful changes.

Here we will concentrate more on common reasons for overeating, which may be the result of emotional hunger, which is controlled by automatic negative thoughts (ANTs) and feelings. When we are under pressure, frequently we self-medicate with a low-nutrition food which is pleasing to the palate.

Obesity is a disease that affects body organs and causes mental weakness. Overeating of low-nutrition foods leads to diabetes, inflammation, high blood pressure, and heart problems, all of which damage the body's self-healing function and brain activity. An obese person is prone to bacterial, viral, and fungal infections, ulcers, and wounds that are slow to heal. All organs are overloaded, are the joints, which have to carry excess weight. Natural interstitial spaces in the body are filled with fat, preventing the comfortable functioning of internal organs.

Dental health is affected, leading to ulcers, tooth decay, and gum problems, as well as difficulty in wearing a denture. Psychological suffering begins to deepen, and depression, low self-esteem, poor self-image, and low confidence are common. This in turn intensifies the uncontrolled behaviour of unhealthy eating, and the obese person finds himself dancing endlessly to this damaging tune.

When energy is low, motivation and determination to achieve any goal may be fragile. Relationships can be damaged, and having a social life may be difficult. Obese people may become prisoners in their own homes. I have attended many patients who were unable to move from their own room or their own home for months at a time because of their obesity.

So why it is so difficult to change and become fit and active again?

If you suffer from ongoing overweight and want to change it, I want you to stop for a moment and think about it. If you have read this book from the beginning, you should recognize by now that only by being totally honest with yourself will you be able to change the self-destructive pattern of thinking that causes unhealthy eating.

The main factor in your overeating is your negative thinking and out-of-control feelings. Therefore, only you can admit that your present eating pattern doesn't work for your body and that you lost control over your eating at some point in time. You need to be willing to make the necessary changes to how you think, feel, and react if you want to be in control of your eating pattern again.

An unhealthy eating pattern is a product of long-term conditioning arising from automatic habitual eating and the negative thoughts associated with it. To change this, you need to unwire the old pattern of thinking and learn a new, healthy approach, until it becomes automatic.

I am sure you want to scream out, "I've tried everything, and nothing has worked!"

It is true, and you are not alone. The real problem comes when you try to stick to the parameters every day during your busy life. However, the fact is that the foregoing behaviours are the only ones you need to commit yourself to if we want to regain a healthy weight and achieve a healthy level of fitness.

Here the beauty of the mind comes to the rescue once again. Working more on the unconscious mind during hypnosis will help you make positive changes in your thoughts and emotions in a relatively short amount of time and with longer-lasting results.

Therefore, making it a goal to tune the mind to a healthy eating pattern is the starting point and the most important factor in securing your health and feeling good about yourself.

Following are a few examples of sound goals to improve eating patterns:

1. "I learn about healthy food so I will know what nutrition my body and mind needs."
2. "I eat only when feeling hungry. I stay in control of my ANTs and emotions."

By repeating these positive statements in your mind over and over, you will turn your attention to becoming more automatically selective with regard to what you eat and when. By repeating the affirmation to choose healthy food and persistently visualizing yourself as you want to be (healthy, active, feeling good about yourself and your body), you will soon turn your thoughts and feelings in this direction and resist any temptations along the way.

By doing these things, you will sensitize yourself to choosing foods which are good for you and in line with your specific metabolism. Supplying the right nutrition will prevent psychological disorders as well, for example anxiety, compulsive eating, and feeling guilty, hopeless, and out of control.

A body filled with good nutrition will automatically eliminate real hunger. The mind will send a signal: "I am fine. I am full. I am happy."

Again, it is the incredible potential of the mind helping to rescue you from the frustrating cycle of losing weight and putting it back on. Starting with all the exercises described in Part IV, you will open the door to learning how to control your emotions, increase your confidence, make sound goals to be fit, and follow a new eating pattern.

Working on the foregoing goals one by one will make you stronger mentally and will help you get on track to lose weight and maintain a balance in your mind and body function. It will replace the destructive negative Trio Mind and lead to a constructive, creative positive thinking pattern.

Positive mood and thoughts will increase your motivation to eat well, stay healthy, and lose weight and will turn your attention towards the benefits you will enjoy upon reaching your goal. Making yourself mentally stronger and reducing stress will eliminate the compulsion to engage in emotional eating in difficult situations, one of the main factors of having a poor diet.

Start by transforming ANT into a positive healthy eating pattern.

The most important point is that you must have the willingness to make permanent changes to your thinking and eating patterns. Deeply root these in your mind so you can form new healthy habits.

Start by identifying the main things that cause you to eat badly, without feeling ashamed of it. Take full responsibility for making the right changes. This will help you go in the right direction to reach your goal to be healthy and feel great about yourself and your body. Make a list of ten reasons why you gain weight or eat badly. This will improve your awareness of your present situation and stimulate your mind to find ways to correct it. If you do not know the reasons, read this book again or seek professional help.

Below are some common factors leading to obesity, many of which you may recognize:

- Lacking or ignoring basic knowledge of food and metabolism.
- Poor health, grief, stress, living in denial, living in an unstable home, being abused.
- Mental weakness, low self-esteem, poor self-image, and low self-confidence.
- Frequent dining out and eating huge portions of processed foods.
- Careless buying, weakness to resist ads, not checking the ingredients in foods.
- Buying too much food without making a shopping list of only fresh, quality food.
- Constant snacking and irregular or late meals.
- Jumping in desperation at any new suggestion of a miracle diet.
- Lack of basic physical and mental activity.
- Lack of commitment, self-discipline, and honesty with yourself.

Starting by overcoming denial, including a *"but"* attitude and other negative thoughts, you will gradually find a positive approach to this situation. Once you have the feeling of being in control of what you eat, this will trigger the positive Trio Mind. It will increase personal willpower and self-esteem, leading you to look for a new approach to fight overweight, get or stay fit, and enjoy life.

Below are examples of essential conditions necessary for building a new eating pattern:

- See the true picture of the problem: "I change to a healthy eating pattern."
- Take responsibility: "I take responsibility for my health and what I eat."
- Include your motive: "By being healthy, I enjoy activities, have a social life, and reach my goals."
- Have vision of the final result you want: "I look well and feel well."
- Review your beliefs and thoughts. Erase the old beliefs that convince you it is impossible to lose weight and be healthy.
- Control your emotions. Stay calm. Reduce stress and set boundaries.
- Work on your self-image and self-esteem: "I believe that I can do it."
- Stick to your new plan until you reach the goal: "I enjoy this challenge."
- Make a goal to stick to nutritious food: "I am the best cook for myself."
- Enjoy activities by doing what is comfortable for you: "I can do what I want to do."
- Share your success, and have a supportive social network: "I share my success with others."
- Celebrate your achievements. For example, make own "five-star" healthy dishes.

Again, to be successful in your goals, you need to take action and be persistent until you reach your goal. Successful people never give up; they try again and again, using different tactics. They keep going until they reach what they want. There is no failure in starting again and learning from previous experience. It is true that many people lose weight only to gain it back, but it is also true that many people are successful in losing weight permanently.

Knowing how to work more deeply on the unconscious mind, you should see yourself among the successful group from now on. Practising self-hypnosis will speed up the transformation and will improve your self-discipline and motivation to stick to your programme. It will help you to trust your unconscious mind to deliver the necessary resources for reaching your goal. Self-hypnosis can work like magic and lead you to accept the new conditions more easily and make healthy behaviour more automatic. Generally, hypnotherapy's aim is to restore the full balance of body and mind with long-lasting positive outcomes, including healthy body function. If you have an image of your goal in your mind, your unconscious mind will work to find the way to reach it, even if sometimes the route is a zigzag. Those who succeed in keeping their body in a healthy condition accept that permanent changes in diet and lifestyle are necessary to have lasting results. Changing only one factor or starving yourself will not make a significant lasting difference.

It is important to keep your new approach simple and logical. It must easily fit with your budget and daily duties. Turning to healthy eating should be a pleasure, not another must. Keep it simple and look for facts. Using logic and intuition is always the wisest and healthiest approach to what is better for you.

Although this book is about the potential of your unconscious mind, I would like to provide a summary of the fundamentals and proven tips for a lifestyle of healthy eating.

There are many healthy diets, and each person has a different preference. Now we know that each of us needs a different approach to weight control, depending on our metabolism, hormonal balance, genes, lifestyle, mental state, and age. For some, a lower-carbohydrate diet is better suited than a diet lower in fat or some other nutrient. Our beliefs and cultural habits play a significant role as well. Experiment to find what is best for you—what brings quicker results and makes you feel good.

Being willing to learn more about food and its preparation will improve your ability to choose the right food rich in micronutrients, protein, fibre, and healthy fats. The human body needs a full range of vitamins and minerals to supply the whole body and the brain with the essential micronutrients to function properly. When the body has a sufficient amount of nutrients, it does not crave for extra food and snacks.

Changing to good-quality food is the most important step to take. Choose fresh organic foods free from chemicals, antibiotics, and hormones to avoid continuous poisoning of the body. These types of food can be found in many local stores at the right price.

1. Protein and essential fats have been the primary staples for as long as the human race has been in existence. Organic meat, fish, eggs, and dairy products in healthy proportions (e.g. an eight-ounce glass of milk, a matchbox-size chunk of cheese, and a palm-size portion of meat) supply essential protein, healthy fats such as omega-3, minerals, and vitamins.
2. Healthy fats such as grass-fed butter, cold-pressed olive or coconut oil, and nuts (only one handful per day) supply essential oils to encourage the healthy functioning of all the organs.
3. Fresh fruits and vegetables. The newest recommendations are seven portions of veg and fruits a day according to research on over sixty thousand men and women in the UK. Vegetables and fruits can be eaten as snacks without limit. A variety of organic vegetable and fruits, both raw and cooked and of different textures and colours, every day will automatically stimulate the metabolism, detoxify the body, and guarantee positive nutrition.

   A practical way to supply minerals and vitamins is to have a medium-size bowl of multi-coloured vegetables and fruits ready in the fridge or on the table. This makes a perfect snack for the whole day, for the whole family. You may be surprised by how quickly such a bowl will become empty. It is a fact that the reason many people do not eat enough vegetables is because they have negative thoughts about preparing them. Home-made salad dressing based on olive or coconut olive, herbs, and lemon juice will satisfy your palate and reduce your salt and sugar consumption. It will prevent overeating and will supply the body with micronutrients, minerals, and vitamins.

Logically, a reduction in sugar, starchy food, and salt is the right choice to make. Using your imagination to create healthy desserts to celebrate your achievements with family and friends may become a new hobby or a profitable business. For example, frozen fruits can be the base for healthy ice creams, smoothies, and pudding.

4. Eat the food that you know is nutritious. You do not need special superfood only available in different parts of the world such as the Himalayas or Uganda. The fact is that healthy essential food is available in every part of the world. We are very lucky to trade in food from different countries, and as a result we have more choices, but starting with healthy food from your region is always a wise move.
5. Here is the only must that is acceptable in starting to implement a new eating pattern: having three meals a day as a rule. Between meals, you can enjoy healthy fruit, a piece of dark chocolate, nuts, and healthy drinks.
6. However, given the modern lifestyle, it is not always possible to eat at the same times every day. According to the physiology of our body and digestive system, the first meal of the day should be consumed twelve hours after the last meal and should be the richest in protein and healthy oils. Examples of foods that fit this requirement are eggs, yogurt, berries, nuts, and vegetables. These supply energy for the day and suppress cravings for unhealthy and sugary snacks.

   The last meal should be between 5 p.m. and 7 p.m. to give you a break of twelve hours in digestion. It is proved that having the nightly gap from the last meal of the day to the first meal in the morning improves metabolism and increases the fat-burning process.

   Top athletes have a sixteen-hour break between their last healthy meal and a competition. Therefore, a late dinner may be an excellent social event a few times a year, but on a regular basis it will lead to weight gain and sleeping problems because during the night, the metabolism slows down.

Use your logic and intuition to make a practical eating plan.

7. The way you serve food plays an important role too. You can start by serving well-balanced meals on small plate and in the proportion of 25% of proteins, 60% of carbohydrates and 15% of healthy fats will make a visible change in your body and improve how you feel.
8. Some foods are known to boost metabolism and should be eaten regularly. These include black coffee (1–2 cups a day), green tea, herbs, mustard, cinnamon, prunes, and grapefruits. Fermented foods such as plain Greek yoghurt and kefir will supply the necessary healthy bacterial flora to the digestive system.
9. Creating a friendly atmosphere and eating slowly will prevent overeating as well. It takes twenty minutes to send a signal from the stomach to the brain that you are full, so slow down. Make a goal based on each of these techniques, and visualize it for five minutes a day.

   Following are some affirmations to improve your eating pattern. These can be transformed into goals:

- "I trust my intuition and all my senses to choose the right food."
- "I am in control of my body and mind. I choose only healthy food."
- "I know that nutritious food in proper proportion is essential to being fit."
- "I carefully prepare my food and eat at regular times."
- "I choose a variety of foods to stimulate metabolism."
- "I am in control of my thoughts and emotions. I control my eating habits."
- "I am confident that I can be in control of my food choices."
- "I eat only when I am hungry, to nourish my body and my mind."

Like in everything else, using logic and balance is crucial to have a healthy body. But being flexible and treating yourself on special occasions with family and friends with your favourite ice cream or birthday cake is part of a healthy lifestyle as well. This "but" should be acceptable to celebrate any achievement to the fullest. It is the fruit of your commitment to have a healthy and prosperous life.

Warnings:

- Severe obesity may have a medical or psychological basis. For example, excessive weight gain can be caused by a dysfunction of the hormonal system or internal organs. If you have a condition like this that leads to weight gain, you should be under the supervision of a medical professional. If you honestly believe that you put on weight despite your healthy diet and lifestyle, contact your doctor for a consultation. Such cases are rare but need urgent attention and treatment. Hormonal imbalance; other medical conditions such as diabetes, iodine deficiency, and adrenal disease; and psychological eating disorders should be eliminated or treated if diagnosed. These conditions must be treated by a specialist. Professional hypnotherapy is very helpful in such cases, so ask your doctor about it.
- If you are overweight and have a problem making a list of at least ten reasons for it, you may be living in denial or may already have a food addiction. If this applies to you, read the next chapter to find more on this subject and learn how to find professional help.
- There are same serious conditions characterized by total avoidance of eating, such as anorexia, or by compulsory overeating, such as bulimia. These are complex psychological problems leading in the long term to serious medical conditions such as multiple organ failure or even death. If you think you may suffer from one of them seek a professional assistance without delay.

Sixty-seven

Poisoning Your Brain and Body

We are living in an age where the consumption of poisonous substance has increased and our awareness of it has decreased. Common substances that cause damage to brain cells are alcohol, narcotics, and many prescribed medications including sleeping pills, many over-the-counter drugs, sugary foods, preservatives, and a variety of energy-boosting drinks. The main organ, our brain, which controls our mind and body function, thinking, and behaviour, is voluntarily poisoned with chemicals every day!

Chronic poisoning of the brain brings serious consequences to physical and mental health and causes organ malfunction. Associated diseases are heart failure, poor circulation, cancer, diabetes, obesity, high blood pressure, and stroke. Alcohol can lead to brain and other organs damage, as will narcotic use by poisoning the whole body.

Being deprived of sleep and staying awake on caffeine and other stimulants may lead to a nervous breakdown or to some form of psychosis and addiction. Addictive substances cause many psychological changes in brain function. This means that whether the person is currently addicted or not yet addicted, his or her thinking and behaviour patterns are affected. The normal brain function is out of balance, jumping from high arousal to unpleasant emotional pain and irrational thinking.

For those affected by addiction, they know it is like being trapped in an octopus's arms for years, in excruciating physical and emotional pain, all day and all night, without the hope of being free again.

When the cycle goes on and on, the body screams for more of the addictive substance, only to take the suffering to a deeper level when the substance is once again ingested.

In turn, the nervous system is affected. Unbearable pain, both physical and emotional, makes it difficult to get through the day. Every day an addict craves for the addictive substance, powerless over it. Finally the addict loses everything, destroying his or her professional and personal life.

All these things happen because the brain is systematically poisoned and shrinks. The shrinkage is clearly seen on a brain scan. Normal brain function and connections with the whole body are disturbed and systematically reduced. Addiction involves a process of dissociation between different parts of the mind. Reasoning, thinking, and behaviour become irrational. One part of the mind says, "I need the substance," and associates it with a feeling of relief; the other part says, "Don't use it again," feeling guilty about the consequences that inevitably come about. This battle may last for many years, and it seems that there is no solution to the ongoing dilemma. This provides the addict with an even better excuse for self-medication. Finally, the addict loses the power to fight back and is pushed to the bottom full of darkness, without hope of being free again.

The person's awareness of his irrational thinking and actions is seriously diminished over time. Reality seems to reside behind tinted glass, and neglecting of responsibilities is common, leading to many problems such as interpersonal conflict, anger, abuse, and damage to one's family life.

So why, when we know all the aforementioned facts, are we still willing to deny the effects of addictive substances? What is happening in our lives that cause us to become willing to lose our assets and logic?

Some people use substances as part of their social life; others, to kill emotional pain. In fact, poor stress control, ineffective coping and problem-solving strategies, damaged confidence, and emotional scars are frequent reasons for turning to a chemical to feel better. Drug and/or alcohol use is a common remedy for those who feel hopeless and disappointed. Simply put, for many, it is a door to forgetting and escape. The fact is that we are tempted to self-medicate when we are losing control over our lives. This happens especially when we are emotionally hurt, going through a difficult personal or professional experience, or being ignorant, thinking, "It will not happen to me."

Whatever the reason for willingly taking addictive substances, surprisingly, within a short period of time, it is likely to lead to destructive and uncontrolled behaviour. As one's personal and family situation deteriorates, the emotional pain increases, and the addict will do anything to get the next dose to relieve the pain. With time, the mind becomes preoccupied with negative feelings of guilt, anxiety, and psychosis, even when the addict believes herself to be in control to some degree. These conditions are quickly progressive and, if not stopped, will lead to permanent brain damage and perhaps death.

Those who live with an addict know of the never-ending mental pain of witnessing a loved one losing control over their life or dying. Sadly, I have to say that according to my experience, it is difficult to find someone today whose life is not affected, either directly or indirectly, by this devastating condition. It affects addicts, their family, their friends, and society as a whole. An addict is someone's child, parent, and/or friend. It is always very hard to see a loved one helplessly going downhill and being destroyed by the disease of addiction. It may be shocking to see a brother or sister, mother or father, child, or friend going downhill rapidly, leaving you hopeless, and not knowing what to do.

New-born children suffer and are affected by the mother's addiction. Older children suffer abuse, neglect, or poverty because of a parent's addiction. Millions of children are hungry and cold because of a parent's addiction. The mental pain that arises from bad childhood experiences frequently leads to addiction itself, and the cycle continues. The whole family lives in fear, praying for mercy and hoping that one day things will be better.

Once more I say that I do not know which is more painful, for the mother to see an addict child or for a child to see an addict mother.

Sometimes when someone starts to talk about addiction, immediately we hear defences such as, "Yes, I know, but that person is weak" and "Everyone uses that drug."

We discussed in previous chapters that we can speed up the process of learning effective strategies to cope with daily demands in a hypnotic trance. But it is interesting to note that while many people are afraid of hypnosis, they are not afraid of taking toxic and addictive substances, knowing that these substances will for sure take control of their body and mind. We all know that many people die every day from alcohol or drug abuse, but still many people say, "Everyone is using drugs for recreational purposes."

Therefore, those who are more aware of this dangerous condition and know how it develops are in a better position to protect themselves and those close to them from this destructive family disease and lend a supportive hand to those who already suffer.

Practising self-hypnosis will help you to build a strong personality and may prevent you from developing this devastating condition or help you to recover from it.

Sixty-eight

Alcohol Addiction—Is It Fun or an Escape?

> When you wake up and the first thought you have is drink, you are alcoholic.
>
> Richard Burton

For centuries, social alcohol drinking has been a custom around the globe, taking place at home, work, parties, celebrations, and sports events. Drinking relaxes people and allows them to have a good time. For many it is OK to have a drink at lunchtime, at dinner, in the evening. In many places, alcohol is available for purchase twenty-four hours a day! Everything seems to be OK until something drastically changes your life or the life of someone close to you.

Here we come to the dark side of consuming alcohol. It may be a car accident caused by a drunk driver, or someone being jailed for abusing another person while under the influence of alcohol, or a terrified child who is hungry, cold, and neglected because her parents are alcoholics. The worst happens when someone loses control over their alcohol intake and thereby loses everything in their lives. To make matters worse, all these things may come suddenly, as a surprise to all involved.

Statistics show that in the United States, nearly 10 per cent of the population has some problem with alcohol. Out of those who drink socially, 10 per cent develop all the symptoms of alcoholism. This means that the lives of about twenty million people are affected by alcohol. So, with an average family of four, the number of lives affected by alcohol in the USA is eighty million! This means that almost one out of every four people is affected by alcohol, either directly or indirectly.

Studies show as well that one out of ten social drinkers become alcoholic. Getting drunk once a month significantly increases the risk of becoming alcoholic. Statistics around the globe tell a similar story. Unfortunately, many do not want to see the real picture of this growing problem and prefer to live in illusion.

Alcohol is a mind-altering substance; therefore, it alters brain function anytime one has a drink. In small amounts, alcohol has some positive effects, such as reducing physical and emotional tension and improving mood. However, frequent use and in higher doses, without exception intoxicates the brain and leads to destructive changes in the body and mind.

It is proven that as little as two drinks per day for women and three for men can lead to alcoholism. One drink is equivalent to five ounces of wine, one and a half ounces of liquor, or twelve ounces of beer. We all know that for many, this is not the average amount of alcohol consumed daily. New research from the United Kingdom indicates that there is no safe amount of alcohol to consume and that each drink increases the risk of heart attack.

Alcoholism is characterized by excessive drinking and an inability to stop, and it has devastating social, occupational, and family consequences. We now know that blood relatives of alcoholics are more prone to becoming alcoholics themselves. Young people are more at risk of becoming alcoholics as their brains are still in the developing stage and therefore are more sensitive to poor nutrition and toxins.

One of the differences between alcoholics and non-alcoholic is that non-alcoholic are more affected by the toxic effects of alcohol. After drinking a considerable amount, a non-alcoholic feels too sick to drink more because of acute alcohol poisoning. Alcoholics can drink much more without feeling intoxicated. It is as if they have no off switch to stop them. They poison their brains constantly and experience increasing cravings to increase the amount of alcohol consumed daily.

When an alcoholic stops drinking for any reason, withdrawals start twelve to forty-eight hours later, leading to tremors. This happens because the part of the brain that coordinates movement (cerebellum) is damaged. Weakness, sweating, nausea, seizures, and hallucinations are common signs of alcohol withdrawal. Hearing threatening voices and experiencing delirium tremens (DTs) are serious symptoms. All these symptoms may occur as soon as ten to twelve hours after not drinking. Alcoholism leads to chronic organ failure and necrosis of the liver, kidney failure, high blood pressure, impotence, and severe brain poisoning, which are primary causes of death.

Long-term psychological problems from abusing alcohol are anxiety, confusion, sleeplessness, nightmares, and depression, including suicidal thoughts. Fear, illusions, and disorientation are common. Blackouts lead to short-term memory loss.

Dependence on alcohol is no respecter of persons. It happens to the poor and to the wealthy, to movie stars, to ignorant people, to ambitious young people, and to innocent children. A dependence to any kind of alcohol, whether spirits, wine, beer, or cocktails, develops in the same way, contrary to popular belief. Anyone may be affected and lose control at any time. And when this happens, it is a one-way street, very difficult to find one's way back from.

Neglected or abused children are frequently victims of alcoholism themselves. For them alcohol may be the only thing to relieve the emotional pain or fear. Later they fear alcohol and feel powerless over it the same way as their parents did.

Contrary to popular belief, alcoholics have some awareness of their condition. They suffer and feel guilty but are still unable to say no to drink. In fact, no one wants or chooses to be alcoholic, stripped of all dignity. Every alcoholic once was an ordinary person who could drink socially to have fun, relax, ease physical or mental pain, or escape from life's disappointments. The facts show that regular drinking is progressive and gradually leads to changes in brain function. This leads quickly to the different stages of alcoholism without the person recognizing it. These phases will vary for everyone. Some may stay in the transitions stages for a longer or shorter time than others. This will depend on many factors such as family situation, health, personal strength, and motivation to change. Finally, without help, it will reach the stage of suffering, which is unbearable to all.

When alcohol changes the brain function, the affected person shows complex mental weakness and starts to live in denial and develop madness. They are afraid to admit that they have a problem and are unable to help themselves. Because an addict's life is out of control, they develop negative emotions such as anger, hate, pain, and resentment. The consequences of abusing alcohol are serious, from neglecting personal and family life, to killing people on the road, to abuse, all of which are very common.

The tragic thing is that when this disease affects one person, it affects the whole family, especially children. The whole family is left with fear and confusion, and the worst-case scenario is when physical or verbal abuse is present daily, when an alcoholic begins losing control over her thoughts and actions. Financial and family problems develop, bringing with them hopelessness, fear, shame, or anger.

Members of the alcoholic's family tend to pretend that everything will be OK, hoping that tomorrow the alcoholic will come to his senses and stop drinking. But in most cases, this does not happen. In the meantime, the family covers up the damage caused by the alcoholic, for example by paying back money, lying to bosses, or creating stories to hide the situation from other family members and friends. Because nothing changes, soon the family loses hope and isolate themselves from friends, afraid that the truth of their situation will become known to all. They are left in darkness, hoping that one day the alcoholic will wake up and stop drinking. The fact is that the alcoholic does not stop and the problem deepens, even if there is a short break from drinking and some short-term improvements. After a few days, a few weeks, or even a few months, the alcoholic starts drinking again, and each time the problem progresses more rapidly and becomes much deeper.

Confronted alcoholics will automatically say, "I can control it," or "I am not stupid," or "What's wrong with you?!"

So, the question is, if they think that they are responsible and in control, why do they do it? They do it because alcohol destroys rational thinking, and addiction is the only winner.

In the light of this fact, we see that alcoholics are the victims of alcohol addiction and need professional help, not enabling or counterproductive criticism. Alcoholism is a serious disease, and for sure alcoholics do not want to feel hopeless and in fear of losing their lives. They feel emotional pain from hurting their families, they lose dignity, and they feel ashamed of themselves. They became addicts because for some reason they missed or ignored the first symptoms of addiction and believed, as many do, that it would be OK because "everyone drinks".

Unfortunately, there is no test available to tell whether you will become alcoholic or not. Frequently it is shocking to see someone close to you becoming hopelessly trapped in the octopus' squeezing arms.

In the box, I present a true story of becoming alcoholic.

Cuba: "Just One Beer"

Cuba was a smart, handsome guy who loved his caring family and had a lot of friends. He was a responsible, funny fellow with great ambitions for his professional life and family life. His unconditional love for his son was known to all. Occasionally he had a drink outside the home, or he enjoyed social gatherings with his friends at home. Sometimes, after too many drinks, he did not go to work. Everything seemed to be normal, until one day his boss gave him a warning to improve his performance. Cuba went for a drink with a friend to share his frustration with someone. After a few shots, he felt better and forgot about the problem. The pattern started to repeat itself, each time after he'd had a stressful day. Soon he began to think about a drink after work, and he started to blame everyone for everything in his life and spend less time with his family. He always had an excuse to go to another party, saying he'd had another stressful day and needed something strong too relieve the pressure. Soon he developed financial worries, so a friend took him out for a drink to cheer him up. The next day they drank while watching football. After that it was another late night, another row at home, and another absence from work. Cuba's son stayed silent, nodding his head, wondering, while Cuba's wife was shouting, "What's wrong with you?"

The next day she called his boss, saying that Cuba was sick again. Cuba's ego was provoked. *How dare they accuse me of drinking too much? I just had one beer.* He couldn't tolerate it and had to go out for fresh air … and one whiskey. The pressure was building up at home, at work, and with friends, and soon the only quiet place was the pub, where'd he have one more drink with a stranger, the only "friend" who understood him. One day everything was closed to him: his job, his home, and his family. He felt guilt and shame and had no place to go. Finally, he apologized to his family and promised to change. After three silent days, his apology was accepted. What a relief!

Three weeks later, he met a friend again for one beer—only one more—and conflicts developed at home again. Within four years of ups and downs, he lost everything and still was unable to accept help from his caring family, who prayed to have a sober Cuba come back home. Cuba's only friend was the bottle. Nothing else was important to him. He wanted only one drink, despite knowing that one day, that one drink would kill him.

One day Cuba was found dead on the floor, alone, with an empty bottle at his side. He was forty years of age. His son shook his head, wondering what had happened to his beloved father who promises to be for him forever. He was such a nice polite man.

Common factors leading the alcoholism are emotional or physical pain, child neglect, abuse, grieving, professional failure, a broken family, and misfortune. Others cases show irresponsible thinking, lack of interest, boredom, etc. Many are just naive and believe that regularly drinking alcohol will not affect them. Others simply say that they do not care, only because they are hiding their secret pain.

The problem is that there is no clear line between alcoholics, controlled drinkers, and heavy drinkers. The most accurate definition I have found is that it is not important whether you drink or not but how alcohol affects your life and what consequences arise from it.

Young Women Having Fun

Alcohol addiction is increasing among teenagers. I would like to express my concern about this new phenomenon of having fun which is spreading across the world.

Clubbing is very popular these days, and there is nothing wrong with that. What is bizarre is that groups of young women make plans to go to the pub, have a few shots of strong alcohol, and get drunk as soon as possible. Drunk and unconscious girls are found lying in the road with no recollection of what happened to them.

TV reporters asked one of them why they do this. The answer was simple: "It is fun."

Surely losing total control over one's body and mind and waking up on the street, not remembering what happened the day before, is something that a rationally thinking person wouldn't call fun. Even more difficult to understand is what happened in the lives of these young people to cause them to believe that "fun" comes from being stripped of human dignity and being abused. Why are so many youngsters prepared to risk their lives, health, and dignity only to get drunk and forget? What is so terrible in their lives that they want to erase it from their minds? Why, at the age of sixteen, don't they enjoy a typical teen's life and challenges? What destroys a teen's enthusiasm for rewarding activities and the company of friends to have real fun?

What we know is that none of the girls interviewed was involved in any kind of hobby, sport, or other activity after leaving school at the age of sixteen. The only place they would go after work was the local pub, where their parents used to spend evenings and weekends. Many teenagers started to drink because they had come from a broken family. None of them had any quality time with their families or friends. London has beautiful parks and different attractions free to everyone, but these girls hardly knew where they were located.

One viewer commented on their bizarre behaviour by saying that they are sixteen and have a right to do what they want. Such statements are even stranger to me, especially when a young girl's life and dignity is in great danger. For some reason, these girls have started out in their adult lives in the most dangerous manner, with severe and long-term consequences. For some reason, they believed that what they were doing was fun.

The tragedy is that they were only teenagers, and there was no one to show them that they could find excitement in real fun activities and gain satisfaction from their own achievements. The sad thing is that they are our daughters or granddaughters and one day will be mothers to a future generation of kids and a role model to their children.

Being drunk is not fun. It is not social either and will destroy the dignity and the lives of many people.

Sixty-nine

Drug Addiction

> Drugs are like witches, promising you paradise but taking you to hell.

One would expect that we all know the danger of using narcotics and many other drugs, but in reality this subject is a very sensitive one, with people defending the use of drugs with, "But everyone tries them for recreational purposes!"

So let's start with the facts. Drug addiction happens more rapidly than alcohol addiction and is more devastating in nature. Damage to the brain is very severe and frequently permanent. Recovery is very difficult and painful, relapses are frequent and death from overdose is common. In Canada, official statistics show that four thousand people died from overdose in 2018. The USA has declared an opioid epidemic.

The situation is similar around the globe with illicit drugs such as marijuana, cocaine, opiates, methamphetamine, ecstasy, amphetamines, and phencyclidine, and with prescription drugs such as benzodiazepines, Adderall, oxycodone, barbiturates, methadone, and tricyclic antidepressants.

The most commonly used narcotics are opioids (codeine, oxycodone, morphine, pentazocine, and hydromorphone). One of the strongest opioids is heroin, and the cheapest variety currently available is fentanyl. Access to opioids is easier these days, and more youngsters are exposed to them every day and everywhere, even at school.

Clinical and scientific studies prove that drugs of any nature are especially dangerous for young people and that even one dose can kill. Moreover, continuous use for three days frequently causes people to experience severe physiological and psychological addictive changes.

It is fact that every day thousands of teenagers taking their first dose of drugs ever die. No one is strong or clever when it comes to drugs. Drugs kill without mercy. They kill celebrities, the rich and the poor, young people and adults, parents and children. The first dose, whatever the drug, puts the user at significant risk long-term suffering and loss of freedom, dignity, and life.

Drugs alter the mind and the functioning of the whole body and present the danger of developing addiction. Taken before the age of twenty-five, drugs may damage brain function permanently, even after one dose—including marihuana. Narcotics always work in the same way. After a short period of "highs" and "sparks" from the brain, the dark side comes, dragging the person down more and more every day, demanding more of the addictive substance, like an octopus squeezing its arms tighter and tighter every day.

Those affected will have withdrawal symptoms immediately, which are far-reaching and extremely unpleasant, both medically and psychologically, if they stop using the drug. The initial euphoria and pain relief will turn to suffering, urging the person to do anything for the next dose of the addictive substance just to stop the unbearable feeling.

Blood pressure can be lowered and lungs affected by fluid retention. Neurological problems start to develop due to brain damage caused by inadequate blood supply. Brain scans show shrinking and permanent damage to the brain.

Poisoning the mind with drugs leads to mental changes such as irrational thinking, depression, anxiety, anger, guilt, and suicidal thoughts. Addicts feel lost, confused, and hopeless. Their dignity, their freedom, and even their will be taken away sooner or later—without exception.

Drug addicts are aware of the damaging condition and are afraid of it, but still they are unable to stop using the substance. The dependence is so profound that it is impossible for them to help themselves and stop themselves from taking another dose. After losing everything, frequently they isolate themselves. Death on the street is very common. They scream in pain for another dose and will do anything to get it. They will lie, cheat, and manipulate without mercy. They will turn their backs on their friends and family members. They become willing to prostitute themselves and allow themselves to be manipulated, only because they are unable to exist without the drug. Their fear of being cut off from the drug is so intense that they refuse any help—and the addiction is the winner again.

Still it is frequently seen that people live in denial and falsely believe that everything will be OK, until family tragedy strikes.

Some are lucky to wake up in fear for their lives and finally ask for help. Many don't and die without having a chance to fight for freedom and regain an enjoyable life.

This type of tragedy is a family disaster because addiction brings pain for those who live with an addict. Some children are born affected by drugs. Others suffer abuse, neglect, or poverty because of a parent's addiction. The facts clearly show that many children are hungry and live in fear because Mummy or Daddy is an addict.

The mental pain from bad childhood experiences frequently leads to addiction itself, thereby continuing the cycle. In any event, the addict is someone's child, parent, or friend. It is always very hard to watch hopelessly as a loved one is knocked down and destroyed by this devastating disease.

One person affected by addiction causes the whole family to live in fear, praying for mercy and hoping that one day things will get better. I do not know what is more painful, for a mother to see her child addicted or for a child to see his mother addicted.

We need to open our eyes and see the true picture of this growing problem that affects us all. There is only one truth—any drug will affect brain function each time it is taken. Therefore, drugs should only be used in exceptional medical conditions and only with professional supervision.

Before taking any drug, ask yourself if you want to volunteer to be in the position of being addicted? If this has happened to you already, don't surrender to drugs. They will squeeze you like an octopus's arms, without mercy. Don't suffer alone. Ask for help. There is hope and help available for you to start a much better life. Don't miss your chance. Get help! You need to wake up, stop living in denial, and stop falsely believing that everything will be OK.

As I said before, we need to open our eyes and see the true picture of this growing problem that affects us all. Any drug will affect brain function each time it is taken. Even so-called "recreational" marihuana may drastically change a person's brain function and personality and put that person on the road to hell.

Seventy

Hypnotherapy and Addictions

> We think that an addict's problem will not affect us,
> but it does every day, everyone, and everywhere.

It's hard to find a family without someone affected by this disease directly or indirectly at home, school, office on the street. Unfortunately, there is still no formal treatment from the government's health service for people addicted to alcohol or other drugs, so those affected will have to find their own way to fight it. Private treatment is very expensive and often too short to bring long-lasting results. Therefore, there is no guarantee that it will be successful.

However, there have been some positive changes as alcoholism is now officially accepted as a disease.

The fact is that every day millions of people of all ages go to rehabilitation and addiction centres for help. They believed in the past that they would be able to control their social drinking or that they would be OK using drugs. They took the chance and proved themselves to be wrong.

Those who were successful in recovery now are grateful to be alive and able to start a new rewarding life. Because of that, many have committed themselves to spreading the message and helping other addicts. Although no one can handle another person's addiction, we all can make many changes to help an addict recover.

Addiction is a complex psychophysiological disorder, and treatment must involve many facets. Family and professional help is always beneficial, and there are many well-organized group therapies. AA (Alcoholic Anonymous) is well-advertised and has centres located in many areas. Meetings run several times a day, 365 days a year, and are free for everyone who has the desire to stop drinking. Those who wish to stop taking drugs may find similar support at Narcotics Anonymous, NCBI.

Amazingly, these groups grows stronger every year. It has existed for 75 years in more than 150 countries. Addicts go to group therapies meetings every day in desperation to find help to save their lives. Other places that are open so late are pubs, nightclubs, and restaurants selling alcohol—nowhere else. Is this a coincidence?

Before rehabilitation, addicts used to go to bars to have fun with friends. Now they go to addicts meetings hoping to survive and find a way to have an enjoyable life. They go there because their lives had become unbearable and they had lost the power to fight back. Group and individual therapies are based on different approaches and everyone can chose what is the most appealing to them. There is an "Accept and Commitment" approach, based on internal experiences, changing cognitive diffusion, clarifying personal values and taking full responsibility from now on. Living in a moment approach, focus on psychological therapy to improve well – being and psychological flexibility towards themselves and external relationships.

For more spiritually minded AA and NA will direct them to seek help for their diseases to follow simple 12 steps program adopted from Oxford Christian Group.

Hypnotherapy is an effective way to break any addictive pattern of thinking and behaving. It is a comfortable tool to use during recovery, helping addicts to get through the difficult period of withdrawal and learn a new way of living. During hypnotherapy, it is much easier to deal with past bad experiences in a more relaxed way. Hypnotherapy helps a person to identify negative emotions change them into positive emotions. Hypnotherapy and practising self-hypnosis will help to eliminate many of the common shortcomings and the irrational thinking of addicts and those who live with them.

Learning self-hypnosis helps an addict to find the motivation to get better, extend the positive changes brought about by therapy, and reinforce these changes daily in the person's new life. It will help to prevent relapses and strengthen an addict's belief that they can have a normal life again and be in much better control of their health and personal life.

A True Story

"I am an alcoholic." A young engineer with high ambitions for the future had been struggling with alcohol addiction for years. Alcohol was the remedy to ease emotional pain connected with his unresolved conflict with his father and later with his broken family.

When the officer's first addiction episode exploded with suicidal thoughts, his recovery period of three weeks in a rehabilitation centre, followed by AA meetings for six months, was unsuccessful. His addiction and suffering continued, bringing much more damage to his life over the course of a number of years.

Following many ups and downs, his addiction hit its highest level. He was drinking round the clock and was facing death every day. One day he was found unconscious with bruises all over his body. He had no recollection of what happened.

This time he agreed to have hypnotherapy and attended AA meetings again. His recovery was like magic from the first day of therapy, increasing his motivation to recover and rebuild all the things he destroyed in previous years, the things he remembered as if looking through a dark glass.

He started to enjoy life as never before, skiing and travelling. His family life drastically improved, and he enjoyed being a good husband, father, and brother again. His grandchildren adored him, and they loved to spend time together as he was such fun to be with.

He continued his recovery for years, appreciating his sobriety every day to the fullest. He was very proud of himself and even more dedicated to helping others. He used to repeat over and over again, "Keep it simple. Don't drink today. Tomorrow will take care of itself."

If you are taking drugs or abusing alcohol and your life has become unmanageable, know that there is always hope and help. Hypnotherapy will not only help you recover from addiction but will also help to prevent relapse. Don't miss the opportunity to meet friends who understand and share. Go to AA, or NA, they are there to help.

The whole family of addicts can seek similar help from a family doctor, and there are many individual and group therapies and spiritual/psychological programmes in almost all countries, cities, and small towns, easily to find on internet or from doctor. Therapies will help people understand the problem of alcoholism and drug addiction and how to deal with this condition better than before and to take better care of personal life.

Seventy-one

Hypnotherapy in the Prevention of Addictions

Addiction is a very complex matter, so it is very difficult to find simple answers on how to prevent it. In the past, authorities attempted to prevent alcoholism and drug addiction by introducing prohibition and later legalizing certain drugs. Both methods proved to be controversial.

The biggest problem is that addiction is on the increase and many of us still have the tendency to ignore this fact, even despite the increasing number of children affected every day by addiction. We live in denial, saying that addiction is not our problem, falsely believing that it is the problem of the addict, the "weaker" person. Unfortunately, such a belief is far from true, because we all are affected by addiction. And there is an increasing risk that it will happen to a member of your family.

Therefore, we all must take these facts seriously and be aware of the hidden danger presented by alcohol and drugs to people even at an early age. Ignoring the devastating power of addiction is like playing with fire. You may get burned, and then drugs and alcohol will be the winner, taking everything in its wake without exception.

Unfortunately, there are many innocent young people who do not understand the high risk involved in taking drugs and consuming alcohol. Many are lacking in fundamental education and human values. Some are looking for friends who care, or they just do what others do. Others just believe that they will have fun if they drink or use drugs. Their friends may say it is "good stuff", and unprepared youngsters who are gullible and easily manipulated may be convinced to try it. Teenagers can be easily tempted from people outside the home and do not have a developed sense of danger or responsibility to know what the right thing to do is. They are curious about everything and are easy targets as well.

There was a comprehensive study published in the US showing a significant link between getting drunk as a teenager and becoming alcoholic. In the UK alone, more than three hundred children under eleven years old were admitted to emergency departments last year with alcohol-related problems. An increasing number of teenagers are going to rehabilitation centres, AA, NA, Al-Anon, and Al-teen around the world!

My questions are: Why are our kids scared or looking for something to make them feel better? From whom did innocent children get a drink or a drug in the first place? Are they well prepared to say no with confidence? Where is the idea of having fun with heavy drinking or drugs coming from?

The answer is plain: they learn from what they see around them and from what life brings to them. They are victims of our silent acceptance of the dangerous worldwide problem of abusing alcohol and other drugs.

Some young people simply follow what they see others doing in their close environment. Others are too weak to refuse what is offered to them outside the home. Unfortunately in many families the children see a drunk parent on a daily basis. In many homes the adults use drugs in front of the children. Many parents know that their children are taking drugs, but they take no actions until it is too late. One terrified mother said, "I knew my daughter was taking drugs, but I thought it was normal because everyone tries it." Her daughter was eighteen years old and was on the street facing the worst from addiction—abuse and death. I witnessed a case where Mummy and Daddy felt sorry for their teenager sitting for an exam and gave her a dose of a drug to reduce the stress!

The fact is clear: what we present to our children is what they will follow.

We must express the facts that drugs and alcohol damage the brain and that addiction is cruel and merciless. There is a long list of great talents such as Whitney Houston, Michael Jackson, and Amy Winehouse who left this world much too early because of their dependence on alcohol or drugs, or both.

Some addicts are lucky to find help and support from their loving family, and many go through a long, expensive, and painful rehabilitation programme. In other cases, the addict does not recover. For people like this, the physical and emotional pain gets stronger day by day. One day they may wake up in hospital from an overdose. Frequently they don't wake up at all.

Every recovering addict will tell you how quickly the problem started and how difficult it was to accept that they had been stripped of any control over their life and had lost their dignity. They still remember that after a high, the pain and guilt monster comes to tell them how bad they were. They feel ashamed of spending the last penny they had on drugs when their children had no shoes. It hurts an addict to know that his mother cried every evening and his wife could not sleep at night because his addiction. It is always painful for the addict to accept that after having grown up with great expectations, they found themselves forced by the addiction monster to steal or prostitute themselves. They will share with anyone who cares to listen that addicts lose jobs, are expelled from school, and are stripped of their medals. Addiction ends many promising sports careers. The only winners are drugs and alcohol again.

Therefore, it is our responsibility to give a clear message to our children to protect them from the biggest problem humans face now, the self-poisoning of the brain and body, before the problem starts. We all must talk openly and teach them about addiction and substance abuse. Above all, we need to give them examples of how to approach this issue and how to find satisfaction in life without stimulants or depressants.

Children need to know that someone may approach them with drugs and say, "Take some of these. They're fun." They must know that their first contact with drugs could happen at school, with friends, with someone at home, or at a party. Children need understand that those who present drugs to them are just manipulators, thinking about their own business. They must be given the message that there is no "but" for taking drugs and that there is no safe drug. Above all, we should tell them that using drugs may cost their freedom and later their career.

"Four teens shared with their mother worries about their school friend, who turn to drugs and alcohol. The mother wondered – how it could happened. The fourteen years old teens answered – "You see Mom, the parent never been for her, as you are always for us." So, stay sober for your children to show them how to enjoy real life experiences, instead of illusions."

The simplest way to prevention addiction is to stay away from drugs. Think many times before you try any drug, and remember one thing: one dose leads to another, and soon there will be no end—just endless excruciating pain. Many believe that marihuana is safe. In fact, it changes the brain function even after one dose, leading to serious changes in thinking and behaviour, especially when taken before the age of twenty-five.

Self-poisoning of the brain always involves the risk of losing independence and finding all doors closed to you.

I want to enlighten everyone by saying that you have the opportunity to learn how to enjoy life to the fullest with dignity and satisfaction by expanding your natural gift—your mind.

The choice is yours now.

It is my hope that by reading this book, you will understand that there is a better way to enjoy life. Hypnotherapy and self-hypnosis are wonderful tools for learning how to stay healthy, feel good about yourself, enjoy challenges, reduce stress, and solve problems, and increase creativity and performance. By using it for a few minutes each day, you can enjoy sailing to the port of your choice.

Be smart—don't let others take you into a dark, cold cave.

Exercising common sense and being aware of the growing problem could be the turning point for making a change in your attitude towards alcohol and drug use. Learning to have fun, feel happy, and control emotions and pain without stimulants is crucial to putting a stop to the epidemic of addiction.

You can start by learning to be more sensitive to the first significant signs of addiction to alcohol and drugs. An addict shows repeated behaviours such as the following:

- Needing the addictive substance as a remedy to feel better, to kill the pain, or to have fun.
- Choosing stronger substances over time and showing the desire to have more of the substance of choice.
- Using the substance on a regular basis and getting angry without it.
- Spending money on the substance even if they cannot afford it.
- Showing irrational thinking, making bad decisions, and neglecting commitments.
- Exhibiting increasing problems with relationships at home and at work.
- Living with denial and lies and possibly withdrawing from close relationships.
- Being willing to do anything, even leaving family or friends, for the addictive substance.
- Showing aggressiveness when fearful of being cut off from drugs.

When such symptoms are present, confrontation is the wisest action. Seeking professional help, or help from organizations such as AA, NA, may save the addict's life. It is a time to wake up to this problem and take it seriously.

The whole family needs to make changes and cease tolerating drug addiction and alcoholism. It is better to go public or share the fact with the rest of the family and with friends than to suffer pain and feel guilty that you did not stop the addict in time.

Many celebrities share their experiences publicly. That is a responsible thing to do.

There is an increasing number of people who enjoy going to parties and having fun without alcohol. They choose to be sober because they are looking for quality fun, hoping to return safely home and have good memories the next day, instead of having a hangover and being ashamed when recalling the previous night. It is good to see recognition and a positive attitude towards addiction problems from the young generation as well. More and more young people confidently reject alcohol and drugs.

Recently, Katy, Duchess of Cambridge, visited a non-alcoholic bar in Liverpool as part of her charity mission. In the UK, the government recognizes that the problem of addiction is out of control and is introducing more restrictions on alcohol consumption. There is a new policy that hospitals can refuse emergency treatment to suspected addicts who refuse to get help with their addiction.

We all need to wake up to this problem, spend more time on the prevention of addiction, and stop making excuses, saying that it is OK to drive after one or two drinks or that everyone tries drugs, so it must be OK to do so.

It is time to look at this issue from a more rational point of view and stop tolerating abuse and violent behaviour from addicts. When an accident happens, it is not an excuse to say that it occurred because the person who caused it was drunk and lost control. Similarly, it is not OK to excuse a mother who forgot to feed her child because she was high. The addict may be the most loving person, but when under the influence, he or she is a danger to others and must be stopped.

Being drunk or high is the primary cause of accidents, abuse, broken lives, and neglect of minors. Young people need to learn what social drinking means and be able to recognize the first danger signs of becoming addicted.

One day I met a young man who refused alcohol during a party. He said, "Drinking makes me crazy, and I don't want to be seen like that." That was a mature statement from a man who made the right choice to be in control of his life.

Making positive changes at home regarding alcohol consumption can be a turning point. Serving alcohol sensibly during special occasions, and rejecting uncontrolled drunken behaviour, will make huge changes in this country and beyond. Knowing symptoms of addictions can help to recognize it and take earlier actions towards our selves or those close to us.

The message must be spread now and repeated by parents, teachers, and media to protect people, especially young people, from being victims of a devastating addiction. We need to erase the old 1950s image of an attractive man and woman with a glass of alcohol at an early morning business meeting, or a surgeon or pilot on duty after having had a lunch which included alcohol.

Whatever your problem is, there is a better way to solve it without shrinking your brain. Instead, you can expand your mind to achieve your goals, whatever your position is right now. Drugs and alcohol may take you only to an addicts' community, put you in a coma, steal your freedom, and start the cycle of endless pain and suffering. It may be as a one-way street; there is no way back. In many cases, there is no escape from it. Addicts no longer find pleasure in anything other than the substance they use. Nothing stops the pain, and there is no hope for them. Don't be fooled, thinking that because so many people are taking drugs, they must not be that bad.

Think twice before you try any drug, because one drug leads to another, and soon there will be no end—just endless, excruciating pain.

Be smart—don't let others take you to a dark, cold cave. Instead, build your self-esteem in order to make better choices, and say no and yes confidently in any situation. We all need to understand that for any decisions we make, there are consequences, and we must take full responsibility for our actions.

We all can be more efficient, improve our performance, be in control of our lives, and enjoy life and our achievements. Happiness comes from the inside, from our attitudes, our appreciation, our personal values, and above all our achievements. Being involved in more rewarding or challenging things in your life will give you more satisfaction than having fun while being drunk and then having a headache and bitter memories or no memory the next morning.

Alcohol and drugs change thinking and emotions in an unexpected way.

In contrast, professional hypnotherapy will help you to develop your natural defences and improve your self-esteem and problem-solving skills to help you cope better with your daily demands and stay in control of any situation. You can learn to enjoy the feeling of satisfaction instead of covering your problems with a mist of alcohol or other drugs.

Practising self-hypnosis helps to prevent many psychological problems and change old habits. Changing to a positive pattern of thinking, behaviour, and emotions gives you a confident platform from which to make the right choices. Increasing ambitious and systematic goal achievement gives you the feeling of being in control and brings great satisfaction. This way there is no need for self-medication by drugs, alcohol, or harmful medications.

This natural tool is beneficial and available to all of us, regardless of age and the situation we are in at the present time. It is the wisest, quickest, and least expensive way to manage one's private life and professional life and any relationship. Mastering self-hypnosis will improve self-discipline and efficiency, significantly helping you to reach your goals.

Expand your mind so you can be a winner and take all.

It is your life; it is your choice. Be smart enough to choose the real fun.

Seventy-two

Trance—the Platform of Comfort and Creativity

> The ability to discover the beauty of this world makes life great.

At the beginning of this book, I promised to give you the best navigation skills to maximize comfort and safe sailing. I hope that I kept my promise. It should be clearer to you now that it is not about hypnosis but about which suggestions we accept or reject during our life's journey. Now you should have begun to believe that you can be the master of your mind and control your thoughts, beliefs, and emotions to make things right – trance will help you to do that.

Now that we are near the end of this book, I want to give an answer to a common question about hypnosis and hypnotic suggestion: is it safe?

Generally, it is proved and accepted by scientists that hypnosis is a natural mind process that is safe. We all experience trance to some extend every day, when reading, watching movies, or letting our minds float. The fact that trance slightly increases the rate at which we accept suggestions is leveraged in medical hypnosis to persuade patients to accept positive therapeutic suggestions aimed at bringing about good feelings and a positive change in health, thinking, or behaviour.

However, in an unprofessional situation, or when playing for fun, the results of hypnosis may be different. An unskilled person or manipulator trying to perform hypnosis may, purposefully or not, apply harmful suggestions which may be accepted by the person under hypnosis who is going through a difficult time such as grieving or trauma, or who shows confusion and irrational thinking.

However, even in such cases, an inappropriate suggestion given during hypnotic trance will only be accepted when it aligns with what the person believes and values in a waking state of mind.

Otherwise, such a suggestion will be rejected, and the trance may be automatically ended. Remember that during hypnotic trance, you are in control and are able to initiate or terminate trance immediately when feeling uncomfortable with any suggestion or condition.

Some people are more hypnotizable and more open to suggestions, but the main indicators of which suggestions you accept or reject is your mental health, how strong your trust in yourself is, how confident you are in your ability to cope with everyday tasks, and what are you looking for.

The fact is that we are all bombarded with different suggestions from media, authorities, family, and friends and we respond to them according to our beliefs. The simplest answer would be that we accept or reject suggestions according to how we interpret any suggestion at the particular time and how mentally strong we are to say yes or no confidently to the suggestions we face every day, in hypnotic trance or not.

People going through tough times and with unhealed scars from past events may desperately look for anything to make themselves feel better and therefore may expose themselves to suggestions without carefully analysing them, for example the suggestion to take drugs or drink alcohol. Therefore, when facing some problems and seeking help, it is important to look for registered medical or psychological practitioners. Such therapy will involve building up your human values, your beliefs, your self-image, and your self-esteem to make you feel confident and improve the essential human values and skills presented in this book.

Practising self-hypnosis will extend the process of changing bad habits and building strong values, including better problem-solving skills and coping strategies. The "new you" will show significant changes in your physical health and performance, prevent you from losing your rationally thinking mind, keep you from living in a coma, delusion, and/or denial, and prevent you from being stuck behind a rusty gate.

Being mentally strong means being able to recognize what is important to you and safe for you. By being able to stay calm and in control, you will be able to think rationally when facing difficult situations and develop better coping and problem-solving strategies.

A stronger personality prevents you from losing sight of the light even in stormy seas. Regular relaxation of your body and mind will help you keep a healthy balance between body and mind, as discussed in this book. Conscious logical and analytical planning and unconscious searching for resources enabling you to make better choices is a natural and effective way to be in control and have the life of your choice. Now you can accept or reject the chance to use your mind to its fullest potential and be in control of your health and achievements.

Following is a summary of the conditions necessary to gain satisfaction from life:

- Keep the image of who you are and what you want in your mind.
- Be aware of your present position. Be honest with yourself.
- Learn from the past, and then let it go so you may be free to move on.
- Review your thoughts. Eliminate rusty beliefs and negative chronic emotions. Stay calm.
- Keep your mind open to new ideas, and be willing to learn new skills.
- Build belief in yourself. Believe that you can. Keep a treasure box of your achievements.

- Have a clear vision of your goals. Motivate yourself to achieve them, and set deadlines to reach them.
- Work on each goal. Never doubt your ability to reach your goals. Be persistent until you reach them.
- Work on your self-discipline, creativity, and personal growth.
- Build your social network, and set strong boundaries.
- Trust your intuition. Follow it at once, and never doubt your abilities.
- Expand your mind—don't let it waste away.
- Enjoy your voyage. Make your dreams come true.

Reward yourself.

INSTRUCTIONS TO EXPERIENCE LIGHT HYPNOSIS AND WORK ON A SPECIFIC GOAL

The following script leads you to experience the natural state of mind of light trance, allowing to work on your selected goals while in closer contact with your unconscious mind.

You can record it or ask someone to read it to you, when you sit down in a safe and comfortable place. Reading should be in a slow monotony but in normal tune. Or simply you can read it and memorize it to repeat it, when you ready to experience trance. With time and more experience, you can make your own suggestions, using your favourite style as presented in Chapter 6. Being more familiar with experiencing trance, you can start to use shorter version as well, instead of repeating the long inductions and deepening techniques. Just make sure you include all the parts of hypnotic suggestions as presented in this script.

The script includes the following components:

- Induction – Modified Eye Fixation, breathing and relaxation exercises.
- Two deepening inductions using counting and imagery of a private place.
- Ego – Strengthening as "from now on I control my feelings, etc."
- Therapeutic /goal suggestions as degree, buying a car, staying calm, etc.

- Posthypnotic suggestion to enhance the work after ending the trance.
- Suggestions to re-experience the trance at any time you wish.
- Awakening suggestions to end the trance with suggestions of feeling good.

HYPNOTIC PROGRAM

Never use this or any other hypnotic program when driving or when are involved in activities requiring concentration, and using any tools.

If you are ready to experience this natural and pleasant state of mind, chose one of affirmations or goal you want to work on now. Detach yourself from any other tasks, make yourself comfortable in a safe and quiet place. Sit comfortably upright with your head, back and legs supported and your hands resting on your laps.

INDUCTION – MODIFIED EYE FIXATION, BREATHING, AND RELAXATION

Sitting comfortably now, you can start by fixing your eyes on some spot high on the ceiling for a while, till your eyes start to feel tired and wants to close at their own time, while you deepen your relaxation to increase your comfort and your concentration on your breathing in and out …, in and out …, in and out.

> And each time you breathe out, say to yourself," *Relax now.*"
>
> Take a second breath, and when breathing out, say, "*Relax deeper now.*"
>
> Take the third breath, and when breathing out, say, "*Relax deeper and deeper now.*"
>
> Take the fourth breath, and when breathing out, say, "*Relax all muscle now.*"
>
> Take the fifth breathe, and when breathing out, say, "*Relax every cell in my body from the top of my head to the tips of my toes.*"

Now, start to count backwards from zero to minus twenty, or imagine that you are going down the stairs to the garden, or to the valley, whatever feel the most comfortable for you. With each step you take, just repeat suggestions of deeper relaxation. Do it slowly with a pause between each one, but in your own natural rhythm. You can join each suggestion with the previous one with, "and, as, while, because of that."

For example; "as I concentrate on my breathing, I relax so deeply, and now I can …"

Continue as follow;

"Relaxing so deeply now increases calmness coming to my mind and my body, letting me to concentrate on my thoughts and my inner feeling, while leaving the outside issues behand for a time. And feeling calmer gives me a nice feeling that I can be in control of my feelings, and my thoughts, just by breathing in relaxation, and by exhaling the tension from my body.

And it is nice to know that by staying calm, I can let my body and mind relax even more by relaxing my muscles now, smoothing every muscle from the top of my head, down to relax the muscles around my eyes. The muscles surrounding my eyes become tired now, and starts to blink slowly from time to time and it may be a moment I feel like to close them, to relax even deeper. And it is nice feeling to let them close now, when they wish to close, to spread the relaxation to my cheeks, mouths and chin, and down to all the muscles in the neck area supporting my head.

Breathing regularly in and out, I can feel the relaxation spreading into my shoulders now, and to my arms and hands. Feeling the relaxation spreading through my body, I can relax now my chest muscles, surrounding my lungs and heart, supplying oxygen to my body with each breath I take.

Now I can spread this relaxation to my abdomen area, relaxing the muscles supporting my vital organs in upper abdomen …, my stomach area, and down to the lower abdomen …, the pelvic muscles smoothing every part of my abdomen, when breathing in and out comfortably.

Feeling comfortable in my body now, I can relax muscles in my legs, from my hips down to the thighs, calf muscles and every muscle in my feet and toes. Relaxing so deeply now I can relax them too, and let go of the tension from the top of my head, down to my feet, and out of my body and my mind.

And it is good to know that if an emergency situation should arise, and I need to be fully alert, I can recognize what is important for me to do at that moment. And if necessary, I will be able to end this trance immediately all by myself and be fully alert, to take appropriate action, as I would normally do.

And if any disruptions or noise will come from outside when I am in trance, I am able to reason what is more important for me at that time, and if I chose to stay in trance, I will use the noise to relax even more. So knowing that, now I can deeply relax now and learn something in this special relaxation state of mind, increasing my imagination."

DEEPENING —CREATING YOUR SPECIAL PRIVATE PLACE

Continue as following:

"As I am relaxing very deeply now, my imagination and creativity increase. And it is a nice feeling to imagine that I am walking in the park, enjoying the freshness of the air, the beauty of surrounding trees, shrubs and plants, and above all, the peace of this special place."

While I am walking in this peaceful place, feeling increasingly comfortable in my body and mind, I can create my own very private place there. The place where I can be closer to my unconscious mind, the deeper part of my mind that takes care of me from the first day of my existence, when I am awake and when I sleep, regulating my breathing and my body functions all the time, helping to go through many everyday challenges without my awareness.

This is the deep part of me which knows me very well, storing all my experiences, good and bad, protecting me, and above all being willing to provide me with resources to ongoing situation, when I need it. And it is so reassuring that my unconscious knows what is the best for me, and is willing to supply the necessary ideas to find the best way to reach my goals, or to make positive change to how I think about myself and my ability to do what I want to do.

Waking and relaxing now, I can see to the right of me, a secure and pleasant place where I can go right now, and make myself comfortable. This place may be somewhere inside or outside and it is my choice where I want to be right now, at home, garden, on the beach or in the mountains. I just need to follow the image coming to my mind while enjoying this deep relaxation, as my unconscious mind knows what is most suitable for me right now, and will allow me to find anything I need there.

Relaxing so deeply, my creativity increases as well, and I can customize this special place according to my own desires and comfort level. I can put anything that would be beneficial for me there. Using my unlimited imagination, I can organize the place to my liking. I may wish to put everything I need, I can add my favourite colours, sounds, or no sounds at all, to increase the comfort of my body and mind, which is supported comfortable on the sit I am sitting on now."

Make a pause now and take your time to build your imaginary special place.

Visualize this place for a while and continue as follow. End of deepening one.

EGO – STRENGTHENING

Continue when ready;

"And it is nice to know that from now on, I can come to this comforting place at any time I wish, where nothing and no one can disturb me, or bother me. And in this comforting place I can relax quickly, stay calm, and make changes to how I feel about myself, as feelings are just feelings, and I can control them, they do not control me.

And it is a pleasant way to sort out my thoughts, find resources to deal efficiently with past and ongoing experiences, boost my creativity and unlimited abilities, to be used in the future. In this relaxed state of mind, I can recall all happy memories, learn from them and use the knowledge in the future similar situations."

Being closer to my unconscious mind, I start to believe that I am a great human being who has much to offer. In this special place I can work on how to find the best way to reach my goals, realize success, achieve independence, improve my health, and above all, find myself and discover what I want to achieve in my life.

While I am feeling more comfortable about my abilities, my confidence increase. Feeling good about myself increases energy and enthusiasm to go what I want to achieve. Staying calm and in control I am more open – minded to new ideas helping me to spot more opportunities along the way and achieve my goals one by one in shorter time.

End of deepening two. You should be in a light trance now just let it go. Make a pause for a moment, relax deeper and let it go.

APPLYING SPECIFIC SUGGESTION OR AFFIRMATIONS

Being in a light trance, you can start to work on your desired goal now.

Use the present tense. For example to improve domestic organization skill:

"From now on I am better organized every day. I prepare my clothes the day before. I practise self-hypnosis every evening; therefore, I sleep like a baby and wake up every morning feeling refreshed with energy and enthusiasm to start my day." "Enjoying deep relaxation, I can take the opportunity to get rid of any unwanted feeling and change it to a positive one to feel better about myself and immediately I can concentrate on the things that are important to me right now, and do it at once, till is complete, etc."

Visualize your success. Create a vivid picture of the final result of accomplishing your goal and all its benefits. Feel the satisfaction and all the benefits for you and those close to you. Take as long as necessary to work on your goal. Enjoy it.

When you decide to end this trance, first use post hypnotic suggestion to extend your work in awaking state. Frame these in the future tense: *"I will."*

POSTHYPNOTIC SUGGESTIONS

"In this natural, special state of mind, my unconscious is willing to do anything that is beneficial and acceptable to me to help me accomplish my goal. And the process of searching for new ideas will continue long after I end this relaxation session. From now on, these positive feelings and the reassurance that I am in control of my feelings and better organised every day in everything I do, will stay with me no matter where I am or when."

POST HYPNOTIC SUGGESTION TO EXPERIENCE TRANCE

"And each time I wish to re-experience trance to relax or work on my goal, I can do this simply by closing my eyes, taking three deep breaths, and when breathing out saying to myself, "Relax now in my private place. "And immediately I will find myself in my private place, relaxing deeply as I am relaxing now, and I will be ready to work on my goals."

Practise this three times.

You can reinforce this effect of entering trance by making a fist with one or both hands, and when breathing out and saying "*relax now in my private place*," releasing the fist and dropping your hands on your laps. You can use any physical anchoring as crossing your fingers, putting hands together, etc.

AWAKENING

"When I am ready, and when my unconscious mind has processed everything I've learned today, I will gently end this deep relaxation and bring myself back to my room and back to my routine activities by counting from one to five. At the count of five I will open my eyes, and be wide awake, feeling very good about myself, and ready to put into practice what I've learned today. And this good feeling will stay with me long after I open my eyes.

So I'll start counting now: one - waking up; two - be more aware of surroundings; three -waking up more and more; four – opening eyes and coming up; five – eyes wide open, feeling fully alert and good about this experience."

After that first experience of hypnosis, each time you want to practise self-hypnosis, you can do it quicker without going through the whole long induction. You can do it just by closing your eyes, taking three deep breaths, and when breathing out, using your clue and saying to yourself your, *"Relax now in my private place."* Take your time … let it go. You should experience trance and can proceed to work on your selected goal. With practice this will become easier every day, and you can start to use a short version of muscles relaxation when concentrating on your breathing as follow;

"When I breathe in, I relax the whole body now and when I breathe out, I release the tension from my body and mind. Now I relax the muscle of my head. Now I relax my shoulders, arms and hands … legs, feet, etc."

Just make suggestion to relax the muscles from the top of head to the toes when breathing in and release the tension when berating out.

You can use short version for building your private place, which can be different for different goal. For example;

"By breathing in and out and relaxing I can find a specific place where I can relax and have close contact with my unconscious mind to find resources and solutions to ongoing situation."

This will give you more precise surroundings to work on particular issue.

Short version of ego – strengthening

"From now on I can control my feeling, my thoughts and I trust myself. I believe that I can do what I need to do. I feel confident in any situation, I learn quickly what I need to learn, and I am open – minded, etc."

If all these above methods turns out not to be enough to re-enter trance, after closing your eyes and breathing in and out three times, you can try to count slowly from zero to minus twenty and say to yourself, after each count *"relax deeper and deeper."* Upon reaching twenty, just apply your cue to enter the trance by saying *"Relax now, in private place."* If you lose track of the number, just start from the last one you remember and repeat the whole script. Even if you are not sure you are in trance, continue the whole work on your goal and use post hypnotic suggestions to be awaken, as presented above.

Sometimes you may not feel like in trance, but you may be, therefore ending any attempt to enter trance with awakening suggestions are important.

Practicing the above few time, be patient and let it go, to enjoy it.

If you still have a problem entering trance, listen to the full script of hypnotic program "Inner Wizard," which can be downloaded from my website. It include built-in suggestions to experience trance, ego – strengthening suggestions, instruction to re – enter trance at any time you wish, post hypnotic and awakening suggestions.

However, it is an educational book, so reading it multiple times will help you better understand each step of practicing self - hypnosis.

AFFIRMATIONS

Following are some affirmations which may help you to make a positive changes in your life. Work on them in a waking state of mind or in self-hypnosis.

- *Every day I look for ways to improve my life.*
- *I exercise my body and mind. I take regular breaks and get good sleep.*
- *I stay calm and confident in any situation.*
- *I know that to be in control of my life, setting goals is important.*
- *My goals are constructive and challenging, and I believe I will achieve them.*
- *When I concentrate on my goals, nothing and no one can disturb me.*
- *I am open-minded to look for resources through all my senses.*
- *I learn from every experience.*
- *I am well organized and preserve my energy for the most important tasks.*
- *I enjoy everything I do, as I find every task a challenge.*
- *I communicate with people in a calm and respectful way.*
- *I easily express what I want to say and share my point of view.*
- *My communication skills are improving every day.*
- *I am a good negotiator and public speaker.*
- *I share my knowledge and success with others without limit.*

If you made notes when reading this book, you should now have a full set of goals to work on. This list will be very useful as you start this new journey to reach your desired destiny. Practise achieving your goals by reading your list and analysing each goal to be reached according to your satisfaction. Soon you will notice a difference in your thoughts and actions. Whatever you want to achieve, you can speed up the process by waking up to hypnosis.

LIST OF PROFESSIONAL HYPNOSIS SOCIETIES

The British Society of Medical and Dental Hypnosis (BSMDH) (established 1952)

The British Society of Experimental and Clinical Hypnosis (established 1977)

The American Society of Hypnosis

European Society of Clinical and Experimental Hypnosis

The International Society of Hypnosis has twenty member countries with nineteen hundred individual members. There are a significant number of professional hypnosis organizations many countries as Australia, Canada, and Sweden. There are many organizations associated with hypnosis, such as the False Memory Foundation in the USA and the British False Memory Society, etc.

To find more information about medical hypnosis, look online for medical, dental, and psychological hypnosis societies in your country.

REFERENCES

Alman, B., and Lambrou, P., *Self-Hypnosis* (New York: Brunner/Mezel, 1992).

Bandler, R., and Grinder, J., *Patterns of the Hypnotic Techniques of Milton H. Erickson*, (Cupertino, California: Meta Publications, 1975).

Barber, J., *Hypnosis and Suggestion in the Treatment of Pain* (New York: W. W. Norton & Company, 1996).

Barber, T., *Hypnosis: A Scientific Approach* (New York: Van Nostrand Reinhold, 1969).

Barber, T., Responding to 'Hypnotic' Suggestions: An Introspective Report, *The American Journal of Clinical Hypnosis*, 18 (1975), 6–22.

Barber, T., and De Moor, W. A., Theory of Hypnotic Induction Procedures, *The American Journal of Clinical Hypnosis*, 15 (1972), 112–35.

Barber, T., Spanos, N., and Chaves, J., *Hypnosis, Imagination, and Human Potentialities* (New York: Pergamon, 1974).

Braid, J., *The Power of the Mind Over the Body* (London: Churchill, 1846).

Cheek, D., and Le Cron, L., *Clinical Hypnotherapy* (New York: Grune and Stratton, 1968).

Cooper, L., and Erickson, M., *Time Distortion in Hypnosis* (Baltimore: Williams & Wilkins, 1959).

Erickson, M., Self-Exploration in the Hypnotic State, *Journal of Clinical and Experimental Hypnosis*, 3 (1995), 49–57.

Erickson, M., *Hypnotherapy: An Exploratory Casebook* (New York: Irvington Publishers, 1979).

Erikson, M., and Rossi, S., *Hypnotic Realities* (New York: Irvington Publishers, 1976).

Fromm, E., and Nash, R., *Contemporary Hypnosis Research* (New York and London: Guilford Press, 1992).
Hartland, J., *Medical and Dental Hypnosis* (London: Bailliere, Tindal and Cassell, 1966).
Hilgard, E., *Hypnotic Susceptibility* (New York: Harcourt, 1965).
Hilgard, E., and Hilgard J., *Hypnosis in the Relief of Pain* (Los Altos, California: Kaufmann, 1975).
Kahney, H., *Problem Solving* (Philadelphia and Buckingham: Open University Press, 1993).
Lancaster, G., *The 20% Factor* (BCA with Kogan Page, 1993).
Lynn, S., and Rhue, J., *Theories of Hypnosis* (New York and London: Guilford Press, 1991).
Lynn, S., and Rhue, J., Dissociation (New York and London: Guilford Press, 1994).
Ornestein, R., ed., *The Nature of Human Consciousness* (San Francisco, Freeman, 1973).
Rossi, E., *The Psychobiology of Mind-Body Healing* (New York and London: W. W. Norton & Company, 1993).
Rossi, E., and Cheek, D., *Mind-Body Therapy* (New York and London: W. W. Norton & Company, 1988).
Sheehan, P., Hypnosis and Manifestation of 'Imagination, in E. Fromm and R. Shor, eds, *Hypnosis: Research, Developments, and •Perspectives* (Chicago: Aldine–Atherton, 1972).
Tart, ed., *Altered States of Consciousness* (New York: Wiley, 1969).
Wester, C., and O'Grady, D., *Clinical Hypnosis with Children* (New York: Brunner/Mazel, 1990).
Yapko, M., *Trancework* (New York: Brunner/Mazel, 1990).

Printed in the United States
By Bookmasters